The Journals
of
Sydney Race
1892–1900

Goose Fair, Nottingham, 1904, looking across the Market Square

The Journals

of

Sydney Race

1892–1900

A provincial view of popular entertainment

Edited and introduced by

Ann Featherstone

First published in 2007
by The Society for Theatre Research
P.O. Box 53971
London SW15 6UL

© Ann Featherstone, 2007

ISBN 978 0 85430 0740

General Editor: Professor Richard Foulkes

Volume Editor: Dr Vanessa Toulmin

Printed and Bound by CPI Antony Rowe, Chippenham, Wiltshire

For Sydney Race

(1875–1960)

'A Nottingham lad'

Contents

List of Illustrations

Acknowledgements

My first expression of gratitude must go to Nottinghamshire Archives and the Principal Archivist, Mark S. Dorrington, for permission to publish selections from Sydney Race's journals, to the Society for Theatre Research for supporting my proposal for the book, and to the Arts and Humanities Research Council (AHRC) for supporting the larger project – 'An Alternative History of Victorian Entertainment' – of which this volume is a product.

In trying to interpret and understand the detail of Sydney Race's journals I have been forced to trespass upon the patience and goodwill of many busy people. Their good-humour in answering my sometimes obscure, often patently obvious (to them) enquiries is much appreciated. In particular I want to thank Dr John Turner, who answered my circus enquiries; Professor John McCormick, who offered his thoughts on the Goose Fair's marionettes and theatrum mundi; Professor David Mayer, who pointed me in the right direction over toga plays; Dr Richard Crangle, University of Exeter, who knows about X-rays and magic lanterns and Richard Shenton at the Media Archive for Central England (MACE) at the University of Leicester, who answered my query about Boer War films. Matthew Lloyd, descendant of the great music hall artiste Arthur Lloyd, kindly made material available to me on the production of *The Belle of New York*. His website http://www.arthurlloyd.co.uk I unreservedly recommend.

Patient and knowledgeable staff in the Local Studies Library, Nottingham, and the Nottinghamshire Archives (in particular, Nick Clark) have fetched and carried volumes and boxes, and have answered my questions on old Nottingham with interest and expertise.

Colleagues at both the University of Manchester and Royal Holloway, University of London have been supportive and sustaining over the past twelve months. My good friend Maggie Gale read and commented on the manuscript and offered many practical suggestions as well as her special kind of encouragement when my reserves of energy were at a low ebb; Jacky Bratton was wise, kind and a fount of knowledge, as always. Richard Foulkes, General Editor of Publications for the Society for Theatre Research, and copy editor Amy Myers were particularly patient and full of sound advice.

Special thanks must go to my family: to my father, Dennis Featherstone, who painstakingly proof-read the manuscript more than once, and was interested enough to talk about it with me when we walked the dog; to my mother, Joan, who arranged much-needed distractions; and to my son, James, who smiled, nodded, and made cups of coffee.

Finally, I owe a great debt of thanks to Dr Vanessa Toulmin and her staff at the National Fairground Archive, University of Sheffield, in particular Ian Trowell, who produced many of the images. Vanessa's expertise in matters of fairground history and the cinematograph are well-known, and she has shared her knowledge and the resources and wonders of the Fairground Archive (including permission to reproduce rare images from the collection) with enormous generosity. As editor, her insight into not only the complexities of the material but also its presentation have been invaluable, and her willingness to respond to my requests for advice unstinting.

Ann Featherstone

Introduction

by

Ann Featherstone

Sydney Race first made himself known to me over ten years ago when, sitting in the Local Studies Library in Nottingham, I read his account of an impoverished portable theatre in Sneinton Market and the unfortunate woman performer sporting a blackened eye who 'had always to stand with the other facing us' on the outside stage.[1] Fascinated, I lost no time in locating his notebooks and other materials in the Nottinghamshire Archives, and spent many Saturday mornings at first avidly reading, and then transcribing them. I wanted to capture, reread and savour Race's descriptions of how people were entertained not only in the theatre, but on the fairground and at the circus in Nottingham at the end of the nineteenth century. Inexperienced scholar though I then was, I knew they were unique.

Race had his first public outing with me at a conference on 'Theatre and Politics in the Age of Reform' at Homerton College, Cambridge in 1999; it was my first academic conference, and I gave a paper entitled 'Illegitimate theatre at the Goose Fair, 1895', talking about portable theatres (of which I then knew little) and shop shows (of which I knew even less). Since then, Sydney Race has made appearances in my doctoral thesis, in undergraduate lectures and academic journals.

It is time, I think, he had the stage to himself.

Details of Race's family and career are scanty. The 1881 Census reveals that he was born in Manchester in June 1875, the youngest child of Roger and Nancy Race. His father was an engineer, rising to foreman engineer in a cotton mill when the family moved to Nottingham at some time between 1875 and 1881. They lived in the working-class suburb of Radford. Race attended Nottingham High School for Boys, a privileged education and, at age 15, was employed as an office boy at the Gas Company. By 1901, aged 25, he was an insurance clerk. After Army service during the First World War, he was employed in the Nottinghamshire Education Department, and remained there for 38 years.

Race had two older sisters, Emily who was nine years and Annie who was eight years older than him. Both worked in the Nottingham lace mills. Sydney was a late arrival in the family, and this may account for his bookishness: perhaps he was a child used to being alone and amusing himself by reading, later discovering an interest in history and architecture, literature and religion. The Nottingham Mechanics' Institute provided him with male society, and also satisfied some of his intellectual needs. Undoubtedly he was preoccupied with self-improvement, and seems all his life, to have been a frustrated scholar. His need to read, research, uncover and explore, his interest in literature, history and the theatre, and above all his writing signal a lively and enquiring mind: he would, no doubt, have been an able

[1] See p. 48.

1

university student. It is not surprising, therefore, that he was a regular contributor between 1930 and his death in 1960, to *Notes and Queries*, that resort of the autodidact and antiquarian; he wrote on such subjects as the first performance of *Twelfth Night*, the location of Byron's heart, the journals of Mrs Hutchinson, wife of Parliamentarian Colonel John Hutchinson, the church of St Bartholomew the Great, in Smithfield, London, and his life-long investigation into the Shakespearian forgeries and fakeries of John Payne Collier.[2] His antiquarian impulse was further satisfied by contributions to the *Transactions of the Thoroton Society*, the journal of Nottinghamshire's principal historical and archaeological society, and the articles he continued to write for publication in local newspapers on subjects such as Nottinghamshire mummers' plays and Nottingham history.

Sydney Race's surviving notebooks begin in 1890 (when he was 15) and continue until 1952.[3] Those covered by the present selection (1892–1900) are written in cheap, paper-covered ruled exercise books (half foolscap, 8 x 6½ ins), many emblazoned with Britannia on the front cover, and Arithmetical Tables on the reverse. He uses pen and ink, and occasionally pencil, writing in a clear, neat, small hand. His spelling and grammar are accurate, though he frequently omits punctuation, particularly commas and apostrophes. Over the years, he develops an individual style; his early efforts show a tendency to dense description and commentary and self-conscious reflection, maturing to the more studied voice of the diarist and an increasingly reflective tone.

Whilst there is no indication that Race ever intended these notebooks to be read or published, there is no doubt that he was, in a sense, practising and was aware of writing 'apprentice pieces'. Entries in 1895 show that he has aspirations to be a journalist and to this end he sends an essay entitled 'Tours in Town and other Sketches. St Edwards Blue Bell Hill' (about a Sunday evening visit to a local church) to the editor of the *Nottingham Argus*. Race is pleasantly surprised when it is printed, 'word for word as I had written it'. He allows himself a little self-congratulation – 'To think that I have been walking these streets for six days not knowing that I had a column and a half in print of my own!' – quickly followed by self-criticism – 'Truth to tell I find the St Edwards account very poor reading with its writing crude and unpolished.' He reflects that he has better work inside him, and this small success gives him the confidence to continue. Self-reflection is rarely within Race's make-up. A single occasion, however, illuminates his notion of practice and process in writing:

> I have lately been very negligent with my diary and have omitted to chronicle several important occurrences. I must keep myself more to the point; for writing here is very good practice at composition though I am very careless in what I write. When I write for print I take much more pains, polishing up a great deal; but it would be better, I think, if I could write with fewer altera-tions.[4]

In fact, the notebooks show that he makes revisions as a matter of course. Writing a response to Wilson Barrett's performance of *The Sign of the Cross*, he notes in postscript: 'I did not like the latter part of this account at all on re-reading, and have

---

[2] So substantial are his notebooks and articles on Collier, that they are now held in the Shakespeare Institute Archives, Stratford-upon-Avon.
[3] The collection is held in the Nottinghamshire Archives and extracts are reproduced here by kind permission of the Chief Archivist.
[4] 8 July, 1897.

altered it considerably. Had it to appear in print, however, its form would need much further alteration.'[5]

Although Race calls the notebooks 'my diary', they bear scant resemblance to the usual notion of a daily record. They contain little that might be termed 'domestic', and if he does chronicle incidents from everyday life, it is the remarkable and extraordinary he selects: the death of the family dog, the release of his pet fox, the illness of his mother (captured in a single phrase).[6] Race's impulse to write is driven by the significant moment and not the obligation to diarise. In his teens and early twenties, it is often scenes and events which strike his visual sense – new sights and experiences on his annual holiday or trips to London, the Goose Fair, extraordinary performances and spectacles – and these he documents with a careful precision, avoiding literary excess. As he gets older, it is the theatre that preoccupies him, and in the 1940s he writes regularly about the progress of the war with Germany.

What is remarkable about Sydney Race's journals, and what drew me to them all those years ago, is the originality of his observation. I have written elsewhere about the 'tourist gaze' which he employs when surveying a circus procession – a paradoxically distant engagement with the scene, which enables him to serialise the moment.[7] His naïve eye witnesses and registers incidents which, in retrospect, are seminal: the early displays of the cinematograph on the fairground, for example, where he documents with precision what he sees, whilst showing sensitivity to the process and product of showmanship (in the exhibitions in shops and at the Goose Fair) through which he contextualises and rationalises the entertainment. His 'tourist gaze' is the lens through which the reader can see and make sense of the moment. His innate curiosity takes him behind the scenes, both literally when he visits a portable theatre, and reflectively when he 'sees through' the scams and tricks practised by showmen – and describes them. He reflects on what he sees and communicates his intense delight (or irritation) at circus performances and minstrel shows.

Race's observations are, finally, snapshots of provincial entertainment on the cusp of change. At the turn of the century, film exhibition was struggling out of the fairground and the shop show and musical comedy was the sophisticated 'thing' in the theatre. But freak shows were still commonplace, Sir Henry Irving, Ellen Terry and the Kembles still performed old-fashioned dramas, and the portable theatre occupied fields and market-places as it always had. When he died in 1960, Sydney Race left behind him a unique record of culture and spectacle in a period of enormous change, images of entertainment that were soon to disappear.

---

[5] See p. 126.
[6] See p. 84.
[7] Ann Featherstone, '"There is a peep-show in the market": gazing at/in the journals of Sydney Race', *Early Popular Visual Culture*, 3:1 (May 2005), 43–57.

Transcription and editorial approach

From Sydney Race's notebooks, I have extracted his accounts of popular entertainment during the years 1892 to 1900. Within these dates, his accounts of visits to churches and castles, attendance at religious services, civic processions and holidays in Scarborough, have perforce had to be omitted. Since they are interspersed between his accounts of visits to the theatre, circus, and the Goose Fair, and since the usual indication of omission ('…') might appear intrusive, I have offered a more or less seamless transcription.

A major editorial decision was to extract and divide the material into three sections dealing, broadly, with Nottingham, London and the Theatre. This seemed to be a useful, focused means of presenting the material, and also enables the reader more easily to track developments and changes. Race's understanding of and response to the theatre can be seen to develop and mature more readily when the writings are contained within a single section, and the significant changes to the Goose Fair – the increasing number of rides, the disruption caused by improvements to the Nottingham topography, as well as Race's maturing attitude towards it – are similarly clearer.

For economy of space, Race used '&' for 'and', 'Co' for 'Company', 'Exhn' for 'Exhibition' and other standard abbreviations. Having no such restriction, I have reinstated the full version. I have also used italics to denote the titles of books and plays where Race used inverted commas, and have corrected the (very few) errors in grammar and spelling. He used apostrophes and commas sparingly; I have respected this, and have only inserted punctuation where it is necessary for clarity. I have indicated the few occasions where words are unreadable.

Any errors in transcription and interpretation, I need hardly add, are entirely my own.

Finally, Sydney Race was living and writing in an era when it was still acceptable to refer to African-American performers (and white performers 'blacked-up') as 'niggers'. He also often demonstrated a critical distance and objectivity in looking at exhibitions of the physically different – 'freak' shows. Since the journals clearly represent a moment in history, I have not made any adjustments to the expression of his point of view which, in our more enlightened times, would certainly be regarded as offensive.

Figure 1. Dancing bear in Goldsmith Street, Nottingham, c. 1890

1

Goose Fair, Minstrels and Shop Shows
Sydney Race's Nottingham

Sydney Race devotes most of his journal reflections during the period 1892–1900 to visits to fairs, shows, portable theatres and circuses in and around his home town of Nottingham. Although his social life was perhaps not as eventful as that of today's young people, Race's attendance at the Mechanics' Institute and performances at the Albert Hall, the attractions of the annual Goose Fair and any shows that happened to open in the Market Place or in one of the vacant shops around the city centre, shows a varied menu of live entertainment.

The Nottingham Mechanics' Institute was always an important part of Race's life, from his early years – he joined at the age of eleven – to becoming a member of the Institute Committee and Secretary of the Lectures Sub-Committee, and co-writing (with James Granger) its updated history in 1912 and 1928.[8] As a young man, he attended concerts, theatrical entertainments and lectures in the Lecture Hall, took classes in literature, and used the library and newspaper room. The 'Mechanics'' was his 'club' and retreat and where he evidently felt comfortable and at home.

Outside, Nottingham was undergoing enormous changes.[9] The face of the old town, in which many eighteenth-century buildings had remained and where rookeries and slums still proliferated, was being modernised to reflect the town's renewed prosperity. Whole blocks of streets and dwellings surrounding the old Market Square were demolished, and replaced by new commercial buildings. Race reflects upon this, as each year the old boundaries and perimeters of the Goose Fair are changed. New streets such as King-street and Queen-street appeared, and the waste ground that had been claimed by showmen for their stalls and rides swiftly disappeared under bricks and mortar. With the change of topography, Race also notes the changing dynamics of the Goose Fair, as rides gradually outnumbered shows, and technology dominated art. His final entry for 1900 – his last journal reflection on the Goose Fair – is a reminder, not only that he had outgrown the Fair of his youth, but also that the Fair itself had come of age.

Two essays published in the Nottingham Argus *– 'The Circus' (January 1896) and 'Shows in Shops' (April 1896) are reproduced in Section 4 (pp. 153–161). They relate specifically to popular entertainments in Nottingham, and illustrate not only Race's now-matured writing style – one nicely attuned to the style of a provincial journal – but also the eclecticism of his interests. Here he describes the audience at the circus and the phenomenon of the shop show, aspects of popular entertainment which receive scant attention elsewhere. These two essays and the range of amusements covered in the rest of his writings offer the reader a rare glimpse of*

---

[8] James Granger, *Nottingham Mechanics' Institution. A Retrospect* (Nottingham, 1912) and *The Nottingham Mechanics' Institution. Fifteen Years' Record, being the History of the Institution from 1912 to 1927* (Nottingham, 1928).
[9] See Roy A. Church, *Economic and social change in a Midland town: Victorian Nottingham, 1815–1900* (London, 1966).

performances that existed both within and, more importantly, outside local licensing laws and conventional theatrical and exhibition venues. Shop shows, to which Race was a frequent visitor, existed in every major British city during the nineteenth and early twentieth centuries, but lie so far outside the scope of journalism and published anecdote that the detail of performers and performance has up to now been scanty. Similarly, Race's evident fascination with the portable theatre and the ghost show allows him to record in detail not only theatrical performance, but also the particulars of back-stage conditions and his conversations with the showmen and proprietors. The cinematograph seen through the eyes of this spectator, presents the new entertainment phenomenon in its embryonic form as a sideshow novelty in the vacant shops and fairground tents of a provincial town.

1892

Thursday May 12th

There is a peep show in the market. Made of small shells and represents Canterbury Cathedral. It stands on wheels in a glass case and there are two men with it one rather aged who wears a sailors peaked cap with gold braid round. It is certainly a well made affair – the shells worked round in proper fashion. You pay 1d to look inside but the interior is rather disappointing – very narrow some small dolls about and a little procession (the figures can't be properly made out) is drawn across the front. It is supposed to represent a wedding party and you hear the bells ring. The fellow puts his hand underneath to work it. The windows are of coloured glass.[10]

Friday May 13th

The conjuror I have before mentioned is again in the Market. I saw him do 3 tricks, viz. the 3 tins and balls; money catching in the air; and some half pence placed on the table, covered with a little cup disappear and come out underneath, etc. All neatly done. He is a clever palmer and a decent fellow. He carries a little table about – covered velvet and red fringe round which stands on 3 sticks (the sticks fold up together). He has a big head of hair, large boots, trousers wide, coat loose, pointed billycock turning green – not [an] over presentable figure.[11]

As I come home to night see two Italians going down Derby Rd with a small bear. One of them carried a long pole. A crowd of children was following them but I didn't see a performance.

Saturday May 14th

To see Bohee Bros at the Mechanics'.[12] Their performance is out of the run of the ordinary minstrels and of a first class character. There was a well arranged curtain all

---

[10] Although Race identifies it as a peepshow, this may be a mechanical illusion. See Richard Balzer, *Peepshows: a Visual History* (London, 1998).

[11] The cup and ball trick is one of the oldest methods of conning the unwary out of their money. See Sidney W. Clarke, *The Annals of Conjuring*, ed. by Edwin A. Dawes and Todd Karr (Seattle, 2001).

[12] Negro minstrels George B. (b. 1857) and James Douglas (1844–97) Bohee, originally performed with Haverly's Minstrels, and from 1880 had their own troupe, a combination of coloured and white performers. See Harry Reynolds, *Minstrel Memories. The Story of Burnt Cork Minstrelsy in Great Britain from 1836 to 1927* (London, 1928), pp. 201–202. Situated on Milton Street, the impressive porticoed building of the Nottingham Mechanics' Institute was erected in 1844 and rebuilt after a fire

Figure 2. The Mechanics' Hall and Institution, Nottingham, c. 1890

round and on a whistle being blown the band came in. Seven in it including a bass fiddle and a harp and a very energetic and good violinist. Then another whistle and three gentlemen in evening dress followed by six ladies come in. The interlocutor sits in the middle on a raised chair, on each hand a gentleman and three ladies. The latter were in evening dress and rouged. Two were young (one very tall and good looking) and one of the others was a mulatto. Of a good girth as also one on the opposite side. Then the band play and the corner men[13] came in creating a great row and dancing and knocking their tambourines about. At each end sat two, blacked, in brown velvet suits, knee breeches, and next them a fellow in evening dress, tight trousers, and red wig. The song and jokes of the first part were all good. Several of the ladies sang ballads and there was a well sung quartet. One of the end men sang 'She danced at the Alhambra' in which the other end men danced all in a row and another 'Ta ra ra doom de ay.' He sang the song and they all joined very mournfully in the chorus. For the last verse the lights went down and he sang in a very troubled voice and the others looked at one another as if in amazement. At the last line the band made a terrific row, the tambourines and bones ditto and the end men stepping forward.[14] Then there was a cats chorus by the nondescript end men, very amusing in which they sang like cats and then did a fight. The first item of the 2nd part was a performance on various musical instruments by these same men. They played Church bells on bells, on the concertina ('The Blue Bells of Scotland' with one hand), the hautboy, tin whistle, etc. One of them pretended to be very simple and the other addressed him as 'Charley'. They asked each other riddles and Charley was told that 'going to Church was affecting fire insurance for the next world'. Next was a sketch. A nigger in white clothes ditto hat and stick and bent with age came in and told of his troubles with his wife Sue. Then he danced and lime light was thrown so that his shadow appeared on the curtain. Then Sue came in and blew him up. She departs and then the old man sings. His voice is cracked with age and emotion. At the end of the verse – the chorus is sung by some[one] hid out of sight. The illusion is very good – the voices appear a long way off. Then the old woman comes in and weeps on his shoulder and forgives him. There is then some dancing and posturing and other fun by three niggers – very well done.

Now appeared the Bohee Bros. They first played in a banjo duet together. Then one sang 'A boys best friend is his mother.'[15] He had a sweet voice. Then the other gave variations of 'Home Sweet Home.' Exceedingly well he played this – I have never heard as good banjoists they get a lot of music out of it. The Bohee Bros are negro. Up to now they were in ordinary evening dress but now they come on as jockeys. In red satin – short trousers and caps. They sing a plaintive little song accompanying themselves on the banjo and then step dance. Lime light is thrown on them and it has a very pretty effect.

---

in 1869. The complex of buildings contained a lecture hall, library, newspaper room and class rooms. At the height of its popularity, it had over five thousand members.

[13] The minstrel troupe included corner and end men, interlocutor, as well as musicians, all of whom had discrete functions within the entertainment which consisted of humorous and ballad songs, parodies, riddles and sketches. See p. 44 for the Livermore Minstrels.

[14] 'She danced at the Alhambra' was a song also in the repertoire of the Mohawk Minstrels, and links with 'Ta ra ra doom de ay', a parody on the recently popular 'Ta ra ra boom de ay' (1890), an American song, taken up by Lottie Collins in 1891, and performed with an energetic dance at the Tivoli, London.

[15] The signature song of the Bohee Brothers, sung by George Bohee, written by Henry Miller and Joseph P. Skelly (1883). Their reputation rested upon their banjo playing. James Bohee was the banjoist.

A violinist named Paganina [sic] Redivius[16] should have been the next to appear but as he was ill he could not come on. I saw a little of another sketch *The Lady of the Lake* but could not stay to see it all. A good entertainment rather out of the ordinary way and the place well filled.

Monday May 16th
As I am coming home to night I see the little bear off Mount Street drinking a mug of beer and apparently enjoying it – it would not allow the man to take it from him. On Ilkeston Road was a big bear. It walked along on its two legs carrying a long pole as a soldier, dancing round its master (very quaint and rather pretty) and turned a somersault. It was fastened to its master by a long rope. Another man (they looked like Italians) went round with a hat.

Tuesday June 7th
In evening again go into Sneinton Market.[17] Here was one show. A fairly large tent … with a red curtain for an entrance but no pictures or platform and only a clown who did not announce the programme.[18] Inside filled chiefly with children. The performance took place at one end but there was no stage. Here was a table covered with a white and gold embroidered and once expensive cloth. On this were placed coloured balls, plates, etc. The clown who had a whitened face with mouth and eyes red wore a good dress of black shiny cloth ornamented (worked) with sunflowers and stalks and leaves. He had black stockings and the breeches to his knees and puffy and a big white collar. At one side was a curtain placed to form a retiring place. He made his entrance with a somersault and began telling a lot of jokes – rather clever ones – and tales. Then he got on some short stilts and walked about pretending to tumble and turning a somersault with them on and he came clean upright again. Also performed with hats. Then he twirled a mop about very funnily and his wife came on. She had worn a long cloak outside and appeared to have an ordinary dress on but she had been sometime behind and now had on a dress of white and brown silk, flesh tights, skirts to knees and bodice cut low. She was about 30 years old and still rather pretty. At a distance she would look very young without doubt. She stood on a large ball and walking it about juggled with various things small gold balls, large ones, plates on sticks, 3 on sticks in one hand all going round and two balls in other and knives and lighted fire brands. This was done well. Then she stood behind the table and juggled with three bottles. As the bottle came down she knocked it on the table. This was being done well when one of the bottles fell and [as] it broke into bits the performance was terminated – the bits were dangerous.[19] I had a little chat with them afterwards.

---

[16] Paganini Redivivus: i.e., Paganini brought back to life.

[17] Approximately one mile from Nottingham's Market Place, and a site used by itinerant shows of all types. It also accommodated the 'overflow' of rides and shows during the October Goose Fair.

[18] Many shows had an exterior stage, platform or parade, on which an abbreviated performance would be given to attract an audience inside. This was frequently decorated with paintings depicting (often fancifully) the entertainment within. Since it is not competing with any other performance, this show has dispensed with the outside attractions, and inside the lack of a stage and the curtain which is thrown up to facilitate 'wings' suggests that it might be a poor specimen, despite Race's claims for the owners' superiority. The performance is suggestive of both circus and music hall. The clown wears regulation costume: motifs such as sunflowers, roses, stripes and spots were customary.

[19] The 'perfect' performance was not always expected, and certainly not in the circus, where acrobats and equestrians in particular often had multiple attempts at a feat before they achieved it. This seems to have been an occasion where the performers 'cut their losses' before an undemanding juvenile audience.

The man said he was doing this for only a week and spoke as if he had been higher up in his profession. A very decent man. I also had a few words with his wife and she seemed superior. I raise my hat to her on leaving.

Friday July 15th
This morning in Burns Street saw a player of many instruments. On his head he wore a brass helmet round which were bells and on his back was a big drum which was played by the stick strapped to his arm. On this drum were a triangle and clappers worked by a cord attached to his boot and in his hands he carried a bag pipe. The music produced was far from melodious. The occasional jingling of the bells, and the tingle of the triangles, the clapping of the cymbals, and the beating of his drum coming joining [sic] on his bag pipes with good effect. He was an Italian and had two boys with him – one to play a clarionet and the other to collect. These men are rather rare now. It must have been 5 or 6 years since I last saw one.

Saturday September 17th
This evening to Sangers Circus[20] located in Meadow Road. The arrangements were the same as last time namely an enormous tent with the regulation ring in the middle, an oval shape ring outside it, the sixpenny seats on the flat round, and further back the rising seats of the higher prices. The tent was supported by a number of poles all round on each of which was a paraffin lamp and on the two centre and main poles were iron rings round which were hung a number of like lamps. This was the programme:

Mr Joseph Craston in white trousers military braided coat and round forage cap rides one horse then two and finally 3 horses, all bareback and standing up.

The Bros. Levardo dressed as clowns with enormous trousers perform on the 3 Horizontal Bars. Their business is for the greater part comic but they are very skilful nevertheless.

Two little twin ponies each ridden by a monkey go through some tricks such as kneeling down, sitting, lying as if dead, standing on tubs etc. The monkeys don't seem to enjoy themselves much however.

Mr Craston again. This time he has a jockeys cap and silk jacket on. He goes through the usual business including dancing on the horse, and running at him and getting straight up on his back. He also turns a somersault on him as his horse trots round alighting safely on his back.

'The Charming Emmaline' on the balancing trapeze. She is dressed wholly in pink and appears very good looking. The trapeze was hung from the top of the tent. On this she swings without holding, kneels and performs like feats. Also places a ladder on the bar and then stands on without any support.

---

[20] For circus biography and also menagerie personnel, particularly animal trainers, see John Turner, *Victorian Arena. A Dictionary of Circus Biography*, vols. 1 and 2 (Formby, Lancashire, 1995 and 2000), and the associated website http://www.circusbiography.co.uk. Circus history and a detailed description of the acts can be found in George Speaight, *A History of the Circus* (London, 1980).

Now is some comic business by two clowns but it is rather feeble. They engage too in a mock boxing glove contest.

Herr Parker with his thoroughbred horse 'Knight of the Garter.' His horse looks something like a race horse or hunter and he is turned out smart – high boots, light speckled trousers, gentlemans riding coat and tall hat - and the pair look very rich. His horse enters the outer ring first, makes the circle backing round. Inside they both bow and thus it goes the various feats. Such as marching very peculiarly, legs thrown far out, dancing to the music, etc. Its master dismounts at the finish and then the horse shoves him along by nudging him in his back with his head.

Race by three jockeys in racing colours.

Race by three boys on ponies. One of the riders was small and young and a long way behind the greater part of the race though he came in winner. It was evidently a made up affair as one could see the others pulling up. I remember the same thing happened last time.

Mdlles Topsy Violet and Rose on the *Corde de Elastic*. This was ordinary walking on the tight rope and dancing and falling and quick jumping on legs again on same. First with long balancing pole and then with flags. The 2 first each did this and then a wooden pole with rounded end was place in front of ones neck and on the back of the others. Then Rose a little girl stands on the middle of this and they all three go merrily along. They were in tights.

Vaulting by three gentlemen from a spring board over 2, 4, 7 and 11 horses. The head of the horses were however placed together so the distance was not so great. Also over a man seated on a horse. The clowns here created much fun.

Steeple chase by three ladies on horseback.

A troupe of lady acrobats who form pyramids and various other figures. There were four ladies and 3 girls I fancy – two of the former rather pretty all dressed in a white suit of knickerbockers and with a pale blue sash on. At the end of each figure they throw themselves into groups representing statuary.

Quadrille by four ladies and the like number of gentlemen on horseback. The former are dressed in ordinary ladies riding costume and the latter as field marshals with red coats and cocked hats. This was rather pretty.

The clown Holloway and his mule.[21] After some comic business youngsters from the audience are invited to try and ride the mule but they get thrown. The mule was so fat that there seemed nothing to get hold of. One big lad at last with very long arms managed to stick on for a while but he had to give away before long.

A black man and a white man each riding two horses astride have a race. They are dressed in a Roman costume and ride very quickly.

---

[21] Riding the bucking mule was a favourite means of inviting audience participation.

'The Beautiful Georgina (formerly Emmaline) in her thrilling aerial ascension.' She walks the tight wire placed very high up balancing herself with a Japanese umbrella. Also blindfolded and a sack over her head. She concluded by carrying a boy on her back right across. The youngster was left to himself to get back and so dropped into the net. A daring lad.

Mdlle Caroline[22] – the daring Equestrienne. Mademoiselle is getting rather on – to be more correct, very old. She is well painted wears an abundance of false brown hair and is dressed in a fetching costume of white and green including a [very] short and even more fetching skirt. She does the usual feats including that of jumping on a horse as he is trotting along.

Chariot (2) race. These chariots are wooden things very clumsy and make a rumbling sound. Each had a pair of ponies in the shafts, the drivers were dressed in Roman costume.

The Thiers Family on the Double Ladders. These, now dressed in red trousers with white bodices and sailor collars, appeared as acrobats before but there is now a gentleman with them who stands up the ladders to hold them. These ladders are placed together in different ways and the performers hang from them in different styles forming various combinations.

A cage containing 4 full grown lions is now drawn in. A man enters the cage and puts them through a performance for a minute or two. The lions go round him and also over a board but this was a poor performance when compared with what I saw at Wombwells.[23]

'The lovely sisters Annie and Ino' perform on the trapeze. Their performance is very clever including a lot of hanging by the teeth. One sister hung by the legs from the trapeze and held the other by a belt attached to a cord hanging from her mouth – then she swings her round and round. They had a very curious contrivance for passing from one trapeze to another. Attached to the top was a wire ladder, which would not have been seen but for the lights shining on it and by this they went along their feet in the [straps]. This gave an appearance of walking on the ceiling.

The last item was Prof. Clarks 4 performing elephants. This [sic] pretends to be lame, walking round with their feet drooping down, round on one another, sat on tubs, etc. A clever performance from such monster animals.

Sangers Circus is well worth a visit and I enjoyed seeing it.

---

[22] If this is the original Mme Caroline she would indeed be rather long in the tooth, since Caroline Mellilo had been performing since at least the 1840s, when the Duke of Wellington made several visits to see her!
[23] Wombwell's Menagerie, where there were displays of 'animal training'. See J. L. Middlemiss, *A Zoo on Wheels: Bostock and Wombwell's Menagerie* (Winshill, 1987).

Monday September 19th

This dinner time go down to Sangers field and watch the formation of the procession.[24] Most of the caravans were harnessed when I got down about quarter past twelve and the horses were ready who were ridden in by the various characters. The horse tent was a long oblong one with the horses down each side, at one end was a waggon and a lot of clothes on it and on this the men dressed. At a little after half past twelve a bell went and all the men trouped out falling in as they arrived in the lane outside. I saw the lion get in the car. The cage containing them was brought under it and a man went in and got hold of the lion by a chain brought it out and left. It walked up an inclined plane to its place and seated itself as coolly as you could wish there. It was waiting to go out, you could see, before the man fetched it and as it went up the lane it dragged its chain loose so it could have jumped down had it so wished.

This was the procession.

Man on horseback dressed as Russian with crown (on top of which was a little cross) on

Large gilded band carriage drawn by 10 horses (2x2)

Musicians in coloured uniform and gold cardboard hats

18 men riding on horseback. These like nearly all the men in the procession were dressed as Spaniards … The former of gold paper, the latter like a Scotch bonnet with crease down middle

Little boy standing up on last of 6 ponies who were 2x2

2 blackmen each standing on last of 2 horses of 6 (2x2)

2 chariots, heavy rumbling things drawn by 2 ponies each

4 large elephants, 3 ridden by men

Man on horseback

3 camels

Spanish gent riding

8 ladies riding. Some of these were the acrobats in the performance and I recognised Mdlls Topsy and Violet. Two or three were decidedly good looking one though painted especially so

1 black woman riding on last of 2 horses

9 Spanish riders

Band (10) on horseback. These were dressed as Turks with blue coats and red trousers and tasselled caps.

Now some caravans drawn by 2 horses each and containing animals

Caravan (this drawn by 10 ponies) containing some dogs

2 monkeys and a crocodile in glass case

2 kangaroos

3 ostriches? other birds like big ducks (2)

Deer and 2 smaller animals

4 animals something like goats

2 bears and man sitting inside with them

3 lions and man in military dress seated inside smoking a cigarette

Closed caravan drawn by 4 horses

Open carriage on springs drawn by 4 cream ponies with red harness. Two men

---

[24] For Race's fascination with watching and recording parades, see Ann Featherstone, "'There is a peep-show in the market": gazing at/in the journals of Sydney Race', *Early Popular Visual Culture*, 3:1 (2005), 43–57.

HENSON & CO., PHOTOGRAPHERS.

ALBERT HALL, NOTTINGHAM.

(Destroyed by Fire April 22nd, 1906.   This Photo was taken April 18th, 1906.

Figure 3. Albert Hall, Nottingham, 1906

(one in livery and other as Spaniard on box seat) and a lady inside with cocked hat on

Large gilded caravan drawn by 9 horses (3x3) round which seated 6 men. On the top a girl (rather pretty) dressed as Britannia. At her feet the aforesaid full grown and whiskered lion. Over him stands a man in military dress with helmet and plumes and drawn sword.

Great high caravan drawn by 9 horses round which are seated 8 or 9 men one at the very top.

This was the procession and a great length it was.

Thursday September 21st

This evening go to Mr Buxtons Diorama and Neapolitan Choir in the Albert Hall.[25] He is a Nottingham man and has only been in this line a few months though they performed privately before. For the first part of the programme the choir all sat round in circle. The older girls (4) and the pianist were in ordinary dress though of a fanciful design and cloth the other girls, younger, were in 'baby' costume (dresses without waists and big white bonnets). The young men were in black coats open waistcoats, knickerbocker trousers and light blue stockings. The singing was very fair. Little Gerty sang 'Pickaboo' nicely and two of the others gave a song and dance well. There was a cornet solo and also instrumental pieces.

The views were of Switzerland and Italy, most[ly] photographs and described by Mrs Buxton, a very good looking lady. She however had not much to say about them and more could have been made of them. I noticed the pianist Miss Hadden whom I had seen play before and in the town often: a pleasant girl. Some views of the Crucifixion, Last Supper, etc were also thrown on the screen and during them Miss Buxton sang 'He was despised.'[26] There were also charming scenes representing the Rock of Ages at sea to which clung some people, the Choir singing the hymn of that name behind meanwhile.[27] A very fair entertainment though Mr Taylor, my music master, thought the singing poor. There was also a comic sketch by Mr Buxton junr. He was made up in old clothes and had a funny tale to tell. Every now and then he would stop in the middle of a sentence to say 'how do you like my flower' pointing to an enormous button hole, which made the people laugh heartily.

[October]
Wednesday before the Fair
Most of the shows had come in and were arranging when I went down tonight. Observed the method of fastening the uprights of the sides to the ground. At the bottom of the pole was an iron [*word missing*] and through the part at the bottom where are the dotted lines was a hole and a big nail would be placed through it to

---

[25] The diorama made its first appearance in London in September 1823. Invented by the Frenchman Louis Daguerre, it displayed, through massive painted landscapes onto which and through which light was projected, the illusion of a three-dimensional image. Poetry and music often accompanied the visual display which grew in sophistication throughout the century. See Stephan Oettermann, *The Panorama: History of a Mass Medium* (New York, 1997). Nottingham's Albert Hall, originally designed as a temperance hall, was opened in 1876 as a general purpose venue. Built in the Gothic style, it had a capacity of around 3,000 and hosted a variety of entertainments from tableaux vivants, to Louis Tussaud's 'All the World in Wax', as well as choral and musical entertainments.
[26] Aria from Handel's 'Messiah'.
[27] 'Rock of Ages, cleft for me', popular hymn, words by Augustus Toplady.

secure the pole to the ground. Walls[28] came in last night. Noticed the living carriage they had. It was very long and stood on short wheels so that it was but 2 or 3 feet from the ground. In the window were some plants and nice and snug did the van look.

Thursday October 6th

Have no holiday to day but am down in the fair early at night having also had a look round at dinner time. First go in and see Polly O'Gracious the Irish Fat Child. The front of this show was painted to represent a cottage with windows doors thatched roof, etc all complete and with pigs and beehives in front. Polly was a mulatto and shown by her mother a negress. She had an ordinary sized face but arms were thick and she was big about the shoulders but had or appeared to have a big belly which gave her a large appearance. She was dressed in ordinary clothes and after her mother had told us her history sang us a verse of 'Annie Rooney' and did a shuffle called dancing. Also she was asked to point out the gentleman she liked best in the crowd and she singles me out for that honour though I did not appear to appreciate the favour.[29]

Next go in Birchs American Midgets, Major and Madame Mite. They were about 4 feet high I should say and looked 21 or so old. The woman had some [*word missing*] features and had an older look than the man who was rather pudgy. They sang 'All very fine Maye' after being described and then their daughter was brought out. She was about 6 years old they said and was a little less in size than they. When her father had hold of her hand she looked intelligent but afterwards a very vacant stare came into her face. The Major and Mrs were afterwards driven round in a very small cab drawn by a little pony and driven by a small boy in coachmans dress and tall hat. This was quite a nobby turn out and was said to have been presented to them by Barnam [sic] by whom they were exhibited a few years back.[30]

Now go into Johnsons Circus the same which was here last year but smartened up a lot and performers increased. Outside were 2 gymnasts, 2 clowns, a man masquerading in womans dress and who kicked high at hats held by clown now and then, 3 girls in tights and the mother of the family in short skirts who danced with the rest and also one or two other men. The performance inside was commenced by a girl walking on the tight rope. She performed with a pole dancing running jumping lying down etc on the rope and also did the same feats without the balance. Next a boy on the swinging rings, a clever performer. Then somersaulting by the Company and a performance by the aforesaid masquerader. He seemed to have no bones in his body and twisted himself into all sorts of shapes, with his legs over his head and round it, etc. The entertainment was concluded by some foolery of the clown with a pony who wouldn't jump over a stick three times for one though he would for another and so on but they did not treat him very kindly at all. The clowning on most of the performance was good, the old joke about chalking the rope underneath to prevent the lady falling up being of course brought on.

---

[28] Wall's Ghost Show, a stalwart of the Goose Fair, vast and spectacular, and always located at the bottom of Market Street. For a history of the ghost show see John Phillips, *The Ghost! the Ghost!! the Ghost!!!* (London, 1998) and Kevin Scrivens and Stephen Smith, *The Travelling Cinematograph Show* (Tweedale, 1999).

[29] See Robert Bogdan, *Freak Show. Presenting Human Oddities for Amusement and Profit* (Chicago and London, 1988) for a solid perspective on the exhibition of 'human oddities', although concentrating on the American fairground.

[30] Nobby: smart. Barnam: P. T. Barnum, the great American showman who did indeed recruit British human 'freaks of nature' for his American Museum and circus.

Last of all went into Parkers Ghost Show. This does not seem to be in a very prosperous condition. I fancy Mr Parker must be dead, he looked very ill last time he was here. The performance is not so good as it was and the performers are old and the dresses older. Besides a black man of the stage and the usual men were three dames, old, especially one in tights, and not particularly good looking. The first part was *The Stowaway* which I have seen and described before. In the next a master engages a servant a black man to mind the house and the latter has some adventures. Embraces his master for a maid who had appeared ghostly like, hits him for a ghost who had also mysteriously appeared, etc. The transformation scene was rather poor there being only two or three pictures, one representing Father Christmas in the snow, on which coloured lights were thrown.[31]

Friday [October 7th]
First go in 'Mexy' the American Shooting Codys Show. 'Mexy' who was a lady of about 30 or so, still retaining much of her good looks, and dressed in a red arrangement with like coloured tights and a wide hat shot at little square glasses stuck on a board some dozen or so feet away. This she did in various positions, backwards with a looking glass, bending back, leaning over a chair, etc. Also did the same feats when the board was on the swing. She was a clever shot in this line and only made one miss. As the admission was only a penny (!) 'Mexy' came round for a little more 'encouragement' a cheeky piece of business I thought.[32]

Next into 'Ferrari Boscoes' or Pearsons Menagerie also here last year. The animals were – in a cage to your left – 2 big bears in one compartment. And a hybrid and Canadian wolf together in the other compartment. In the cage in the centre a lion and the remaining cage 3 wolves in one compartment and a dog and 3 monkies in the remaining portion. A man first entered the bears den made them walk round and round and also jump over a board. Also one of them took some lumps of sugar from his mouth. A little girl next entered the wolves (3) den and made them run round and round the cage and also jump over a board. One of these animals was a very tame but poorly spirited one. Then the woman whom I saw last year, entered the lions den. She had a lot of trouble to get in. He snarled a lot and dashed at the door but at last she managed it and chases round and round a man firing a pistol etc. This represented a 'lion hunt'. After she had got out the lion got very savage running at the bars and showing his teeth. He was said to have attacked her a few weeks ago and to have torn her shoulder a lot at the time.[33]

Now into Radford and Chappells Ghost Show. The performers outside are numerous, 2 men in armour, 2 clowns, 2 little girls in tights and 2 older girls and 2 women in ordinary dress. These 2 girls I remember when they were little dots now they are quite tall, one of them rather pretty but the other not so good looking as she was. Then there's the old clown, just the same but he is getting old. It's funny how you remember these people and take an interest in them. The show is fairly well fitted

---

[31] See Phillips, and Scrivens and Smith above. Also Vanessa Toulmin, 'The Cinematograph at the Goose Fair, 1896–1911' in Alan Burton and Laraine Porter (eds.) *The Showman, the Spectacle and the Two-Minute Silence. Performing British Cinema Before 1930* (Trowbridge, 2001), pp. 76–86.

[32] The Wild West show was a fairground favourite in the latter decades of the 19th century. The reputation and tours of Buffalo Bill (from 1887 until 1904) enhanced the popularity of sharp shooters such 'Mexy'. The adoption of the name 'Cody' added authenticity. See the National Fairground Archive's essay on Wild West Shows – http://www.shef.ac.uk/nfa

[33] A rare description of the interior of a fairground menagerie, including the arrangement of the cages, and of the animal trainer, working the wolves and bears in the cage. See below, also, Race's description of Day's Menagerie, the cages and the animal trainer.

up and performance very decent. First a man comes on and as he tells a tale you see the pictures come. There is a duel. The death of one, the weeping woman, and the angels over her. This was called 'At the Swords Point or a Sisters Honour'. Next the old clown does some fooling – places a box on a pedestal opens it and there is a head. Takes the box away and the head still rests on the chair. Takes this away and the head remains in space talking in a faint voice. A pretty transformation scene to conclude. [34]

Saturday [October 8th]

Go down in the afternoon and have a look at the round abouts. George Lodge, one of my playmates in the old times, a pleasant fellow now – wander about with him a while and then we go in Days Menagerie. This was in Sneinton Market last year but one though it seems to have changed hands since. A Frenchy looking man performed with the animals, his name was Martina Bartlett. There were 5 caravans, 2 on each side and one in the middle filled as follows.

No 1 to your left. 6 parrots in separate cages and 2 hawks, 2 swan like birds (pelicans?). No 2 cages jackal, small zebu animal,[35] middle compartment, 4 monkies and 2 hounds, end compartment, two monkies together, one ditto by himself, and a foreign pig, and 2 parrots. No 3 car in middle lion and lioness together and splendid full grown lion to himself. No 4 big sheep and wolf. Another compartment of same 2 wolves. No 5 2 lions and hyena (latter alone). No 6 divided into 2 compartments each of which contained 2 bears. There were also 2 camels near entrance.

Bartlett first entered No 5 caravan and performed with the 2 lions there. They were the tamest I have ever seen and allowed him to fondle them and place them about anywhere. One of them jumped over a board and his companion being lazy was lifted over the same. Also they kissed him and sat together on a chair. He finished up by putting his face inside of the lions jaws which latter he did not hold in any way. Then he entered the lions den. The animal had been growling a lot and it took some time before Bartlett could get in. The lion roared and snarled at him and had to be driven into a corner with red hot bars so that the tamer could get in. Then he was driven all round the cage at a big rate, Bartlett firing a revolver several times. At last he was brought to bay in a corner. The performer got out of the cage by a quick movement but the lion rushed at the door lashing about. A man by me said that yesterday the lion came within an inch of the mans hand and which would have dragged him down had he caught him. I noticed that his hair was cut close today whereas yesterday and Thursday he had worn it quite long onto his shoulder. He carried a big club and a dagger at his belt to go in this den though he had entered the other without anything. This performance was quite genuine and I have never seen a lion so fierce before. It showed as the man said 'the difference between lions as was brought up from cubs and a lion as came out of the Forests of Africa.'

Afterwards go in a performing bird and hare show. Some little green coloured birds do some pretty tricks. One walks a tight rope, each time it reaches the middle pretending to lose its balance and flutters for a while, and another climbs some ladders and go down a few steps and back etc. at its masters command. One bird is clothed in a black gown and stuck on a pillar. Another one then walks up to a cannon and by an arrangement lets it off at the first. This represented the Death of a Deserter.

---

[34] The outside show reveals the showman's method of attracting an audience with performers either wearing exotic costumes or, in the case of the women, displaying their natural attractions. The clown, like the negro, was a staple performer on the parade. See Phillips, *The Ghost!* and Scrivens and Smith, *Travelling Cinematograph Show* above.

[35] A humped domestic ox.

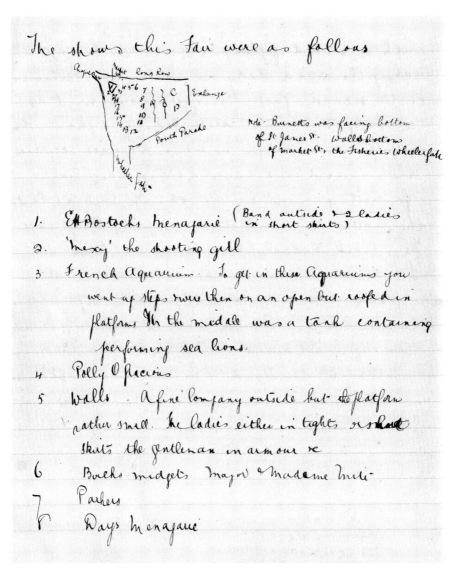

The shows this Fair were as follows

1. E H Bostocks Menajarie (Band outside & 2 ladies in short skirts)
2. 'mexy' the shooting gill
3. French Aquarium. To get in these Aquariums you went up steps aww then on an open but roofed in platform In the medall was a tank containing performing sea lions.
4. Polly O Pracious
5. Walls. A fine Company outside but the platform rather small. the ladies either in tights or short skirts the gentleman in armour &c
6. Bochs midgets Major & Madame Miti-
7. Parkers
8. Days Menagarie

Figure 4. Page from Sydney Race's journal, 1892, showing his sketch plan of the Goose Fair and numbered list of rides and shows

Then a very lanky and lean hare is brought out and gives us a solo on a tambourine held up for him to rap by his master. He also gives a few raps for the ladies, the gentlemen but rushes to do so for the game keeper. The performance is closed by a little pony telling us by tapping the ground with his feet the number of days in a week, etc. He also answers various questions by shaking his head and points out the girl that loves jam, the man that loves his whisky, etc. and also the biggest rogue in the Company – his master.

Last of all the shows I visit is Walls.[36] Again is the front most gorgeous, the inside very neat and the whole performance of the best. The drop scene represented the raising of a village maypole. A little harmonium accompanies the acts. The glass was unusually large and the appearances etc were excellently managed. The usual story for the first part. A man with a sword fighting a shadow, kills it and the angels bearing the dead body away at the conclusion. In the second part 2 niggers come on, sing a song but are disturbed by a ghost who hits first one and then another. At each occurrence the injured one rows at his neighbour for hitting him as he thinks, but at last the ghost, in a white sheet and a skull, lays into them both heavily and at the same time. The transformation scene was unusually pretty there being a number of pictures representing castles and forest scenes which rolled up in turn after coloured lights had been thrown on them and disclosed at last a waterfall. The water of which was rolling over and over and very nice it looked.[37]

The shows this Fair were as follows
Note: Burnetts[38] was facing bottom of St James St. Walls at bottom of Market St, the Fisheries, Wheelergate

1   E H Bostocks Menagerie (Band outside and 2 ladies in short skirts)
2   'Mexy' the shooting girl
3   French Aquarium. To get in these Aquariums you went up steps and were then on an open but roofed in platform. In the middle was a tank containing per-forming sea lions
4   Polly O'Gracious
5   Walls. A fine company outside but the platform rather small. The ladies either in tights or short skirts the gentleman in armour, etc.
6   Birchs Midgets, Major and Madame Mite
7   Parkers [Ghost Show]
8   Days Menagerie
9   Performing birds and hares
10   A Fisheries exhibition
11   Fine art gallery[39]
12   French aquarium
13   Fisheries exhibition (Burwoods)
14   Swimming Exhibition

---

[36] See p.18.
[37] A rare and detailed description of a ghost show performance.
[38] Professor Burnett's Military Academy was a regular feature of the Goose Fair.
[39] The Fine Art Gallery may have been an exhibition of tableaux vivants or waxwork. See Kathryn A. Hoffmann, 'Sleeping Beauties in the Fairground. The Spitzner, Pedley and Chemisé exhibits' in *Early Popular Visual Culture* 4:2 (2006), 139–159. This old-fashioned roundabout, known as a 'dobby', had a nostalgic appeal for Race, amongst the noisy new steam-driven rides. See Fred Fried, *A Pictorial History of the Carousel* (New York, 1964).

15   "   "
16 Johnsons Circus
17 Radford and Chappells Ghost Show
18 Pearson or Ferrarie Boscoes menagerie
19 Fine art gallery
20 Burnetts military academy

Next in the Market place to the shows were (A) 2 switchbacks lighted by electricity, one galloping horse (elaborate). Then 4 rows of bazaars (B). (C) The Fish stalls and the remaining portion of the market. (D) was occupied by a row of swing boats, a sea on dry land roundabouts (ships going round) and 2 rather common galloping horse roundabouts. Then the vacant ground in Wheeler Gate was filled with shooting galleries and in the Improved Area were, on the ground to your left going up – a rolley polley, a maypole and 3 roundabouts horses, a sea saw and one switchback horse. In the middle portion formed by the roads, 2 switchbacks, 2 galloping horses, 'Venice' roundabout, a rolley polley and 2 swinging boats.

These rolley polleys were large circular platforms fixed to an arrangement in their centre underneath. On this they revolved very much after the manner of a ship tossed on fierce waves. The roundabouts were all most gorgeously decorated with gold paint and small glasses and illuminated by big globes containing the electric light or fanciful patterns of gas lights. The switchbacks were of cars driven round from the centre going round up and down …[40]

The maypole was a number of cars fashioned like swans suspended by iron girders from the top of an iron pole. The pole revolved and the cars were carried round far out. 'Venice' was a very elaborate and highly decorated roundabout. The cars in this case were shaped like gondolas and not only went round up and down, switchback wise, but also rocked from side to side! Inside the gondolas was all lined with plush too.

All down these streets and Long Row and all round the Market were ice creams sellers, cocoa nut galleries, shooting galleries, various games of chance, toy fruit and sweet stalls, phonographs, trial of strength machines, galvanic batteries and the like. These phonographs were new things. Attached to a little centre machine were a number of tubs each having a little bulb at the end to fit into the ear. Then the proprietor placed a little flat circular plate on the machine and made it to revolve by a handle. I had a go at one where you held a cup shaped thing to your ear but thought it a fraud. You could only hear the voice occasionally and then very indistinct. Still this may have [been] owing partly to the great noise around.[41]

Went into Sneinton Market too. Here was a large number of roundabouts also a Fine Art Gallery and a show of performing birds and monkeys. As this latter was not filling well I did not wait to see the performance. Also here was a very old fashioned roundabout. A rather small one, with rather small and old horses and one or two cars. In the middle ran a pony harnessed to the top of the affair, on a soft peat bed pulling the thing round. Of course it did not take much work when once started. I notice the method of stopping him. The master rather an old man who each time ground out 'Ta raa' on a small barrel organ when he though the children had had

---

[40] A clear indication that rides rather than shows were increasingly dominating the fair. For detail on these rides see David Braithwaite, *Fairground Architecture* (2nd rev. ed.) (London, 1976).
[41] Always conscious of the attraction of new technology, showmen offered novelties (here a variant on the Edison phonograph) as fairground attractions. Race mentions the 'noise' at the Fair frequently, especially where it prevents him from following the plot of a play. See p.31.

enough patted the pony as he went past him and immediately the little animal slowed down, coming at last to a stand still. And a very fat and jolly pony he looked and seemed to like the business.

Wednesday October 12th
To Hamiltons entertainment at the Albert Hall. The pictures I had all seen before, consequently they were rather stale. Some however were very pretty notably a View of Rome illuminated on Easter Sunday, Venice, and some Hindoo scenes. All these scenes appear to be well painted and some have cost a large amount to produce. A new feature of the entertainment was a complete minstrel performance lasting nearly an hour. About 7 blacked men, 5 mulattos and 3 young ladies after mentioned sat round in a half circle and detailed the usual jokes and songs. Some of the songs were well sung but the jokes were very old and lacked the 'go' you get at Livermores. Then afterwards was a performance by 2 blacked men of knocking hats down held high up, and various curious gymnastic feats. This rather clever. Also a skipping rope dance by Miss Verne. She was dressed in black tights but being slim did not look well. And a performance by The Musical Serenards, a man with face blacked and two young girls dressed in a loose blue dress. The man played the harp and the girls performed on the guitar, mandoline, dulcimer etc. Also one sang a song in a rather forced and unnatural manner after a music hall style.[42]

The entertainment was not so good as I have seen it and I did not wait to see it finish having had then [sic] from half past seven to ten.

Saturday October 22nd
Tonight go in and see a show 'the greatest curiosity on earth, a child with 2 heads 4 legs and arms and one body' in a shop in High Street. An organ was playing to attract peoples attention, a man was playing a kettle drum noisily and another was pointing out the picture representing the curiosity and inviting people in. But it turned out a fraud as I expected. On a platform was arranged a representation of the front of a house with curtain for the doorway and after the woman has described the exhibit, she drew this curtain aside, whipped a cloth off a large bottle like globe and there was the 'great curiosity' – preserved! A child with 2 heads etc as described which could never have lived, shrivelled up and bottled in spirits. We were given the pleasure of walking round and viewing if from all sides, but what a sell, the picture on the window showed 'the curiosity' to be living and walking about before an admiring audience.[43]

Tuesday December 27th
Have a holiday again to day, as all the shops and warehouses in the town are closed.
In the morning go down to the Mechanics' and then on to Sneinton Market. There are no shows here but I find one in a shop in Goose Gate.[44] … then to Hamiltons. This is

---

[42] Hamilton's 'Excursions', a diorama entertainment, explored entire continents and countries, and included an elaborate accompanying musical and vocal entertainment. Miss Verne's 'skipping rope dance' was a popular music hall and variety turn.

[43] The first mention in the journals of 'shop shows', a form of urban entertainment in which Race appears very interested (see his 'Shop Shows' article for the *Nottingham Argus*, below, p. 157). This shop, in High Street, was close to the city centre and would have been a vacant or, given the improvements taking place in Nottingham at the time, a condemned property, available at a very low rent. The 'greatest curiosity on earth' – a baby in a bottle – is a typical exhibit. See Vanessa Toulmin, '"Curios Things in Curios Places": Temporary Exhibition Venues in the Victorian and Edwardian Entertainment Environment,' *Early Popular Visual Culture*. 4: 2 (2006), 113–137.

[44] Race returns to this – see entry for Saturday December 31st below.

not the same Company as was here before. The scenes I had not seen before and were very good indeed. The chief part of the programme was taken up by the Half Moon Minstrels. These give a performance in the orthodox style of songs jokes etc. and then after more pictures wind up the entertainment by sketches, acrobating, etc. In one of these a man came on four times each in a different lady's dress and looked the character to a T. Then there was a performance by the Musical Lindsays who dressed as clowns played on various instruments. The novelty of the evening however was a 'Baldwin Cat.'[45] An ordinary pussy who climbed up a rope to the top of the building and then swung on to a parachute which was let go and down it came, being caught on a pole before it reached the ground...

Saturday December 31st
At night go down town with Will and into that show in Goosegate. Outside and inside was very dirty as were all connected with the show. A small organ was played to attract folks and the strong man who called himself 'Samson the Conqueror of all strong men' invited the people in with a wonderful account of the things to be shown. On a small platform inside stood Zaeo the strong lady – a buxom young lady, rather dirty both in face and clothes, of 20 or so dressed in flesh coloured tights, trunks of blue and jacket of white linen. After some time the performance commenced. The young lady put a leather strap, at the end of which was a hook, into her mouth and with this lifted big weights, a dumbbell etc. from the floor. The strong man did various exercises with the dumbbell, etc. the concluding feat being for Zaeo to lift up and swing about a barrel said to be filled with weights and stones. We were not allowed to test the weights though they appeared heavy so the performance was rather a swindle particularly as they made a collection inside.

Here endeth 1892.

1893

Saturday April 29th
Arnold[46]
After a wash go down town and into Andertons and Haslams Show.[47] This A[nderton] is the Conjuror but now he does not perform unless the business is slack. Outside there was brought a snake in a box which was got out with much by play and firing of pistols, etc. Inside were cages as follows

1	Conjuring carriage
2	Large bearded lion
3	2 lionesses
4	3 wolves and a bear

---

[45] Named after Professor Baldwin, the balloonist and parachutist, of the 1880s.
[46] Approximately three miles from the centre of Nottingham.
[47] Anderton and Haslam's Royal No. 1 Menagerie. 'Professor Anderton, the King of Wizards' had a touring magic show, before expanding into the menagerie business, which he ran with his sons and daughters.

And along in front of the cages were hung 4 parrots (a dove with one) in cages.

One of the Andertons dressed in Buffalo Bill style entered the wolves den and put them through a jumping performance and also gave a representation of a bear hunt accompanied with much firing of a revolver. Red Hot irons were then brought up to the lionesses den and a Negro quickly entering put them through a short performance. Rather risky this apparently.

Now into Manders.[48] Inside were 5 caravans all very neatly and well got up. Before each hung a large well painted picture. This rolled up when the groups inside were described. The figures were very well dressed and most of them moved though in a very mechanical way. Caravan No. 1 represented The Death of Napoleon Bonaparte, in No. 2 were figures of monstrosities, No. 3, the Queen, Royal Family, and other great personages. Also some mechanical figures. No. 4 Heads of Criminals and Eminent Men and moving figures of Mephistopheles and Negro Flute Player and in No. 5 a group representing Solomon giving judgement over the child claimed by 2 women each as her own. All these pictures and waxwork groups are fully described in a catalogue I bought in the show.

Tuesday

Have the afternoon holiday so leisurely walk down town. Go into the 'Alligator' Show. It was formed of a large caravan in the middle of which was a raised stand. In it, the spectator protected by an iron guard, lay a large crocodile and 3 or 4 smaller ones. A man dressed in sailor costume made them by the aid of a stick open their mouths to show their teeth and he also brought one of the small ones out. The caravan was heated by a stove and was very hot. Admission 1d. Also go into the Waxworks show. You did not pass over a stage to get inside, the caravans being ranged round in a square.[49] All round, seen through a peep glass, were miserable paintings or rather daubs representing some scene in Deeming's, the murderer's, career.[50] At the far end were 3 dimly lighted little cells in one of which Deeming (in wax) was shown digging a grave for a victim and in another shaving off his moustache in prison. Here was also a wax figure of the 'human frog' a cripple with body fashioned somewhat after the manner of a frog...

Thursday July 6th

A shop in the Long Row has lately been taken by the people who exhibited 'The Siamese Twins' fraud in High Street.[51] They have shown now

1   An armless young lady who writes etc with her toes. Also her baby, who is guess contained in a glass bottle
2   The aforesaid twins
3   General Dot – a midget
4   A performing seal with A Fine Art Gallery
5   Miss Flora Bell and her trained dog Shmeider

---

[48] For waxworks history, see Pamela Pilbeam, *Madame Tussaud and the History of Waxworks* (London, 2003) and Paul Braithwaite, 'The rise of waxwork shows: a short history,' *Living Pictures: Journal of the Popular and Projected Image before 1914* (1:2) (2001), 36–58.

[49] Instead of mounting the outside platform, here the entrance must have been between the caravans.

[50] Born in Leicestershire, Frederick Deeming was a nineteenth-century villain of sensational proportions, committing theft, perjury, fraud, bigamy as well as murder, under at least 20 aliases.

[51] See page 24 and 158.

Figure 5. General view of the Goose Fair, 1911, across the Market Square to Long Row, and showing the 'show row' (which includes Kemp's Theatre Unique)

I have not been in to see any of these.

Wednesday August 23ʳᵈ

With Will and W. Whittaker to the Nottingham Exhibition now being held in the Victoria Hall Talbot Street.[52] The interior is lit by the electric light worked by two of our Trent gas engines and there is a fair display of things. The blind are at work making mats and reading and a good band played during the evening. Then Bingley Shaw played on the tubular Church Bells and a number of little boys and girls sang snatches of popular songs. The smaller hall was made up to represent Old Nottingham but it was a poor representation. We had much fun here chaffing the girl stall holders. There was an Edisons Phonograph on view[53] and for 2d you could hear a piece. I had 'The Charge of the Light Brigade' put on for me. The voice was very distinct; it is a marvellous invention.

Thursday October 5ᵗʰ

Goose Fair is once more with us. The Shows this year are more numerous than last but the quality is not so good. Most of them came in yesterday – Walls was fixed when I came through in the morning but Wombwells did not arrive till today. They are as follows

0	Wombwells (ex Bostocks)
1	Polly O'Gracious – the fat girl
2	Walls – 'the only Walls', 'the great Walls'
3	Testos Marionettes[54]
4	Parkers Ghost Show. Norman & Kaspers, late Kaspers
5	Sedgewicks Menagerie
6	Chipperfields Performing dogs
7	Fine Art Gallery
8	Ferrari's Performing Monkeys
9	Holloways Swimming Exhibition (a lady)
10	Burnetts Military Academy
11	Paynes Fine Art Gallery
12	Fisheries Exhibition
13	Crocodiles etc (French Aquarium as described before)
14	Radford & Chappells Ghost [Show]
15	Biddalls Menagerie
16	Aymes Mechanical Exhibition
17	Major & Madam Mite
18	Ashmores Fine Art Gallery
19	Another Fine Art Gallery

– and on the waste ground in Wheeler Gate

20	Johnsons Circus
21	a Whale Exhibition

---

[52] The Victoria Hall, a large central venue, was frequently used for exhibitions and circuses (see below p. 153). The Nottingham Exhibition was a combination of stands displaying the products of local businesses and industries, along with musical entertainments and other novelties.

[53] This was probably a licensed Edison show.

[54] For a detailed history of marionette shows, see John McCormick, *The Victorian Marionette Theatre* (Iowa City, 2004).

22   Stuarts Exhibition of Boxing[55]
– and in King Street
23   Another whale[56]

The Corporation this year have not erected any bazaars but have filled the space with roundabouts as follows:

1   A gondola switchback. In this the boats rocked from side to side.
2   Ditto but without the rocking
3 & 4 Two car switchbacks
5, 6   Two horse switchbacks. All the above are most gorgeous and lit by the Electric Light
7, 8, 9 Three ordinary jumping horse roundabouts
10   A sea on dry land. These are little ships which rock up and down as they go round
12   A long line of swings
13   A razzle dazzle. A long circular platform which goes round with a funny 'boat in a rough sea' motion.

Tonight I go in Radford and Chappells Ghost. On the outside were several men in pirate costumes, one as a clown and another as a nigger making much fun by helping the girls up on to the platform etc and also ladies. Two of the last – somewhat old – were dressed in long pink 'baby' costume with big hats. Inside was performed the story of Uncle Tom who is lashed by his master, comforted by white robed angels, forgives his persecutor when the latter is dying, etc.[57] Part 2 is the unusual performance of the nigger [who] endeavoured to hit and also embrace the Ghost each time coming in contact with his master instead and then a stool is brought on and a box placed on top of it. Then a head appears in the box and afterward on the stool alone and also a young lady and one of the above pink dressed ones comes in and dances and a flame plays all round her. The performance was concluded with a transformation scene in which different coloured lights were thrown by means of a lantern in front.

     Next go into Testo's Marionettes. First was performed the plays of the *Babes in the Wood* by some well managed puppets. Then clown pantaloon and policemen have some fun and clown pulls policeman's shirt out behind. Lastly is a transformation scene. [58]

Friday
This evening go into Walls Ghost Show. This certainly is the A1 of the shows in the Fair. The front is a gorgeous arrangement of gold and other colours and everything is most clean and well arranged. Inside all lined with green baize. Besides a first class

---

[55] For boxing shows, see Vanessa Toulmin, *A Fair Fight. An Illustrated Review of Boxing on British Fairgrounds* (Oldham, 1999).
[56] Over 15 feet long, the whale, which had been washed up in the Humber the previous year, was 'scientifically set up' during the day, and 'lighted up' at night. (*Nottingham Express*, 6 October 1893).
[57] The play is clearly a version of *Uncle Tom's Cabin*.
[58] Well-known plays, pantomimes and music hall acts were popular in marionette shows in the late nineteenth century. Although, by the 1850s, *The Babes in the Wood* was a pantomime in the legitimate theatre, in marionette shows it remained 'a folk drama', where it was part of the repertoire 'longer than any other piece', McCormick, *Victorian Marionette Theatre*, pp. 112–114.

organ to which the performers sing there is a brass band of 9 instrumentalists. Mr Wall who is a short and portly but pleasant little gentleman dressed in evening clothes I heard tell some men that he would have to take £80 before he began to take profits on the Fair. There are four ladies with the performance. Two somewhat old but well made have appeared this year in short skirts, ones hardly reaching to the knee and one of them I noticed once showing some lingerie as she was dancing. Then there is the daughter a girl of 12 or so of one of the above and also the other's sister. This last was dressed in a loose baby costume, but as she has a somewhat sour face, she always kept well behind for the singing. There are in addition of course a number of men, some dressed as niggers and some as cavaliers etc. Part I was a short tragedy as usual but the noise was too great to follow the piece well. Part II two niggers came on with tambourines then sang a song. At the end of each verse the ghost comes on and lays into them. At last they wait for him, apparently catch and struggle with him and as the lights go up we find them with a white sheet (really thrust in from behind), the covering of the ghost in their hands. Part III was a very beautiful transformation scene with pretty views of ruined castles and the line on which coloured lights were thrown ending in an extremely good waterfall.

As is usual with the Fair there has been the usual crush up the Beastmarket Hill. Here all the young would be swells of each sex congregate and go up and down in long rows. At intervals rushes occur and a great block is formed. The only drawback is that wicked policemen have a habit of throwing unruly persons out with violence. However it seems to be enjoyed by those in it and of course it gives an excellent opportunity to a fellow to help a young lady along and to catch her round the waist occasionally when in danger.[59]

Saturday afternoon

… At night I am down in the Mechanics' by six thirty intending to have a few minutes there and then go on to Sneinton Market. However I had not been in long when a very heavy shower came on and lasted till quite 8 without intermission. Borrowing an umbrella I come home for my coat and am down in the Fair quickly though I cannot go to Sneinton.

First I go into Biddalls menagerie.[60] This is said to be its first visit, but I noticed Ferrari Boscoe about, and probably his menagerie has amalgamated with this one. There were six caravans, two to each side. The one to our right was divided into 6 compartments, containing 3 foxes (at least two appeared to be so, but I could not get a proper sight of them), 2 leopards and a kangaroo. Each of the next three had a lion, one of them being a bearded one. Then the next had 3 large brown bears in it and the next was divided as follows

cockatoos	monkeys	monkey
4 lion cubs		antelope

---

[59] The 'rushes', a carnivalesque ritual at Goose Fair, involved numbers of young people linking arms and 'rushing' up or down Beastmarket Hill. In itself it was inoffensive, but to the jeremiahs of Nottingham it was yet another example of the fair's corrupting influence. See Richard Iliffe and Wilfred Baguely, *Victorian Nottingham. A Story in Pictures. Volume 4. Goose Fair.* (Nottingham, 1972).
[60] For a history of the Biddall family, see Frances Brown, *Fairground Strollers and Showfolk.* (Taunton, 2001).

and in one compartment was a penguin and in the other a dog and live wolves. The lion cubs were little bigger than cats and very sportive. It was quite fun watching them play and they allowed one to stroke them which I did. A lady entered the lion in No 2 cage and made him go round and round and afterwards jump over a board. There was no spirit in the performance however. Afterwards a black man entered the big lions den. It was sometime before he could get in as the lion was savage and growled hard. When he got in he chased the animal round and round the cage and then got him in a corner. Then with an ordinary horse whip he lashed the King of the brute creation unmercifully for his previous bad behaviour. The lion growled a lot but did not touch the man. Someday without doubt he will have his revenge.

Then into Norman and Kaspers late Parkers Ghost Show which this year has a big swell who looks and speaks quite like a gentleman. He is dressed in ordinary costume sometimes with a soft hat and others with tall hat and frock coat. He played the kettle drum occasionally and directed the outside performance generally. Also there is a very pretty young lady of about 26 years old or so, the wife I take it of the above who is about the same age. On Thursday she was in a military costume with braided coat and round hat, on Friday she was in a baby costume and hat of pink and as she has golden hair and blue eyes this became her well. On Saturday she had a red plush dress on trimmed with gold braid. All her dresses were long but she stepped and marched nicely and though she pulled her face about a little when singing she was certainly very pretty and genteel. I also noticed another good looking and superior looking lady in one of the caravans but she did not appear outside. Also performing outside were 2 old men in cavalier costumes, a negro and a nigger, a young fellow in Jack Shepherd [sic] costume[61] and two somewhat old women (one ugly with a big nose and the other ditto with a small one) who appeared in tights and skirts.

With the performance inside I was charmed – it was a great improvement on last years. The plot I could hardly follow owing to the noise but a villain appeared to promise vengeance to a fair one (she of the big nose) and a champion for her appears. They fight with swords, the villain is wounded and then we see the lady supported by her defender and an angel pointed them upwards while the villain is rolled over and over down below by a representation of the Evil one who cries 'To hell – to hell!' Afterwards the nigger comes on and when his master has gone out a ghost appears and knocks him about. At last he gets ready for the ghost rains a terrific blow at him but catches his master instead who has taken the place of the ghost as the latter disappears. To conclude a scene was let down of the 'Victoria' and other ships off Tripoli.[62] Then as at Hamiltons and other dioramas the lights in front are lowered suddenly and ones behind turned on and the ship is seen sinking and men drowning etc as took place. This last visit put me in rare good humour with the Fair. I have only been in a few shows this time. All the others which are worth visiting I had seen before but I should like to have paid another visit to the above.

There is hardly as much available room in the land about King and Queen Streets this year as last[63] but I noticed the following roundabouts – 1 switchback car, 3

---

[61] The thief and jail-breaker Jack Sheppard was a popular dramatic figure from the first half of the nineteenth century. His costume doubtless reflected both the period and his romantic character.

[62] A topical reference to the collision between the battleship *Victoria*, the flagship of the British Mediterranean fleet, and the *Camperdown* in the Bay of Tripoli, 22 June 1893.

[63] Major improvements were taking place around the Market Square during the 1890s. Much of the surrounding land was claimed for the building of retail premises after the demolition of 'rookeries' and ancient slums. It was common practice by showmen to build up on waste land, but this was clearly diminishing in Nottingham from year to year.

roundabout horses, 1 ditto in which you rocked the horses yourself and one Flying Swan and a maypole in which the cars are swung out a big distance. Then the place was packed with cocoa nut shies – shooting galleries – stalls of all kinds and the like. I notice one novelty. Two safety bicycles were placed beside one another and could be ridden as usual though stationary. The distance travelled was shown by dummies on a small track in front and so the two could thus race together. This is a patent.[64] There were several Phonographs about.

The shows this year hardly did so well as last owing to the Strike.[65] The bazaars in the Market Place were not put up this year. That the Fair will last many more years unless there is an alteration somewhere I greatly doubt. Already it is nothing like the size as far as shows go as it was 4 or 5 years ago and when the land in King St is built on there will be less room still. It will be rather a pity if it is done away with because there is little any could object to in it. A few indecent photos and books are it is true sold on stalls … but these are all that is objectionable.

Of course there is a great deal of fun in getting up rushes and crushes. On Saturday there were 2 fellows going about, one with a mask and the other with a false nose and both with tall hats on and creating much amusement. Pickpockets of course are about. I saw one woman running after one and crying her purse was gone but he was lost in the crowd in a minute.

Sunday
'Jimmy' Dupe[66] held his harvest festival in the front of Sedgwicks Menagerie this afternoon. He had got a lot of fruit and vegetables and flowers hanging about and a large number of people listening to him. Johnsons, Parkers, Radford and Chappells, and Wombwells are the principal shows left but many, including Walls, and the majority of the roundabouts have gone and the market place has a quieter look than it has seen in a few days.

Tuesday October 17ᵗʰ
To Basford Wakes at night. These are held in a field by the tram terminus. There was any amount of stalls and coconut throwings present, two roundabouts (one a switchback car and the other galloping horses) and three shows, Testos, Chittocks and Sedgwicks.[67]

Testos were acting the play of *Blue Beard*. Outside a man makes 2 dolls walk up and down in a very life like manner and there is also a woman in short skirts but the show suffers for want of a good outside display.

I went in Sedgwicks Menagerie. There were 6 cages with animals as follows

---

[64] See Braithwaite, *Fairground Architecture* and the National Fairground Archive page on the History of Rides http://www.nfa.dept.shef.ac.uk/index.php

[65] The lockout affecting miners in the Nottinghamshire Coalfields.

[66] 'Jimmy' Dupe was born in Leicester in 1827, and was converted during a thunderstorm whilst he and a friend were out fishing – on a Sunday when they should have been at worship! He began his outdoor ministry in Sneinton Market and Nottingham's Great Market Place, holding a harvest festival service after Goose Fair from the 1850s onwards. He was a contemporary of General Booth, founder of the Salvation Army, and friend and partner of 'Bendigo', the converted Nottingham pugilist. See *City Sketches*, 2 June 1898.

[67] Basford, two and a half miles away, was part of the Nottingham run of fairs. Chittock's was probably a dog and monkey circus.

1 Wolf   monkeys   parrots
   2 kangaroos   antelopes (?)
2 ostriches (?they were asleep) a lioness
3 2 full bearded lions
4 4 wolves
5 A black bear. 2 big brown bears
6 Lion and lioness

First a young man entered the 2 bears den and put them through a performance. One of them fired a pistol. Afterwards Lorenzo (who was bitten by these bears a few weeks ago) entered the wolves den and put them through a good performance of jumping and leaping, including through a narrow hoop covered with paper also through a flaming one. At the finish he fed them with raw meat. Then he entered the 2 lions den. Before the door a little cage was fixed to that there would be no danger of the lions getting out. He held a naked knife in his hand and chased the lions round and round. He had a lot of trouble before he could get in and after he was out the lions sparred at one another. It was a dangerous performance.

I notice a very brutal affair in the field. A man had erected a long kind of passage so to speak covered with netting to prevent people getting in. At one end a boy put his head through a hole in a board and under him sat a youth with his face black and a paper cap on. Then you could have 3 shies a penny with fairly hard balls of leather at them. I was surprised to see many having a go too. I saw the youth get a hard knock on the top of his head and several very hard throws went near them. I should like to have given the proprietor into custody.

1894

Monday January 22nd

Coming home from business tonight see a dwarf show in a shop in High Street which I go in after paying my 3d. There was a platform in the interior and on this a little woman – a perfect little doll in appearance – was seated. She was called the Princess Paulina, was born in Holland and was said to be 20 years old and 19 inches in height. Perhaps she was taller than this but not much. She was a mulatto almost in appearance, her features were very small her size in good proportion. She answered several questions in English with a foreign accent, shook hands with me and for a performance coquetted with a fan, lifted a heavy dumbbell and stood on her head several times (she was dressed in short frocks and I suspect gave a glimpse of the interior thereof in this last feat to those who looked as though they would appreciate it). She was well worth seeing and unlike most of the midget shows you came out feeling that you had not been swindled.

Saturday February 3rd

In a shop in Clumber Street go into Violets Waxworks show. This I had seen in High St a year or so ago but the exhibition has been very much improved since then. Many of the figures were new and all had been freshened up and arranged tastefully. Round about were hung some very creditable oil paintings of warriors fighting , etc a lot of red stuff and ornaments etc as the shop had been but newly cleaned and done up the effect was very good. One group represented the capture of a lady and groom by brigands, others the execution of Mary Queen of Scots (the costumes of this being very pretty) and Tropmann [sic] a French murderer[68] attended by a priest. Then there was the grave scene from *Hamlet* with Mr Irving as the Prince and also 'Jo' from *Bleak House* lying on the steps of the churchyard. There were many figures of Kings and Queens, noted and notorious men etc and also a number of working models. The proprietors of this show were most respectable and superior looking. A pleasing exhibition…

Saturday March 24th

In Sneinton Market this afternoon find Rayners travelling Theatre and go into the first performance. The front was a Ghost Show, but the show was much longer. Outside there was a hand organ and a band of about half a dozen, several of them boys. The performers who stalked majestically about but gave no performance were a sailor, 3 brigands (one of them with blacked face) in top boots, skirts and the regulation attire and a little girl in a pretty costume. The ladies were 5 in number – one of them in a mans dress of red tights jacket etc., a very stout dame with beautiful golden hair and a bewitching little hat (!) and 3 others, one of them decidedly pretty in dresses which 'Arriet might wear on Sundays. The admission inside was front seats 3d, pit 2d and gallery 1d. I went in the front seats. The play performed was called *Jack Robinson and his Monkey* and was for the most part very senseless and one or two dirty little tricks were done in it. On the curtain going up Jack Robinson was found work[ing] among hay. He sees a monkey fires at and wounds it. This monkey is then pressed into service and invited to work for its living. Jack however ill treats it so it will do nothing for him but for Miss Eveline (the stout dame aforesaid) it will do anything. However it sets Jack free when attacked by the brigands and also saves some of the passengers of a ship when wrecked on the island and so is not entirely useless. The 1st act concluded with a good tableau of a doomed ship approaching the island. One of the three ladies I have mentioned was weeping over her little boy and appealing to her husband (the lady in tights). The brigands were stalking about in various attitudes of despair and leaning over the sides of the vessel. The black faced villain went into revolt and fought the captain otherwise the lady in tights in a tremendous fight with broadswords. Jack Robinson was played by the sailor with a variety of supposed nautical expressions and attitudes meant to represent a good hearted though careless tar but the characters were very poor.

The performance concluded with a farce. A cruel father wishes to marry his daughter – the pretty girl – to a rich suitor but strange to say she prefers another – namely Jack Robinson. A long string of people come on the stage and are invited into the house and then they all troop off in twos to Church. However, the parson is not in so the ceremony cannot come off. They come back and when they have gone in Jack comes on and laments his hard fate. Hearing him a fairy (a rather old fairy too she was in Whitechapel costume before mentioned) comes on and gives him a magic nose. In a minute the father comes out to speak to him but is silenced by the nose being wafted in his face. And so all the guests in turn are made mute as statues by the magic nose and left standing in various comic attitudes while Jack and the pretty girl go off and this time find the parson in and the happy knot is tied in a jiffy. And so ends the farce,

---

[68] Jean-Baptiste Troppmann (1848–1870), executed for the murder of an entire family of eight.

and the cruel father accepting the inevitable and everybody making merry in a kind of Sir Roger de Coverley.[69]

I intend to visit this show again.

Easter Sunday March 25th

This afternoon go down to London Road and see Sangers Circus arrive. The two best living vans and the elephants and camels had got in before I got down but I saw all the rest come in. The men lay on top of the wagons and some were riding in waggonettes but all looked very dirty and very neglected in dress. About 12 of the ladies were riding together in a glass carriage. The horses were harnessed to the carriages somewhat indifferently and did not look well groomed. I watched them on reaching the field. There was a waggon of hay waiting there and all the horses were let loose and immediately began eating either the hay or the grass. Then different parties of the men commenced putting up the tents and in about half an hour when I left 3 of them were up. The circus had come from Woodville that morning starting at 9.

Easter Monday [March 26th]

… It being near 1 o'clock wait awhile and see Sangers procession. I did not consider it so good as former years but the soldiers looked fine.[70] It was as follows

> Band Carriage 9 bandsmen dressed as Grenadiers drawn by 6 horses
> 10 Turks on horses
> 3 elephants each carrying a gun and a Turk
> An elephant
> 4 camels each ridden by a Turk
> Koh-in-oor – the fire horse – riding under a carved black oak canopy. 3 attendants and 8 horses
> 4 ladies in helmets with shields and spears riding
> Band of 10 Turks riding
> A Field Marshal
> 6 horse soldiers mounted as in Soudan campaign
> 2 " " carrying the colours
> More soldiers
> 7 Lancers
> Gun carriage 4 artillery men and 4 horses
> 2 nurses riding
> Another gun carriage

---

[69] Rayner's portable theatre, established by Samuel Rayner around 1860, travelled the Midland counties. This Ghost Show was probably owned by Samuel's son, Edward (Teddy). The parade, with a selection of exotically-costumed performers and a band, was a feature of 'fair-time' performances where it was necessary to attract an audience. *Jack Robinson and His Monkey*, an early nineteenth-century pantomime-melodrama, was much favoured by the portables for the variety of dramatic effects available, and in particular the acrobatic man-monkey. See Jane R. Goodall, *Performance and Evolution in the Age of Darwin: Out of the Natural Order* (London, 2002). Rayner's was doubtless a bowdlerised version, adapted to local conditions and audience. James Rayner, Edward's brother, was famous for his performance of the man-monkey in his own portable theatre (*World's Fair*, 1 May 1926). Sir Roger de Coverley: an English country dance.

[70] The ritual midday circus procession in which the company parade their animals, personnel and gorgeous cars and wagons, here with the theme of the Sudan campaign, reflected both in the procession and in the performance – see p. 36 and Brenda Assael, *The Circus and Victorian Society* (Charlottesville and London, 2005).

3 Red Cross waggons each drawn by 4 horses and 2 men to each
The fire house drawn by 4 horses with 2 men and clown on it
Horseman
Fire cart - 2 horses and 4 firemen
Open carriage containing 2 lions 2 horses and 2 men
Elaborate and high car with Britannia and a lion at the top. 9 horses and 9 men
     to it
Gun carriage. 2 artillerymen and 4 horses
Another elaborate car but higher than last. 9 horses and 6 men with a
     blackman on top
Open yellow brougham drawn by 4 white horses containing 2 clowns, a lady
     and another
About 30 little ponies kept together by 3 men riding

… After a hasty tea we go down to Sangers. The place was packed when we got there
and for most of the evening I had to stand. The programme was as follows

1   Mr Austin dressed in red trousers with a green coat rides 1, 2 and 3 horses
     successively
2   The Bros. Austin perform on the horizontal bars with the usual funny business
     in which one of them pretends to be a dummy at the business.
3   Our ancient friends Mdlles Topsy, Violet and Rose on the Corde de Elastic.
     By the aid of a big balancing pole, Topsy walks a thick rope, runs, jumps and
     sits thereon and Violet does likewise. Then a pole is laid on their shoulders
     Rose gets on it and then they walk backwards and forwards all together.
4   James Holloway jr appears on horseback as an Indian. He carries a big club in
     his hand and with this he strikes various attitudes and also he imitates the
     motions of rowing with a paddle.
5   A lady contortionist goes through a performance of bending and twisting to
     our great admiration.
6   Professor James does a clever ladder performance. A ladder is placed on a flat
     surface without any support and up this the Professor in a naval costume goes.
     When at the top he makes the ladder dance and he comes down again with his
     face outwards.
7   Mdlle Lillian a pretty young lady gives us an equestrian performance. She is in
     short skirts with plenty of 'lingerie' and goes through the usual performance of
     riding and jumping.
8   The Fire Horse Kohinoor goes up an inclined plain on to a narrow platform.
     Then suddenly fireworks light all round and the horse stands still while they
     burn and several shots go off.
9   Now appears an apparent damsel in very short skirts and golden hair. She
     experiences great difficulty in mounting her horse and chases all the ring men
     about for not helping her up properly. At last they all get together and manage
     to shove her up. Away she goes and gives us an imitation of lady riders with
     extensive and frequent displays of the interior of her skirts. When leaping over
     a flag the golden hair wig suddenly comes off displaying a mans head of hair
     and later part of his skirts come down. This was called a 'parody' but was far
     from good taste.

10 One of the clowns, Harry Whiteley,[71] introduces his singing donkey with which he has some fun.

11 James Holloway brings in his comical mule which upsets all the boys who try to mount it. It exhibits several other pleasantries and runs all the ring men out of the place.

12 The Fernandez Family two ladies and a gentleman give an exhibition on the flying trapeze. One of the girls swings to the gentleman who is hanging from a bar by his legs and by him is caught after a flight of some feet through the air.

13 Mr Austin appears as a Jockey on a bare backed horse and gives a clever performance of riding.

14 A painted representation of a house is wheeled in and into it a man dressed as a woman goes. The thing is then set on fire and through the open doors from one side to another a horse runs several times. He was supposed to bring out some clothing but on this occasion it was thrown out to him and he picked it up in his mouth and so effected a 'rescue.' Presently a fire engine with 4 firemen rushes in and the conflagration is put out.

15 Herr Ulric lies down on the top of a high pole on a convenient small platform and cushion and balances first a barrel and then a long roll on his legs. This was well done.

16 The Sisters Ani and Ino give us a trapeze performance. One of them by the aid of an invisible wire ladder seems to walk along the roof and another hanging from a trapeze swings her sister round and round by the aid of a rope fixed to a belt and held by her in her mouth.

17 A large cage contained 3 bearded lions is wheeled in and into it a man dressed as a Cow boy enters and gives us a very tame exhibition of lion taming.

The performance concludes with some scenes intended to represent the war in the Soudan and Fall of Khartoum.[72] About 20 men dressed as Turks ride in first and are addressed by a black man in Red Indian costume. After these have gone a party of British soldiers comes up and to them a man in the attire of a Field Marshal reads a letter from General Gordon asking for help. In the name of his Queen and Country the Officer asks them to be brave and true and all the men raise their swords and say 'We swear.' Scene III comes in Gen. Gordon with a beautiful damzel in a beautiful dress with Turkish trousers. They are in the midst of a love conversation when in rush the enemy and a terrific fight ensues.

Overpowered by numbers the General is apparently slain and falls over his horse and the lady after one last kiss is led struggling away. However in a few minutes Gordon rises and staggers forward but one of the enemy sees him and finally shoots him dead. Now come in English foot soldiers with 2 nurses. The nurses

---

[71] Probably Henry Whiteley, son of John Whiteley, and part of the Gregory-Matthews-Whiteley family of circus performers. See Jack Le White and Peter Ford, *Rings and Curtains. Family and Personal Memoirs* (London, 1992).

[72] The circus programme often featured short dramas: Astley's Amphitheatre in London was one of the first to feature *Dick Turpin and the Death of Black Bess*, *Shaw the Lifeguardsman* and *Mazeppa*. The circus ring, its spaciousness and the complement of horses and 'supers', also lent itself to more spectacular productions – here the war in the Sudan and the death of General Gordon (January 1885). The colourful costumes on display, the marching, swordplay, noisy gunfire and cheering made, no doubt, an attractive exhibition. For further discussion of circus dramas see Jacky Bratton, 'What is a Play? Drama and the Victorian Circus', in *The Performing Society: British Theatre in the Nineteenth Century* ed. by Tracy Davis and Peter Holland (Palgrave Macmillan, forthcoming). See also p. 153 for Race's account of attending Gilbert's Circus at the Victoria Hall, Nottingham.

examine the General and pronounce him dead and he is carried away shoulder high on a stretcher covered with a Union Jack to solemn music and the applause of the spectators. Then enter the English Army under the charges of the Field Marshal – Cavalry – Lancers – foot soldiers – artillery men with three or four field guns – and several ambulance waggons. As soon as they are settled the enemy appears with elephants carrying guns which are discharged at our soldiers and also with camels which are huddled behind the elephants. Now takes place a terrific combat and after terrific hand to hand encounters, brandishing of swords and firing of guns the Soudanese are totally routed and the performance ends with 'Rule Britannia' and 'God Save the Queen.'

The clowning was very fair – one up to date joke exciting much laughter. The clown was running about and the Ring master asked him what he was doing. 'Going to York,' says he. 'What, New York?' enquires the other. 'No to the Duke of York with a cradle,' replies the Clown.[73]

On the whole I was not over pleased with the entertainment as I had seen nearly the whole of the performers before and I did not consider it up to the standard of other performances I have seen at Sangers at elsewhere.

Tuesday
… At night we [Race and Will] have a walk down town. In the market was Haggars Show.[74] It seemed to be a small kind of menagerie but I did not care to go in. Outside were two girls in Scottish costume generally who gave a regular exhibition of skirt dancing. One of the two – they were only young but they were good looking – I saw from a distance dancing with a tambourine but I did not get an opportunity to watch them long. There were also in the Market Place 2 or 3 Fine Art exhibitions, a Fisheries Exhibition and several roundabouts.

Wednesday
This evening go to Rayners with Will. Outside in addition to the company I saw before there was now a young girl who was exhibiting some very elementary dancing. The play was called *A Ship on Fire*[75] and we were both quite pleased with it. It was a great improvement on *Jack Robinson and His Monkey*. In the first scene was a Wood where a rich young man (the black brigand) was warning a young ladys father (another brigand) that the said young lady was in love with a penniless navy lieutenant (the Fair Eveline in male costume) whereas she was promised to the aforesaid rich young man. Then the father hides in the Wood and presently the young couple come along and there is a love scene. With the Lieutenant is a faithful follower, a hearty and bluff sailor (Jack Robinson) and he also has a love affair. He goes to see his girl (the Captain of the Brigands in a short pink skirt) and finds her mother and her in great trouble. A lawyers clerk is there promising to clear them out

---

[73] Prince Edward (the future Edward VIII) was born on 23 June 1894 to the Duke and Duchess of York.
[74] The portable theatre and cinematograph owned by William Haggar is known to have visited Nottingham, but there is no evidence that Haggars owned a menagerie; Race perhaps made a mistake. For a rare account of life in a portable theatre, see Walter Haggar, 'Recollections. Early days of Show Business with a portable theatre in South Wales', *Dock Leaves* (n.d.), 8–22 and Lily May Richards, *Biography of William Haggar: Actor, Showman and Pioneer of the Film Industry* (n.d.), (Pamphlet held at the National Fairground Archive, University of Sheffield.)
[75] This may be a version of C. Z. Barnett's *The Ship on Fire, or the Loss of the Monarch* (1845) (alternative title *The Ocean Monarch*) first performed at the Britannia Theatre, London, and a great favourite with portable theatres. Its major recommendation is the strong, but simple story line and the amount of 'sensation' and 'action' involved. See p. 34 for *Jack Robinson and His Monkey*.

immediately if the rent is not paid to his master – the rich young man. This rich young man coming in Jack is hidden in a cupboard and hears him make him tell <u>his</u> girl that he loves her. Jack cannot stand this and out he comes and gives the insulter a good thrashing. The rich young man goes off and sends two country yokels to take Jack in custody but meanwhile the clerk has returned and finding Jacks hat on the floor (Jack has again been hurried away) has put it on. The yokels seeing a sailors hat of course make for the wearer and pull him about pretty well. Just as they are damaging him the rich man comes in and explains the mistake whereat Jack rushes and is only prevented from going for him by being held back by his sweetheart. However says the rich man the couple shall be turned out of the house when in steps the Lieutenant and holding out a bank notes says "Here is the money." And the curtain falls on Act I to the discomfiture of all villains and the uproarious applause of the audience.

Scene II opens with a view by the sea shore with Jack strolling about and explains among other woes that his master is in trouble with the Captain. While he is standing here a beautiful fisher girl (the pretty girl who appeared in the farce I saw on Saturday) in a short costume of blue with brown stocking, dark hair done high and altogether a more or less bewitching picture. In pantomime she explains that she has taken a paper from some Pirates. Jack opens it and finds it to be their private signals. In a minute in rush 2 of the pirates and though Jack fights hard and endeavours to save the girl from being touched she is run through by one of the Pirates and falls down dead. Then Jack kneeling over her and raising his eyes to Heaven promises vengeance and so the scene ends amid our hearty applaudits [sic]. The deck of a ship is the next scene the Captain comes (the father of the first scene in another costume) and has his Lieutenant up before him. He is charging him with various offences when Jack appears with the signals and the information that the pirates are now in sight. For Jacks good service his master is pardoned by the Captain and next a terrific fight takes place with the Pirates. After some time a red fire burns and on the deck of the ship the Captain of the Pirates and our Lieutenant are found. After a few passes the Pirate cries hold and then proceeds to explain that he knows the others history. He is he says the rightful heir to the estates the bad rich young man now possesses. After some more information he declares that the ship is sinking and they must both die. The Pirates rush on the Lieutenant and then are again fighting when in bounds Jack and rescues his mate and puts an end to the Pirates amid great enthusiasm. And thus *The Ship on Fire* ends, everybody being highly pleased and satisfied with the turn affairs have taken.

The farce was intended to please the children more than any body. A young man goes up to a cottage and tells the good housewife that his father is dead and she must now pay him rent. She does this and after a little further conversation he explains that his father had said that he meant to come back to earth and haunt the people he knew. Much fun is meanwhile created by a boy and girl the children of the cottager who will persist in fighting each other. The mother continually separates then again but the young man gives them pennies and ha'pennies to go at it again. Shortly after the young man has gone his father appears in the flesh and is received by the others as a ghost. They run him about with [*illegible*] cloths, rakes etc and are only prevented from doing harm by the young man coming back – explains all. He satisfies the father by saying that with that rent he has won £1000 and promises to give his father a good share of it and to pay a years rent for the old woman.

And so the performance ended.

Saturday March 31ˢᵗ

To Rayners again at night. Learn that the play is *Maria Martin* [sic] *or the Murder in the Red Barn* and should not have gone in to see that had I not also been told that this was the last performance here. When announcing *The Silver King* for last Thursday we were informed that the show would stay another week. I should not be surprised if the authorities have ordered the show off. [76]

The place inside was packed but the performance was gruesome. Scene I rose on the Villain (the quondam sailor in a frock coat, felt hat and a black wig) telling Mr and Mrs Martin that he wishes to marry their daughter privately. The old man assents to it and in a voice broken with emotion recites a speech which brings down the house promising a curse if any harm comes to the daughter. Then the two have an interview [and] he gives her some boys clothes to wear and presently the scene rises on the interior of the barn with the Villain in his shirt sleeves digging away at a grave. He struggles with himself but eventually his dark passions get the mastery and the Maria (the fair Eveline) comes in. A pathetic scene follows (Eveline put a bit of feeling into this performance) and then he breaks his purpose to her. She struggles hard and manages to get away. With a pistol he fires after her and then she totters in, her face covered with blood to die. Afterwards Mrs Martin comes in sits down on a chair and sleeps. Then the scene rolls up and behind the murder is again gone through. Her husband comes in and she tells him her dream. The Red Barn is then searched and the body found and next the Villain is arrested in a sumptuous house in London. The last scene I saw was the condemned cell with the Villain in chains lamenting his deed and then being led off to execution.

I was rather glad to get away from such a horrible affair. Woven into the above tale there was some good comic business between a country man and his sweetheart.

Music for the show is supplied by a harmonium occasionally assisted by a cornet and there was some good scenery. I remember now a sea beach, a country view, a woodland scene, a prison, a cottage interior, palace interior and a street and also a practical wood and also an open doorway for the palace and there was also a house side. I did not see the pretty girl or the (lady) Captain of the Brigands this time. (P.S. There were one or two swear [words] and other things in this performance I did not like.)

Tuesday October 2nd

Once more the bills, with their curious endings of "'God Save the Queen' by order of Johnson, Clerk" announcing the Fair have made their appearance and today many of the roundabouts came into the Market Place which was chalked out yesterday. One of these was drawn by a large traction engine. I noticed the method they have of raising the waggons containing the engine and centre the pieces to a height to form the middle of the affair. A platform is erected and long boards placed at one end. Then the waggon is brought up and pulled, in grooves along the woods, by means of a rope and wedges worked behind up to the level in front above where it is fixed with more wedges under the wheels.

---

[76] The mythical favourite of barnstormers, evidence shows that *Maria Marten, or the Murder in the Red Barn* was in fact no more popular than Boucicault's *The Octoroon* or the many versions of *Pizarro*. For a performance history, see Catherine Pedley, '*Maria Marten, or the Murder in the Red Barn*: the Theatricality of Provincial Life', *Nineteenth Century Theatre and Film,* 31:1 (2004), 26–38. *The Silver King* (H. A. Jones and H. Hermann, 1882), a more robust and recent melodrama, was clearly more to Race's taste.

Wednesday [October 3rd]

Most of the shows arrived and were fixed up in the Market Place today. I saw Days when they came in. They have one large elephant and 2 or 3 camels with them this time. I do not think that the Fair this year will be a good one.

Thursday [October 4th]

Goose Fair is with us again to day but it is shorn of much of its glory. The space in King and Queen Street occupied last year is now being built upon and so the Fair is less than it was then. The Shows in are as follows

1   Wombwells (E. H. Bostock's) Menagerie
2   Walls Great Ghost
3   Testos marionettes
4   Johnsons Circus
5   Days menagerie
6   Chittocks performing dogs, etc
7   Williams Fine Art Exhibition[77]
8   Amyes Mechanical Exhib.
9   Buckleys performing birds
10   Ashmores Fine Art Gallery
11   Naval Exhibition of working models etc
12   Coxswain Terry's Crocodiles
13   Paynes Fine Art Gallery
         Shooting Galleries
14   Lewis' Marionettes
15   Radford and Chappells Ghost
16   Biddalls Menagerie
17   Performing Pony, monkeys, etc
18   Kemps midgets
19   Burnetts Military Academy
         Shooting gallery
20   Giant Girl

In the Great Market Place are the following roundabouts:

Rocking Boats
Galloping Horses
Collins Switchback – rocking cars. (These were the most gorgeous in the fair.
     At night each car was lit by 2 little electric lights)
Switchback galloping horses
Switchback rocking cars
     "   cars
     "   "

A Razzle Dazzle of Sea on Dry Land
Switch Back Cars
Switch-back rocking gondolas
Switchback cars, and
A set of swings

---

[77] 'The "art galleries" – an improvement, scientifically speaking, on the familiar "peep-shows" of former years – appeal for patronage on the grounds of presenting correct portraits of the latest murders and their victims.' (*Nottingham Evening Post*, 5 November 1895).

Figure 6. Front of Codona's, late Parker's Ghost Show, c.1880, the carved 'vampires' and goblins clearly visible

In the waste ground in Wheeler Gate was a Roundabout and in addition several shooting galleries and in Ford Street was the Flying Swan machine and also a tiny roundabout. This last was worked by hand and intended for little children only who were strapped on to prevent them falling. It was well patronised in the afternoons and always had a crowd of people round watching it.

King and Queen Street were lined with stalls and so were Long Row and Chapel Bar.

This afternoon Belle and Mr Greenhalgh are over and after taking the former a walk round the Arboretum[78] and neighbourhood we meet Emily and go to the Fair. Walls Ghost Show is as usual at the bottom of Market Street. I have before mentioned the gorgeous front it has (there must have been six great gilt 'vampires' and at least 20 heads, all moveable attached to it) and that besides a good barrel organ it rejoices in a brass band of 10 or 12 performers. This time they have a slight addition to the outside display. There is a cross bar erected at a considerable height and to this a gymnast pulls up by a rope the while hanging by his teeth to one end of it. Then at the top still hanging by his teeth he fires half a dozen shots from a revolver and then lowers to the ground again.[79]

The performance commenced with a recitation from the front by one of the performers and as he spoke scenes were shown on the glass of a boy dying and being carried away by the angels and the grief stricken parents praying by his gravestone etc. Then two little men, they called themselves Little Tich[80] and General Small and could hardly have been 4ft high, gave us a comic sketch. They sang and were knocked off their chairs by a ghost and also went to bed to be disturbed by the same party. This was rather comical. The performance concluded with a transformation scene, the various views which underwent changes of colours by means of a limelight. The last portion of this represented a waterfall in action and was very pretty.

Afterwards we went on Collins's latest roundabout. The cars on this were carved and gilded in a gorgeous fashion and the seats inside were covered with plush. The cars went up and down like a switchback and also rocked from side to side like a ship at sea.

In the evening Will comes for me and … we go into Lewis's Marionette Show which I find to be one of the cleverest I have ever seen. The following figures first appeared in succession:

A pole balancer
A clown with a pole at each end of which was a chair
A juggler (2 balls)
A skeleton which danced firstly as an ordinary skeleton and secondly with separate limbs thereof

All these gentlemen were very clever and the actions of the first three were very lifelike and clever.

Then we have a comic pantomime in which a clown, pantaloon, harlequin, columbine and policeman take up. Clown and pantaloon were up to any amount of

---

[78] Opened in 1852, by 1894 the Arboretum had matured to include gardens, lakes and refreshment rooms. It still survives.
[79] This outside display is quite a spectacle, and was sure to attract an audience. The vampires – carved figures in the Gothic tradition – can be clearly seen in Figure 6.
[80] Doubtless named after Little Tich, the famous music hall performer.

tricks stealing sausages, invading barbers shop, riding a donkey cart and the like and finally fire the policeman out of a cannon. Harlequin and Columbine danced together.[81]

The performance concluded with a transformation scene in which the above five figures appeared and others representing Britannia and fairies were brought on.

Afterwards we go into Kemps Exhibition.[82] A performing seal was first shown. The seal like all his brothers seemed quite human and did some little tricks well. The poor beggar seemed to be roughly treated and was locked up in a box which allowed no light in at all. I was sorry for him for his keeper seemed to think him something like the most ferocious animal which he represented that they had a painting of outside.

Afterwards the Princess Dot and her daughter were exhibited. I should think they were from 3ft 6inch to 4 ft in height. The former had a big head rather out of proportion to her body and looked more like a stunted woman than a midget. Her daughter was more like a real midget, but neither was to be compared with the Princess Paulina I saw sometime back. After having a short history of them declared by the proprietor they walked round shaking hands and then got into a tiny carriage drawn by a small pony. In this with the blinds down they drove to the front to attract another showful of people in.

Of course there was the usual crush up Beast-market Hill. It seems however a somewhat soft game going up and down in a long stream and as every now and then a party of fellows gets thrown out by the police for rough behaviour we did not join in with them.

Friday October 5th
This evening go with Will, who does not want to go into the Fair again, to Livermore's at the Albert Hall.[83] The place was packed but we got a good seat. I have before described, I think, the Minstrels court dress and this time the Company was bigger than ever and there were no less than 5 corner men at each end. The band too was larger than I had seen it before and there were 3 boy singers. Taking it on the whole I did not think the performance was so good as it used to be 7 or 8 years ago and many of the acts were very old. The noise produced sometimes also with a great number of bones tambourines and musical instruments was too great.

The first part of the programme was composed of songs etc in the usual style. There were not many jokes though what there were were very good. Harry Trellis the end tambourine man is a great card and exceedingly comical. There were 2 or 3 fair comic songs – the best being that of waiter in which all the circle placed little boards

---

[81] Lewis's Marionettes: thought by many to be one of the finest marionette shows. This programmeme includes classic figures from the marionette repertoire: the skeleton figure, for example, separated at the neck, shoulders and pelvis, and the pole balancer lay on its back and tossed a pole into the air, which it caught on its feet. See McCormick, *Victorian Marionette Theatre*, pp. 141–3 and 162–3.

[82] A combination of two shows: Kemp's Royal Midgets and Kemp's Talking Fish (the seal was frequently billed by showmen as a 'talking fish'). See Toulmin, '"Curios Things in Curios Places"' above.

[83] The Livermore Brothers Court Minstrels were a black-face minstrel troupe numbering at least 50 performers by the 1890s. The variety and number of separate elements in the programme (from acrobatics to 'drag', songs and comedy) made them very popular, particularly with a middle-class audience who could be confident that no offensive or risqué material would be performed. See Reynolds, *Minstrel Memories*, pp. 172–182.

covered with white cloths on their knees so as to form a kind of table and on this various stale articles including a pipe out of which a rat jumped were placed to our great amusement. The second half was as follows

1   The 3 Ottos dressed as Cooks come on and do some acrobatic feats over chairs and tables

1   Four men appear. They are in exceedingly short dresses [*illegible*] and stooping down and have all appearance of 4 dwarfs. Two are men carrying little sticks (one of them with a false nose and cheeks) and two are women with small parasols and they are supposed to be Africans. Then they sing and dance in a most comical and absurd but natural way. This was a treat.

2   The Great Continental Comedian Mr Howard Baker. This gent had appeared in the first part when he among other things wished to sing us a little b-b-ballad from Sha–kespeare. On he went after an imaginary bee which he caught and put in his pocket where it stung him and he also imitated a train, on its journey through a tunnel, etc, on the kettle drum. He also sang a song or two. He had a funny laugh and was rather comical on the whole.

3   The Bohemian Court Entertainers. These were four fellows in a pretty court dress with white faces (powdered and rouged somewhat and wearing beauty spots) who played the hand bells, a mouth organ and the mandolin. They were good players but looked rather conceited.

4[sic]   The Bros Hearn do some comical business and sing a duet.

4   The Kentucky Force. A number of cooks come on followed by policemen. They are engaged in conversation when the alarm is given that the sergeant is coming. Thereupon the cooks don uniforms and they all drill together. This was very fair but it was not apparent why cooks should come on to don the uniform and further the sergeant did not appear.

5   Henry Zento 'champion bicyclist of the world' does some feats. He rides a safety and also a small 'tall' bicycle doing various feats on them after the style one sees done at circus on horses. He also rides a cartwheel, a cycle with two uneven wheels etc, and also rides a safety on the top of a table top which revolves in the opposite direction to that he goes in. A rather clever fellow this.

6   'A walkround' by the company who come on in various miscellaneous costumes accompanied by a made-up giraffe and a like manufactured donkey.

I should have mentioned that in the first portion of the programme Mr J. Hilton does his burlesque scena of a lady singer and also we have 'Pompey's Excursion by Train' both of which I think I have described before. This time they did not seem so well done.

Saturday [October 6th]

This afternoon go into Sneinton Market. It is filled with roundabouts, stalls cocoa nut throws and the like. Sedgwick's Menagerie is there (I could not go in because a performance was on when I got to it) and also Chipperfields show which latter I saw in Manchester in the early part of '93.[84] It is rather dirty outside as also are two or

---

[84] Chipperfield's marionette theatre – one of many associated with circus families (see McCormick, *Victorian Marionette Theatre*, p. 18). The variety of marionette figures – from the cartoon character Ally Sloper to the bargees – is remarkable. The 'Bombardment of Alexandra' took place during the war in Egypt in 1882.

three men without any special costumes on, who are inviting inside. There are however two girls, dressed in tights with short continuations of the bodice forming skirts, who sing and waltz together and also a boy in a clowns dress.

Pass my penny, and when inside proceed for a like additional sum to the front seats there being rather a rabble present. First one of the girls juggles with balls and then a tableaux of Venice was shown. At the back various state and other barges were rowed in and have little men climb a greasy pole. Also some smaller craft are rowed in – the men working the oars very naturally – and in front a long string of characters goes by. These include a knight in armour, Ally Sloper, a man wheeling his wife home in a barrow, and one-legged man who meets a lady in a sedan Chair whom he salutes, an old woman running after her pigs, a lady who comes on and opens her parasol, and some others which I forget. All these were described by old Mr Chipperfield to the children in a very intelligent and amusing style. The figures are walked in a life like manner. Next a fat old pony does some little tricks, telling the number of days in the week and the number he would like to work, picking out the biggest rogue in the company (his master), lying down as though dead and the like.

When the show was over I had a little chat with Mr C. and he seemed very fond of this pony which he had trained he said – and I believed him – by kindness. He was a nice old man. He told me he had to pay £5 for the show ground for 3 days only. The performance was concluded by a representation of the Bombardment of Alexandria. Before us was shown the city and then warships came in, squibs were destroyed and as a red light spread over, the walls collapse and the place is seen on fire. The show quite interested me and though the figures and scenes were old it was worth a visit.

Next go into a small tent outside of which was hung a somewhat crude painting representing the capture of 2 badgers. Inside were the animals themselves. They were in a small box having a wire front. They were sleeping and the man in charge had to poke them to get them to move. They were 2 fine badgers – a male and female – it seemed a pity to have caught them and to have them confined in such a poor house. They were caught near Grimsby.

Coming back to the great Market Place go into Amyes Mechanical Exhibition.[85] Over the entrance was inscribed 'The greatest of England is (sic) Mans inginuity' and it was rather disappointing to find the interior exhibition so common. On one side was arranged a model of the ship canal and various vessels passed up and down the water. In one place a bridge swung round when a big boat came up and in another the mast of large vessels collapsed to allow them to pass under bridges. Also an express train came along every 3 minutes. But the affair was poorly got up and looked nothing. There were one or two working models including a ship in motion and also some which required an extra penny to make them go.

Down the other side were arranged some coloured battle and like scenes at which one looked through glasses and there were also some magic mirrors, fortune tellers and the like. A poor show.

At night the shows filled as fast as they emptied and business was very brisk. Go into Radford and Chappells Ghost. This is only a second class show as they have but a dingy front and the players looked a trifle dingy also. There are two or three pretty girls in the company. Part 1 consisted of a tale told by a cavalier (one could hardly hear owing to the noise a word he spoke) during which there was represented a duel and one learnt that the cause of the fight was the speakers sister. Then for Part 2

---

[85] An exhibition of simple automata.

we have the old old story of the engagement of a servant by a master and the appearance of a ghost who knocks each of them in turn. Afterwards a head is shown in a box and then on a stool, then in mid-air, as usual followed by, as also usual in this show, the appearance of a flame which encircles a lady dancing, and Part 3 which winds up the entertainment is a transformation scene on which varied coloured lights are thrown from a varied lime light. The admission to this show was 1d.

So ends Goose Fair 1894. It has been a feeble one – at any rate so far as shows are concerned.

Sunday October 7th

Take my usual stroll into the Market Place, as is my custom this afternoon. Wombwells have gone and so have many of the small shows and most of the roundabouts but Walls, Burnetts, Testos, Radford and Chappells and Chittocks and several other remain. On Chittocks Jimmy Dupe was holding his harvest festival in the presence of a large number of people. On the front of the show were hung cabbages and other greens with apples and the like and bread and fancy cakes. It looked quite a brave display.

My diary will henceforth be written at uncertain intervals.

Saturday December 8th

Will learns that a Pavilion Theatre has been erected at Beeston,[86] so tonight we both walked there and find it in the Wakes Field. It is the ordinary timber building with canvas top, but no platform outside; a bell was being rung to announce the performance. Inside there was the usual gallery then the pit and some front seats draped off from the rest. The place was filled at admission prices of 3d, 6d and 1/-. The stage was not a very large one of course and looked a little bit old and worn. Music was supplied by a piano but that instrument gave forth a very feeble tone and could only be heard with any distinctness when the place was quiet.

Tonight the romantic drama of *Firematch the Trooper, or the Striking of the Hour* was being performed.[87] The curtain drew up to an interior. The Cavalier condemned to die sits lamenting his fate; enter a Roundhead, who promises to set him free if he will agree to their children marrying and to the payment of a large sum of money. The Cavalier agrees and calls in his faithful servant Firematch to witness the signing of a deed. Then comes in the Cavalier's little daughter whom Firematch teaches to say a little prayer, asking her Heavenly Father to watch over her papa. But afterwards the Roundhead repents of his bargain, enters with 3 troopers and stabs the other dead. Then Firematch vows revenge, exits and the curtain falls on Act 1.

The next act opens with a comic relief. The keeper of 'The Monkey' public house who is an idle but warm-hearted rogue, is afflicted with an exceedingly talkative wife and a nuisance of a servant girl. Much fun then with the aforesaid wife and the servant girl who is dressed in rags and tatters but is a very vivacious creature.

---

[86] Another portable theatre, this time located in Beeston, about two miles south west of Nottingham. The lack of a parade or outside platform indicates that there was no necessity to 'tout for business'. Despite its shabbiness, this seems to have been quite an upmarket establishment. The front seats, separated by a screen or curtain from the pit and gallery, at 1/- were relatively expensive.

[87] *Firematch the Trooper* (W. H. Pitt, 1867) is an interesting piece, not least because of its resurrection thirty years after it was originally performed. Its appeal to audiences and proprietors alike seems to be its dramatic variety, containing humour and pathos, romance and violence in equal measures.

She will have her Master kiss her and so he is discovered in a compromising attitude by his spouse. Roars of laughter. With them is living a beautiful girl, who is sought by 2 lovers. One is the son of the Lord of the Manor and he orders some of his men to carry her off. Then we find her locked in a room at the mercy of this scamp. But she is saved by the entrance of a stranger and so falls the curtain again. In the last act the stranger turns out to be Firematch who has lived abroad for many years now [and] returns a white-headed and aged man. Then he reveals to the rescued but still strong girl that she is his former master's daughter now grown into womanhood and, out of nearly forgotten memory, he revives some incidents of her childhood and brings back the old prayer to her memory.

Then he calls on the father of the rascal who had wished to ill-treat her and who turns out to be the Roundhead of old and then, in a secret chamber, they have a terrible combat with swords which lasts several minutes. At last, virtue triumphs and Firematch runs his old enemy through. Then enters the daughter and her other lover and as they kneel before him Firematch gives them an old troopers blessing. And so the curtain falls.

The Company is certainly far above the type one would expect to find in such a place. All the performers seemed refined and used no bad language and spoke good English. The acting too was very good. The scenery, though not very grand, was passable. For the leading lady is Miss Clara Cavendish who played the part of the Cavalier's daughter in the second and third acts. She is tall and not bad looking by any means. She wore an ordinary dress of white. Miss Marie Montague (the servant) was, however, a cure. She was chock full of spirits and fun and carried all before her. In person she is small and I rather think (but God forbid) inclined to be just a leetle bit cross-eyed. The other two ladies were not so larking but did their parts (especially the housewife) well. The little girl gave a nice child-like interpretation of her part. The gentlemen of course were not so attractive to me. Mr G. Warden (the trooper) is a nice fellow and spoke well; Mr Collingham (who is clean-shaven in the face) represents a Roundhead to the life and the Keeper of The Monkey (whose name I do not know) is a very comical fellow.

Wednesday December 26th Boxing Day

In the afternoon visit Sneinton market where I find a very old Theatre with a waggon in front to form a stage. On the outside was painted Rayner's[88] in long straggling white letters, and the master of the affair, I recollected as having been in that Company, but things looked as though there had been a catastrophe. The company consisted of (in addition to the one already mentioned) a woman, once good looking and still somewhat so now, in tights, a girl of about 14, two children say 10 and 6, and a boy of about 12 dressed as a clown. The woman had long black hair and looked well, but she had one eye blackened and so had always to stand with the other facing us which upset things somewhat.

Part 1 consisted of a drama in one act. The man and the woman (who represented a man) were in love with the same girl and meet in a lonely wood. They fight with a couple of rusty swords and the 'woman' is killed. The boy later appears on the scene and there is another battle and the murderer is in turn killed.

---

[88] Race is suspicious of this portable theatre being 'Rayner's', both in terms of the quality of the company and performance, and the shabbiness of the structure.

The girl also took part in this and spoke her lines well and the boys had some comical things and sayings (assisted occasionally, I am sorry to say, with a swear word) but it was very poor stuff.

Afterwards a farce (which it was indeed). The boy wants to marry the master's daughter (the little girl of 6, a pretty laughing thing). The master objects, but is charmed into an immovable statue with a magic ring and so are the wedding guests which gives time for the couple to get tied together. Very poor stuff again.

Rayners did nearly the same thing when they were here, but of course they managed it better. The stage was a rotten erection and the scenery was most miserable, nearly all the paint being worn off. This was indeed a 'penny gaff' and I felt quite sorry for the children. The man looked decent too but he was dressed poorly and to have a heart, and I heard him swear once or twice.

Saturday December 29th

This evening to Beeston to the Pavilion Theatre again. The piece billed was the Pantomime of *Dick Whittington and His Cat* but unfortunately Miss Montague has left and she was the best of the lot.

The play opened with an interior of the Evil Spirit's home. The Evil One is there himself. He is dressed in red and carries a bladder attached to a stick with which he lashes his two men who are in grey clothes, with masks on and having tails. Enter the Good Fairy (Mrs Collingham looking very young; she wears a pretty dress, has her hair down her back and carries a wand) who informs them that she will guard Dick and only allow him to do a certain amount of mischief. Next we are introduced to the Mill where more characters come on. There is the lawyer (Mr C.) who is in close fitting black tights and dances about with his long legs and there are also 2 lazy brothers of Dick's who do some tumbling about. Dick himself is a she – Miss Cavendish, in a pretty dress of pale blue and tights. (This is *Nicholas Nickleby* revived.[89]) She looks very nice and gives us several songs and also does a dance. Her cat is a little child in a dress of rabbit skins. Afterwards we see Dick lying down by the Milestone when he hears Bow Bells and an invisible chorus sings. Reaching London he gets employed at a shop, the master of which gives us more comic business. He has a daughter (a girl who had only a small part in the piece I saw before, and who is now painted up to look fairly pretty; she wears short skirts) and with this daughter Dick falls in love. Usual lovers business and kisses. Enter Master. Dick discovered and turned away.

Next for some reason or other we are on a ship at sea. The Crew is composed of about twenty little Beeston girls in blue trousers and white blouses.[90] They had appeared in a previous scene when they had worn a kind of smock over their blouse which had given them a funny appearance and been engaged outside the Mill in various farm duties of digging, wheeling, carrying, etc. These sing and also do some drill business with Union Jacks. Likewise appear the other characters and Dick and his sweetheart. The former has changed her former suit for another of deeper blue and for her short jacket now wears complete tights. She looks fetching. Her girl also looks very nice. Later the Company gets wrecked on an island, and then, one by one, they all struggle safely to shore. Each says as they come on, 'The only one saved' and are surprised to find others there too. On this island was a mad man who sings a song

---

[89] Race seems to be paralleling the Crummles theatrical company who feature in Dickens's *Nicholas Nickleby*.

[90] The involvement of local children was a common practice, guaranteeing an audience delighted to see their offspring on the stage!

dressed in a long gown and gives us a dance. In his underground palace he is next discovered seated with his daughter (a girl in a yellow dress I had not seen before). Then we have a small kind of variety entertainment. The local chorus, some of them now wearing short frocks, gave us more evolutions and a little girl in knickerbockers does a skipping rope dance. She is succeeded by another child who does a tambourine dance. This latter was more clever than her elder sister. (They were termed the Sisters Walkden on the bills.)

As it was getting late and as I had had enough I came out here, without waiting to see the rest or the Harlequinade which was announced to follow.

The above is an account of some of the scenes – there were several others which I have omitted to detail.

The performance was very fair considering, but did not appeal very much to me. Several smart local sayings had been worked into the dialogue.

1895

February

During this month Edison's last greatest invention – the Kinetoscope[91] showing living figures – has been on exhibition in a shop on the Long Row. The figures were contained in a big box and one looked down through a glass and saw them within.

I saw at different times a dancer and a barbers shop the latter with several figures and everything was true to life. The figures appear a brilliant white in outline on a black background but in the barber shop it was possible to distinguish a negro from the white man. The figures have been photographed continuously and two or three thousand of them are whirled before your eyes by Electricity in less than a minute.[92]

Thursday, Friday & Saturday October 3rd, 4th, 5th

Goose Fair has once more come round. This year only the Great Market Place is available for shows and the large roundabouts, though stalls of all kinds are arranged up King Street.

The following are the shows

	1 Wombwells (in its old place)
Down Beastmarket Hill	2 Burnetts (opposite St James's St)
	3 The Mystic Swing
	4 Kemp's Midgets
	5 Buckley's performing birds etc
	6 Radford and Chappell's Ghost
	7 Amyes Mechanical Exhibition
	8 Second Sight Show
	9 Coxswain Terry's Crocodiles

---

[91] See Richard Brown, 'The Kinetoscope in Yorkshire', in *Visual Delights. Essays on the Popular add Projected Image in the 19th century* ed. by Simon Popple and Vanessa Toulmin (Trowbridge, 2000), pp. 105–115.

[92] A very early description of moving pictures. For Edison's films, see 'Inventing Entertainment: The Motion Pictures and Sound Recordings of the Edison Companies' on the Library of Congress 'American Memory' website http://www.loc.gov (accessed 23 February 2007).

Figure 7. Goose Fair, 1904, looking across the Market Square to the Old Exchange, rides now dominating shows

10 Ball's Midgets
11 Diver's and Naval Exhibition

Joining up
the
Avenue

12 Williams's Fine Art Exhibition
13 Johnsons Circus
14 Wadbrooks Ghost
15 Sedgwicks Menagerie

Top of avenue
facing Long
Row

16 Norman's Varieties
17 Marionette Exhibition
18 Walls Ghost

Of course there was a large number of roundabouts. The only novelty among them was 'the Tunnel'. This consisted of a line of rails laid in a circle on which ran a miniature engine drawing four plain wooden carriages. Half of the circle was covered in with painted canvas to represent a tunnel and through this the train went in its journey round the circle. This affair was crowded every journey but the train only went round four or five times and as its length was just half the circle a ride in it was not a very long business. I hear the effect of the tunnel was not very good as there was no ventilation in it for letting out the smoke and fumes caused by the little engine. Most of the roundabouts were lighted with electricity and many of them were very gorgeous affairs, Collins being the chief. They were as follows

Galloping horses
Tossing ships
Collins horses
Smaller rocking horses
Collins rocking, switchback boats
Switchback cars
Collins gondolas
Murphys switchback cars
Twigdons   "
The Tunnel
The Sea-saw 'plain'
A row of swings[93]

All along Long Row from Clumber Street to the top of Chapel Bar were stalls displaying a great variety of 'fairings'[94] and there were stalls also along Smithy and Angel Rows and in Cheapside and on the Parade. Owing to the bad weather many of these stalls were shut up early in the nights and on Saturday evening, when it had been raining since tea time, I found only a small proportion of them seeking business. I suppose that financially the present fair has not been a good one.

In King Street the only novelties were Edison's Kinetoscopes of which 2 exhibitors had 3 a piece.[95] Here were two or three children's roundabouts. These are turned round by means of a handle and in the afternoons it was very pleasing to watch the little dots having their rides round on them.

---

[93] For rides see Braithwaite, *Fairground Architecture* above, and Freda Allen and Ned Williams, *Pat Collins, King of Showmen*. (Wolverhampton, 1991). It is noticeable here how the number of rides is increasing.
[94] Fairings: food, usually sweets and sweetmeats bought specifically at fairs. The particular specialities at the Goose Fair were Grantham Gingerbread and cock-on-a-stick.
[95] See p. 50.

I did not go in for the shows very strongly this time; I am afraid that my interest in that form of amusement is on the wane. I will take them for description in the order I have given before above.

1   Wombwells.
This was lighted with electricity for the first time here, and so was Norman's Varieties. The latter had the engine on the left half of the front working away in our view. Wombwells had theirs at one corner of the oblong their caravans formed and both attracted a good deal of attention from country cousins.

2   Burnetts.
The same old show again, given off it appeared to me, greatly to boxing displays. I forget if I saw the "Professor" with it this time, but at any rate I never observed him haranguing the people outside as he had done in previous years.

3   The Mystic Swing.
This had a dirty appearance and on Thursday people seemed exceedingly shy of entering it. Afterwards, however, it seemed well patronised. They had a little boy in police costume, with a black face, dancing outside, and altogether did not appear to know how to draw people. Will and I went in. Inside seemed an ordinary room, there being pictures hung on the walls which were covered with ordinary sitting room paper. Visitors (about 10 in all) sat on seats laid in rooms with a passage down the middle and were requested to mind that articles in their pockets did not fall out. The platform on which we were seemed suspended like a swing from an iron bar in the middle of the cage and at first moved a little as though we were being swung. Then the motion got faster and we appeared to travel right up and through the air at a great speed. After a while the process was reversed and we fancied ourselves going down and down. In reality it was the room itself (it being a box within a box, as it were, and we saw the inner one which, though it appeared to be fastened easily revolved round and round) which was going round and round being swung by men underneath. The arrangement was very ingenious and the deception perfect. I believe it was shown in London a year or two back at one of the Earl's Court Exhibitions, and that originally it was a Yankee invention.[96]

4   Kemp's Midgets.
Went in here. The midgets were diminutive people about (I should think) four feet high. We were told that they were over 20 years old, each, but the man did not look it; the woman was old. After the Showman had described them they walked round shaking hands with folks and then got into a little cab together. We were also shown a seal, described on the outside as 'The Great Sion Lion' and which went through some tricks. It seemed an affectionate thing but was kept locked up in a long box and treated, apparently, rather roughly. I did not like to see it dealt with in this fashion. This show I had visited before.

5   I did not visit this.

6   This likewise.

---

[96] See Braithwaite, *Fairground Architecture* above.

Radford and Chappells only charge 1d admission and generally seemed down 'the nick' somewhat. Their parade outside is rather lifeless and the front of the Show has become very old. Some of the girls are rather good looking; the performers all appear to belong to one or two families and have homely ways.

7   Took wee Donald into here on Thursday afternoon. A very feeble exhibition indeed of models. One represented the Ship Canal and boats went up and down, and also a train but the thing looked poor.

8   Will and I went into the Second Sight show. A woman was blindfolded and the master of the fair went about touching articles and she correctly gave their names, all done in the usual way of course. W. handed the man a ticket to be deciphered, but the result was hardly a success as she only gave some of the numbers on it, and did not read his profession, and some other particulars it bore.
      A large snake was also shown to us being held up by a girl in an Egyptian costume. This girl was very good looking most certainly. She was dressed in the before mentioned costume which suited her well. Over her face was a veil which partly hid her features. She had wide, loose trousers on. There was another girl connected with the show; she also was in Eastern dress her costume being of a dark blue material. This latter was not so nice looking as the other and was powdered somewhat and had frizzy hair but nevertheless she did not look bad. These girls took the money at the door and also ascended a small platform outside when it was necessary to attract people in. I thought their connection with the show rather strange, particularly as the man's features were not very prepossessing.

9   The Crocodiles I did not inspect this time.

10   This advertised a midget and a wonderful double-headed child. From the pictures of the latter however I knew it was contained in a glass bottle, having been deluded some years ago into inspecting it. I therefore did not go into this show.[97]

11 and 12 The Naval Exhibition I did not go into. The Fine Art Show likewise.

13   Johnson's Circus.
In here the first item of the programmeme was, as usual, a performance on the tight rope (and a very thick tight rope it was too). This time an older Johnson did it and not one of the girls. She was about thirty five and had been in her time good looking. She had retained a great deal of skill in the art and was very expert and lively on her legs. Then we had some flying ring business and after that juggling and knife throwing. For the last named a women stood with her back to a board and first knives then hatchets and lastly knives with burning ends were thrown all around her head and arms and body. This business is not very pleasant to watch. Further there was also a gentleman who had no bones in his body, and he obliged us by getting inside a tub and going through it doubled up and doing like expert antics.

14   Wadbrook's Ghost.
This was their first visit here. W. and I went in twice. The first time there was a drama in which a Rose played a leading part; I fancy I have seen the same thing before. The

---

[97] Probably the exhibition in a shop in High Street that he saw in 1892. See p. 24.

Figure 8. Pedleys Premier Exhibition Fine Art Show, c.1895

lady performer was rather stout and the glass interrupted the sound somewhat but the thing was done well. Afterwards we had a comic farce. It was the old old, story of the countryman who takes a post in a house where dwells a ghost. This first comes in the shape of a young lady whom the countryman embraces and he is enjoying a good hug when he discovers it is his master he has his arms round. This is done by the latter coming in and standing on the spot whereto the audience the girl (on the glass) is visible. Afterwards the ghost reappears in another shape and the countryman gives him a good knock which floors his master as he comes in again. Then we had the usual head in a box. The box is brought in and the speaking head discovered in it. Then it is taken away but the head appears on the table and when that is removed the head remains in space. Lastly a flame appears and dances all round the countryman who vainly endeavours to catch it. In this, one or two indecent attitudes were struck and 'big' words dropped which marred the performance.

On our second visit we saw the tale of Little Jim from *The Collier's Child* depicted in four or five tableaux in the space of about 3 minutes.[98] This was the first half of the programme, it being a busy time on Saturday afternoon. There was a farce to conclude.

15   I did not visit.

16   Norman's Varieties.[99]

Outside were two or three young girls who occasionally performed a jig and one of them was 'elevated,' in the old conjuring trick, on a single support by the proprietor. The interior of this show was lighted with electricity, the first to visit the Fair here. The programme was opened with a very clever second sight performance, the blind folded one being a lady. This lady could tell the name on the post mark on any letter, and she also read any name in a very quick and clever manner. Afterwards we were introduced to a man and woman lying in a trance in boxes very like coffins. There were no footlights to this show but there were rows of small lights up each side and along the top. These were turned out and a limelight in front was turned onto the trance figures. However, the limelight refused to act, though we were put into total darkness two or three times, and that idea had to be given up. Consequently, we could not distinguish the features of the parties very well but they lay very still. It would be quite possible however for the exhibition to be a fraud as the trance figures were quite hidden from view till a cloth was withdrawn from the top of the 'coffins.'[100]

17   The Marionette Show.

---

[98] 'The Death of Little Jim, the Collier's Child' or 'Little Jim, or the Collier's Home' was a popular, improving if melancholy poem of infant death by Edward Farmer, containing the verse, 'Tell father when he comes from work /I said good night to him/And now dear mother I'll go to sleep /Alas poor little Jim.' See *Ned Farmer's Scrap Book; Being a Selection of Poems, Songs, Scraps, etc. etc.* Enlarged and Revised (3rd ed.) (London, 1863).

[99] Almost certainly Tom Norman, the showman, auctioneer and 'owner' of Joseph Merrick, the 'Elephant Man'. For biographical details see the entry in the *Oxford Dictionary of National Biography*, and also Tom Norman, *The Penny Showman: Memoirs of Tom Norman 'Silver King'* with additional writings by his son, George Norman (London, 1985).

[100] Trance exhibitions were popular on the fairground: 'the man and woman in a trance, real "live" corpses in real coffins, form the attraction here, and if the roaring of the lions from Sedgwick's Menagerie next door does not wake them who can doubt that they are really entranced!' (*Era*, 19 October 1895).

I did not go into. A young woman (in decidedly short skirts) and a girl were on the outside dancing.

18   was Wall's Great Ghost, 'larger, grander and more magnificent than ever.' Certainly the front is a blaze of gold paint. Inside is very neatly decorated, a recent addition being a series of small heraldic shields worked in silks and hung all round the bottom of the cloth roof.

Part 1 was a tragedy of course; it took less than 5 minutes to perform and one could not follow the action as the performers could not be heard. Secondly we had a comic sketch from a negro and a little dwarf dressed like an Irishman. There were 2 of these dwarfs here last year, but one has now left and is replaced with a little woman who may be the wife of the present one. The negro was naturally a funny fellow and exhibited his propensities outside in cheeking (in fun) his master and in assisting females along the platform. These two sing seated on a chair each and are disturbed by a ghost as they sing to tambourines. Finally they pretend to catch the interrupter and twirl a white sheet (which had been skilfully handed in to them) in their hands as though they had caught it. To conclude we had a transformation scene which is, as usual, very pretty. I have noticed that in all these transformations an unfailing effect is that of rain falling, with the rain itself on view in golden strings.

Sneinton

In Sneinton Market was a great conglomeration of roundabouts and cocoa nut shies, shooting galleries, etc. and also 4 shows, the original Rayners, [101] Rayner's II, Bentleys Ghost and Days Menagerie.

Rayner's company were not out when I visited the Market, but the next-mentioned had a dray drawn up in front of their old fit-up, and on this 3 girls were trying to dance to the tune of a barrel-organ. I have described this show before. One of the girls is aged about 17, I should think, and was bravely attired in an old-fashioned silk dress. Her mother, who was fortunately sober this time, was turning the organ and the man was directing the operations in general, but the public did not seem eager to visit the inside of the show.

Day's show was ranged facing the Baths, while the other three looked towards Gedling Street. This gave the Market a more compact appearance than it has had in former years ...

1896

Saturday February 8th
[*Race and his long-time friend Will visit Pleasley and Mansfield, two north Nottinghamshire towns about 15 miles away.*]

Having seen bills of a 'gaff'[102] I wish to look in at it. W. takes a walk round the town while I make for it. It lay in a field at the back of a pub, near the Station and was the

---

[101] Rayner's Portable Theatre, see p. 34.
[102] Sometimes known as the Alexandra Theatre, it was a superior portable, owned by George Jennings the father of the leading lady, Viola Jennings who was to take over proprietorship. Her mother, Julia

usual wooden arrangement. Over the proscenium were the words 'All the World's a Stage,' the drop curtain bore a lot of advertisement. I got in in time to hear the closing part of a terrible drama. A young lady was seated at a table in great agony. She seemed to be lamenting the presence of a lover in the place. She rises and after some muttered exclamations falls with a heavy thud to the floor. A curtain is pushed aside and a man enters gingerly. 'What is this? Claris? 'Tis she!' He stoops and raises her up, she recognises him. Enter a swell with a drawn sword. 'Henrique, what do you do here?' 'I have come to succour this woman.' 'Begone, Sir, or your life will not be spared.' 'I refuse to move.' 'Oh Henrique I pray you go, I tell you I married him willingly.' 'Begone sir,' again in a louder voice from the swell. 'Villain, I will meet you,' replies Henrique rushing on the sword, without any means of attack of his own. They wrestle. Henrique is losing but a figure steps quickly in, a shot is heard, and the swell with the sword drops down dead. The figure, a lady somewhat advanced towards middle age dressed, very modestly and very suitably, in knee breeches and other of man's attire, advancing says, 'Thirteen men slew my father; with my own hand I have slain each one of them. Father! (kneeling down with hands and face stretched upwards) Thou art avenged.' Curtain.

This was followed by a Nautical Drama in which a poor widow with a sailor son is being turned out of her house by a cruel hearted landlord. She sends her grandchild (a very pleasant little girl of 14 or so with a nice manner who was received with the applause of a general favourite) to pawn a wedding ring and she had just been stopped by two tramps and a jolly sailor (the widow's son, I suppose) was just appearing in the distance to rescue her when I left. Another chief character in this play was a good hearted, bustling young woman whose prototype I have I think met before.

The company seemed a very good lot of players and I should much have liked to have seen more of their performance. By the bills they seemed to perform a different play each night.

Coming out in the little vestibule I had a few moments chat with the proprietor, a pleasant man of good education and gentlemanly manners. He told me that there were 25 members of the company and that they included in their repertoire *Hamlet, The Merchant of Venice*, and several other Shakesperian [dramas]. The chief star of the company was Miss Viola Jennings (I should have said that the proprietor of the show was Mr Geo. Jennings) of whom there were several photos and testimonials hanging. While I was talking to him a lady (who may have been Miss V.J.) came up. She was very superior, also, in her dress and conversation, and I had two or three words with her. She carried a little pug dog with her. The gentleman sent and fetched one of their bills for me. This I read to W. in the train coming back but on searching for it on Monday I could find it nowhere and have had to conclude that I must have left it behind me in the carriage. I am very mad but shall not do such a trick again.*

I was told that there were a thousand people in the show but though this could hardly be correct there was certainly a large number.[103] Most of them were young lads in the gallery, and older youths and older girls in the other places. Music was supplied by a piano and a violin. Both played well.

(**Thursday February 13th* Joy! The bill has been discovered in a drawer where it had been placed by E. I am glad.)

Jennings, famously played Hamlet as a breeches role. It was probably located in the White Hart Croft, a site frequently used by portable theatres.

[103] An exaggeration, though some of the larger portable theatres had an audience capacity of around 800.

Monday March 23rd

Monday March 23ʳᵈ

Last Friday Tom Hayward told me a 'gaff'[104] had been in Sneinton Market since the previous Saturday. On the following day before coming home to dinner go to look at it. Find the exterior somewhat poor and as I had arranged with Will to go to the Carrington Minstrels's entertainment decide to leave my visit over till tonight when I go down on coming out of my English Literature class.[105] The charge for admission is 1d gallery, 2d pit and 3d front seats and the place was crowded with a very dirty audience composed principally of boys. *The Murder at the Old Toll Gate* was being performed. I see the guard murdered and then the proprietor of the show (Mr Scotton) does some foolery. He is dressed in the raggiest suit I have ever seen with the shirt coming out of the trousers seat, his face is whitened, he wears a battered top hat and he is supposed to be drunk. After some foolery in trying to climb the gate he comes across the murdered body. He tries to lift it and his hands get covered with blood. He wipes them – which act causes great laughter. Then enters the murderer and knocks him down and as he lies on the floor and the curtain is coming down he cries 'all for the sum of one half penny.' The play proceeded on the usual lines only a glass (as seen in ghost shows) is utilized for the showing of the murder to the sleeping wife of the toll gate keeper. This glass was cracked badly some distance from the bottom and took up a great deal of stage room without much recompense. The man who took the part of the toll gate keeper I have seen in some other show though which I cannot remember. *Dread* [sic] was the fare announced for Tuesday. The performance concluded with a farce of which I only saw just the beginning. The gent I have met before (who I was told had only joined the Company the previous day) was a big swell in this.

I had some conversation with a young fellow who was keeping the 'gods' quiet but who I think acts as a [*word missing*]. He was a pleasant and well spoken fellow. The company is about 8 in number, of whom are two ladies, one the wife and the other the daughter of the proprietor. I saw them on the stage – neither was very attractive. I suggested that it was a pity they did not get further female talent but was told these ladies were jealous. The company rehearse at half past six as a rule; at eleven in the morning if the piece is a new one. Most of the plays are those supplied by French – this in reply to my supposition that they had them in manuscript. Jennings's is the top of the 'portables' and sometime gets noticed in *The Stage*.[106] Collinghams is now in Staffordshire. Melville has got a regular company.

Saturday March 28th

Go down to Scotton's again. Arrive there about 8.30 and find there is a performance on but am told it will be over in a few minutes so take a walk up Carlton Road. Arrive

---

[104] Scotton's was not a first-rate portable, admission being very cheap (compare with the Pavilion Theatre, above p. 47), consequently the audience, as Race notes, was composed chiefly of boys. Part ghost show (they use the glass apparatus to show the murder), the piece they perform could have been H. Campbell's *The Tollcross; or, The Murder at the Turnpike Gate 100 Years Ago* (1877) or a version of any number of plays. *Dred* (the earliest versions by F. L. Phillips and W. E. Suter dated 1856) was a popular drama, and was available in a cheap printed edition. Race's subsequent conversation with the gallery-keeper elicits interesting information regarding the practice of the acting company, in particular that, contrary to Race's reasonable supposition that they wrote their own pieces, the company used printed plays, 'supplied by [Samuel] French'.

[105] Race was probably taking his English Literature class at the Mechanics' Institute, which offered a wide range of subjects from book-keeping to music and German.

[106] *The Stage*: a weekly theatrical newspaper, published from 1881.

back in quarter of an hour, but find the audience not out yet. In a few minutes however the performance is over and then the audience come out with a sound something like a train rushing through a tunnel. When the show was cleared nearly everybody went back again, and shortly afterwards I go in. The audience is composed almost entirely of young lads of the rag-a-muffin class with a fair sprinkling of girls and a few grown up persons. We had to wait till quarter past nine before the show began. To relieve the tedium a youngster was sent round with oranges.[107] He was given ten at a time in a basket and required to hand up the cash as soon as he had sold his stock out. At first there were tremendous shouts of oranges from all over the place and the kid had an unhappy time of it. How he managed to get the right money in I don't know as his basket was pulled all roads and several parties made their selections themselves. Afterwards there was a good deal of throwing of the peel. I saw one youngster while skinning his orange keep up a regular fusillade with the peel and before he had time to get the orange into his mouth he sent it bodily at his neighbour who was evidently a regular enemy of his. The fun became so furious that the men of the show made a desperate raid on certain of the rowdies but they came away from them after a good deal of haggling and protesting of innocence without doing anything. There was a lot of bad language used.

I only [saw] the first act of the play as I had arranged to meet W. at 9.45. The scene I saw showed the interior of a castle where after some foolery from the ragged man of the last sketch with the soldier on guard (the travelling proprietor of the peep show) we were introduced to a dumb girl.[108] This was Mrs Scotton who did not look at all bad in somewhat short skirts. This girl protested in dumb show her loyalty to the lord of the castle, the other lady of the company who looked rather fine. She was dressed in a red plush coat, with green trousers and black stockings and had a long flowing cloak hanging from her shoulders and a broad green sash across her breast. As she was tall and rather nice looking and wore her hair in curls over her shoulders she presented a fine appearance. Afterwards three travellers were admitted who were known to the dumb girl as three notorious robbers. These robbers meditated on an attack on the castle and I suppose the dumb girl would frustrate the success of the scheme, but I could not wait for the next scene. I was rather sorry as the play was interesting and what I saw of it had repaid me for the things I had thought of the show while waiting.

Tuesday April 7th
In the Market Place there is a collection of roundabouts and stalls, a wrestling show and Clarke's Ghost.[109] When we went through last night the Fair was still lively and tonight it was quite crowded. Clarke's is a fine ghost show, very elaborately got up and quite clean. Outside Mr C. dressed in an every day suit (well made and wearing a neat bowler) was inviting the people in. He talked well but seemed a bit of a bully. Mr C. jnr was playing a kettle drum and the rest of the company were singing and dancing to the usual organ. The Company consisted of a little dwarf (a man of about

---

[107] Selling nuts and oranges was not an uncommon task for the youngsters in the company: 'I … used to sell oranges at 2 a penny and a bag of nuts at 2d a bag between the acts. My wages for this were 1d in the shilling and I used to make about 7/- to 8/- a week'. (*World's Fair*, 30 June 1956).

[108] It is difficult to deduce what play this might have been, since pieces with 'dumb' parts were regularly included as vehicles for showing physical as well as dramatic skill.

[109] William Clarke's Ghost Show. Race describes at some length the performance on the *outside* stage, emphasising the importance of the exotic, often revealing, costumes worn by the female performers, in attracting an audience.

3ft high), two niggers, a Cavalier or two in long flowing ringlets, painted cheeks and gorgeous dress, a very stout man, tall with a handsome face, dressed in a loose robe in Roman fashion and three ladies. The ladies were the pick of the show. Tonight they were dressed in military costume, brown velvet dresses trimmed with gold braid and little round cavalry hats. On Wednesday and Saturday they wore Highland costume, two in green plaid and one in a red plaid, with bonnets and feathers, kilts reaching to knees, part of leg bare and just a touch lingerie visible in which they looked captivating. One of them was perhaps four and twenty, a wife and a mother, I believe, and possessed of clear blue eyes, a piquant nose, clear skin and good features generally. She took honours for show beauty, easily. The other two were girls of seventeen or so, one dark and the other fair. The dark one had a very nice face. There was another good looking young woman in the company whom I am not sure was not on the stage when we passed on Monday night but whom I have not seen since. A fifth female, the wife of the stout man, I believe, assisted on the stage, but did not appear in public.

On Tuesday when the curtain drew up the stout man was seen sitting at a table to the right of the stage and then a quick tragedy called *The Haunted Man*[110] was performed. The stout man had a rather husky utterance, and so I could not make anything out of the thing. The usual scenes were shown on the glass and then at last two 'Angels' were seen bearing a woman upwards. The tragedy was quickly gone through and then followed a Negro sketch. A gentleman was about to engage a servant and two niggers apply for the post. The usual complications ensued through the blacks striking at the ghost and the master unfortunately coming in just at that moment and standing in the ghost's place etc.

The performance [ended] with a really admirable series of views. These comprised Linlithgow Palace, Balmoral Castle, the Grand Trunk Railway and Niagara Falls, the Crystal Palace, an Indian Encampment and two or three scenes at the World's Fair. Most of these were pained on cloth which rolled up and disclosed the next view but some including the Campaign at Sea, the India Encampment, etc. seemed to be projected onto the other view by a magic lantern and as they dissolved into the other picture the effect was very good. The view of Niagara was also shown by moonlight, and the World Fair was shown illuminated at night. Then one of the younger girls came in and danced for a while and finally, when in a little whirl we had a glimpse of something white, she was lost in a picture of Britannia thrown by the Magic Lantern and then the curtain fell on a transformation scene which ended in a classic pedestal ornamented with the name of Clarke and supported by several figures.

On Saturday (I may as well group my recollections) the stout man had the stage again to himself for the tragedy. This time he was dressed in doublet and tights of red velvet in which he looked handsome. There were again the usual scenes on the glass but this time there was a good fight with swords by the 'ghostly' figures. The negro sketch was better than Tuesdays. A ghost, having a skeleton head and a long white gown on, knocked each nigger down in turn whereat his neighbour was kicked off his chair by the aggrieved party and then he (apparently) knocked them down together at the same time. Afterwards when they think they are embracing the ghost they find they are really holding a figure with an enormous (cardboard) head. Afterwards on the glass the dwarf climbs up a pole which looks very funny and a lady, Mrs Stewart, I think, the stout man's wife, seems to do some acrobatic feats on the pole. She appears to be dressed in a very sparse costume of skirt and short, loose

---

[110] A drama perhaps based on Dickens's novel, *The Haunted Man and the Ghost's Bargain* (1848).

knicks, in brown flannel, but we could not see distinctly. The transformation scene was the same as last time save that I noticed a representation of the bottom of the sea with fish, painted on transparent gauze, swimming about.

In Sneinton Market, on Tuesday, was what appeared to be a Marionette Show. It looked rather dirty inside and as the one or two children who were on the platform outside were the same and the performance was not about to begin I did not go in it. Near it was a small show containing a collection of moving pictures into which I went. There were some good coloured pictures outside and the proprietors (an old man and woman who did not seem regular show people) were describing them. Inside the old man described the pictures which were as follows:

> *Lady Godiva's procession at Coventry with Peeping Tom on the look out
> *Devils having a 'festival' in a church, with attendant witches and skeletons
> *'The Single Life' An old bachelor mending his own stocking etc with various indications of the disordered state of his household and a spinster who wouldn't mind marrying him looking round the door.
> *The Slaying of the Innocents by Herod
> *Daniel in the Lion's Den

The figures were cut out of cardboards and the pictures had evidently not been painted by a first rate artist. After they had been explained the figures moved in a somewhat stiff manner and in the case of Lady Godiva, the celebrated procession went along. Daniel in the Lions Den was an amusing scene. The lions brandished their tails in such a stiff manner and a door at the top of the cave opened and two figures (the King and another) which completely filled the space came up and down like a Jack in the box. In addition there were two rudely painted battle scenes and a working mechanical model of two monkeys, Darby and Joan[111] one offering a drink and the other a pipe to its companion. There were only three or four children in this show.

It was the last night with Scottons and they had a hand organ on a small stage on the outside and a little girl dancing.[112] She had just finished a skirt dance (in one of those loose frocks that stretch right out) when I came up.[113] Mrs S. was out on the platform got up as a young girl with her cheeks rouged a little and her hair hanging down her back. The other lady of the company seemed dressed in a similar fashion but was keeping in the background. Mr S. himself was in coster clothes. The stirring drama of *Deadwood Dick*[114] was being performed and the rest of the men were in costumes more or less (check 'less' for the wardrobe of the show is not an extensive or costly one) suitable for that play of the Far West. This show, I believe, is going next to Beeston.

The Market Place is filled with roundabouts, coker [sic] nut shies etc., a regular little fair is on.

---

[111] Probably a very simple 'theatrum mundi' – in which figures pass in front of a simple panoramic backdrop. Darby and Joan, the archetypal contented married couple, here represented in true carnivalesque spirit by monkeys, may have been automata, or moving waxwork figures. (Thanks to John McCormick for his thoughts on this and other shows.)

[112] See p. 59.

[113] Skirt dance: depended, for its effect, upon a very full skirt. See Katie Vaughan, pp. 120–121, who is acknowledged as its first exponent.

[114] A drama by P. Korrell (1894), but the character of Deadwood Dick, based on a notorious criminal of the American West, existed outside this piece: 'Wild West' dramas had been popular in British theatres for some 30 years.

Wednesday April 15th

This evening go to Sneinton Market to see Clarkes again, arriving there about 7.30. The gorgeous front of the show had all disappeared and the bare wagons with the coverings over them ready for the 'road' were disclosed to view. A single row of lights was all that was left for the Stage, the grand 'military' organ had been moved to near the doors and the beautiful ladies and gentlemen at whom we formerly gazed so longingly were nowhere to be seen.

A board at the side announced that the famous drama *Maria Martin* [sic] *or the Murder in the Red Barn* would be performed at 7 and 9, so I had to wait twenty minutes with a crowd of lads and lassies and men until the first audience came out with a rush about ten minutes to nine. The place was filled again in a very few minutes and then the play began pretty nearly to the time announced.

Inside there were further indications of a speedy removal. The striped red and white cloth which decorated the roof on my last visit, the row of little streamers that then hung down the roof also, and the green baize of the sides had disappeared.
I think I have forgotten to say that the interior was very comfortable. In addition to a sloping wooden platform on the back there were many wooden seats reaching right a way back which also, an unusual feature for these shows, sloped. Music was supplied by a harmonium played by Mr Clarke jr.

Of the play I did not stay to hear much and hearing at all was difficult owing to the 'glass.'[115] The very stout gentleman was William Corder in a slouched hat, light overcoat top boots and a little moustache. He looked very like a 'Cowboy' in this rig. After an introduction the Maria (the lady of the ghost scenes in my previous visits now in a print dress with a white apron) and a little opening out of the plot we had a comic scene wherein my pretty Highlander made love to a country bumpkin. My Highlander was dressed as a typical country lass with a broad picture hat which suited her well. She looked well but opened her mouth a bit too wide and she also disclosed a somewhat broad speech. Then too in her encounters with the bumpkin (a well got up figure this in the regulation slouch) she was not quite so free from – well, a knowledge of coquetry – as a simple country lass should be. I noticed that when the couple hugged the lady discreetly laid her head on the gentleman's shoulder and otherwise indulged in a stage 'embrace.'

Left the show before half past nine having pressing business (i.e. a desire to look at the papers) at the Mechanics'. Besides having seen *Maria Martin* once I have no great desire to do so again.

Tuesday September 29th

The Market Place was cleared and chalked out yesterday and today the roundabouts came out, the shows not being permitted to do so until tomorrow. I saw Mr Wall and several other showmen walking about, so surmise that their establishments are encamped near the town ready to come in as soon as possible. As it takes nearly a day to take down and quite a day to fix up these shows (the roundabouts take longer) it follows that they will only be able to exhibit three or four days a week when on the road unless they can make a long stay at a place. The roundabouts were nearly all drawn by immense traction engines. I saw one of these ponderous instruments of locomotion drawing four loaded waggons after it with the greatest of ease. It seems that since the Railway Companies raised their rates for show luggage the roundabout

---

[115] See p. 40. Unlike the earlier performance of the play at Rayner's theatre, the ghost show 'glass' clearly impeded Race's ability to hear the dialogue.

Figure 9. Living wagon, owned by Wilfred and Jane Turner, 1903

proprietors have taken to the roads again and there they find one traction engine serves them better than a lot of horses. The front wheels of the engine turn on a pivot and are guided by immense iron chains. It was wonderful the ease with which the men in charge directed their engines.[116]

Wednesday September 30th

When went down this morning many of the shows were half fixed. Walls, Wadbrooks Johnsons and Days with several smaller ones are in again. Days have a large elephant and two camels with them. The Market Place is all hickety-pickety, van and cars being in all directions and one wonders how it will ever get straight by noon tomorrow. The showmen when putting their show up look a very ragged and dirty lot. They seem to have no order in working, nor any particular places for the many component parts of the show but somehow or other the work is done very quickly. The horses are in most cases poor looking brutes, appearing ill fed and having ill kept coats. Some of the living cars are very fine. They stand on low wheels and are about eighteen feet long. The interior is covered on each side with mirrors. The women take great care of these wagons, keep them very clean, and are often polishing up the bits of brasswork about. On the other hand some of the old fashioned carts are dirty enough. These stand on high wheels and are short and narrow. Many of these caravans are guarded by dogs who are to be tempted away from their seats on the steps. I saw several fine St Bernard dogs among them.[117]

At night many of the roundabouts had their lamps aglow and Walls, Wadbrooks, Days and one or two other of the shows were also lighted up on the front with, in the case of the Ghost shows, their interiors also open to view.

In the Market Place, as I came home, there was a ring, chiefly of boys and youths, gathered round a man who was stripped to his undershirt. He was going round with a coil of rope inviting any gentleman to step forward and bind him. Whereupon a fellow took the rope and with determined face set to work, first putting the rope in two coils round the man's neck. When the man was bound, and he appeared to have been done so securely, he started on the coin track. He said he generally looked to the gentleman who bound him to go round with the hat, but as the said gentleman preferred to keep in the background, had to do it himself. Then by some means or other or else cleverness, he freed his hands and went round with his old 'moke.' The youngsters round the way now began to jeer and ask him when he would get the rope off his body without cutting or untying as he had promised. The man, after indulging in some clat trap, of which he had given us a lot previously, seemed to get in a broil with the lads who began to close in on him. A cry of police was raised, the man got hustled in all directions, imprecations were scattered about and the meeting broke up in disorder. I could not quite make out whether it was a plant and that the same would have happened if the man had got the money, or whether he would have done the trick fairly had he been left alone.[118]

---

[116] Traction engines provided a more flexible mode of transportation for showmen than the railways. See Michael Lane, *Burrell Showman's road locomotives: the story of Showman's type road locomotives manufactured by Charles Burrell & Sons Ltd* (Hemel Hempstead, 1971).

[117] Race displays a common curiosity about showpeople's living conditions. By the 1890s, the living wagon was both a domestic vehicle and 'a symbol of prestige, status and rank on the fairground', Vanessa Toulmin, *Pleasurelands: All the Fun of the Fair* (Sheffield, 2003), p. 71. See also Paul Braithwaite, *A Palace on Wheels: a History of Travelling Showmen's Living Vans with an A-Z of Manufacturers 1860-1960*. Fairground heritage series; no.4. (Berkshire, 1999).

[118] Moke: from the Romany, a donkey or ass.

Thursday, October 1st 1896 – Goose Fair

When I went down this morning, Wombwell's had just come in and were fixing their caravans. They have 2 elephants; one a fine tall one and the other a young and small one. They were standing together in Market St begging from people on the causeway. The keeper moved off with the first and shouted out, 'Now Bill come on.' 'Bill,' the young one, immediately left off begging and followed its brother! In the afternoon, have a holiday and arriving home find Mrs Greenhalgh here. Stay in talking with her until about three then go down town.

The shows this Fair are:

	1	Bostock and Wombwells in its old position
	2	Salvas Giant child opposite it
	3	Walls Ghost bottom of Market St
	4	Lawrence's Marionettes next to Walls
Going from	5	Wadbrook's Ghost
Long Row	6	Days Menagerie
to	7	Johnsons Circus
Wheeler		
Gate	8	'Wallace' the untameable Lion
	9	Williams Fine Art Gallery
	10	Fat Bullock
Facing	11	Payne's Fine Art
Wheeler Gate	12	Nautical Exhibition
From	13	Joseph Penrith, diver
Wheeler Gate	14	Count Orloff
to St James' St	15	Pauline Nana, Second Sight lady
	16	Deppo. Diver
	17	Radford & Chappell's Ghost
	18	Randall Williams Trance & second sight exhib.[119]
	19	'Madame Pauline' (2 midgets)
	20	Aerial Machine or Flying Ship
	21	Burnetts Military Academy

And in the public house at corner of Queen Street now coming down

	22	Man in a Trance
	23	Armless Lady.

For the sake of easy reference I think I had better take the shows as they stand.

1   Wombwell's.

I did not go into this. They had a band of 10 musicians outside (no organ). I noticed one day a small bear chained to the platform.

2   Giant Child.

This was the same as I visited some two or three fairs ago.[120] I did not go in again.

3   Wall's.

Nor did I find time to go in here this year. One or two old faces had gone from the company including a dark lady whom I have seen with it as long as I can remember.

---

[119] See Vanessa Toulmin, *Randall Williams King of Showmen. From Ghost Show to Bioscope* (London, 1998).
[120] Perhaps Polly O'Gracious, the Irish Fat Child, see p. 18.

Figure 10. Bostock and Wombwell's Menagerie, 1906, 'in its old place', adjacent to the statue of Queen Victoria and the Bell Inn

They have the little man with them again and also the funny negro and for the rest 'they are larger, grander and more magnificent' than ever. In addition to the fine organ there is a band of eight or ten brass instrumentalists. This show always fills as quickly as it can empty and is very neat inside. I noticed old Mr Wall bore a good hand in erecting but when the show is on he stands on the platform merely directing the Company. Then he is in a very smart suit with an up to date silk hat.

4   Lawrence's Marionettes.[121]

Went in here on Saturday night. On the scene going up, the Chinaman was discovered walking on a tight rope with a pole in his hand. He goes through all the regular attitudes of lying on and jumping on the rope, etc. Next is a clown on stilts who drinks freely from a bottle. Becomes unsteady on his legs and is also sick, the last operation being performed to the life. Thirdly, a skeleton which dances in skeleton fashion and suffers no inconvenience when it loses, in turn, its head, arms and legs. Last come two queer looking little 'devils' in shiny coats who danced together and from a little height grow, alternately, to a much greater size. Part 2 consisted of a harlequinade, the characters being clown, pantaloon, harlequin and policeman. This was genuinely funny. The usual bother took place and clown and pantaloon got into hot water with the policeman. One scene was a capital view of the Crystal Palace before which was what appeared to be a garden seat. C. and P. sat on this, and then it opens out to a large bird of which they take possession, one at each end, and then this rises with them, right out of sight. Two or three seconds after the two figures drop down to the ground with a great flap. The illusion was perfect. After these was the usual business with the barber's shop and the donkey and cart and a big gull tossed the two old villains right through a house top.

Business being brisk there was no transformation scene this evening. A capital show, this.

5   Wadbrooke's Ghost.

The performers at this show looked, whenever I caught sight of them on the outside, a very unprofessional lot. I went in on Thursday. First, there was the usual business of the soldier and his dying child as seen through the glass, while one of the Company recited some poetry from the front. A wag in the audience had a little fun. The scene ended with the view of the little child being carried away by the angels and the following line,

'And dwell in Paradise forever.'

"Ne-var" said the wag in a comical voice amid great laughter and the "ne.v.a.r." was introduced several times after with more or less appreciation.[122] Part II the usual business of the comic servant who embraces his master in mistake for the servant girl and is frightened by a spirit wrapped in a great white sheet. There was also the usual appearance of the flaming torch which the comic servant endeavoured unsuccessfully to catch. There were one or two vulgar (or immodest) actions introduced into this business as before. The performance concluded with a rather poor transformation scene in which 'real' water coloured by the limelight rushed over a waterfall.

---

[121] See McCormick, *Victorian Marionette Theatre*. Branches of the Lawrence family feature large in late nineteenth-century and early twentieth-century fairground and itinerant entertainment with, in addition to the marionettes, a portable theatre, ghost show and cinematograph. For a photograph of James Holden's stilt-walking clown, see McCormick, pp. 164, 165.

[122] See p. 56. Perhaps a variant of 'Little Jim, the Collier's Child'.

6   Day's Menagerie.

2d was charged admittance and the place was cleared after each performance just like the other shows. There were seven cages of animals, three on each side and one at the top.

>The first contained two bears and an animal I did not recognise.
>2   Two Asiatic lions
>3   Five or six wolves and 2 hyenas (?), the last in a separate compartment
>4   A young lion.
>5   A Nubian lion and its lioness.
>6   Monkeys in a compartment with a pig and various small animals and birds in separate divisions.
>7   A porcupine and some small animals, parrots etc.

There was a fine Elephant on one side and two camels on the other and a Tattooed man was on exhibition in a separate part on payment of a 1d. Some of the cages did not seem very clean and I think I have seen the Menagerie to better advantage before. The cages are getting old.

There was a capital exhibition of lion taming. A black man put the two Asiatic lions through a splendid performance. One of them seemed as gentle as a cat and allowed him to fondle her and to put his head in her mouth. Her mate was not quite so tame, but the two see-sawed on a plank and jumped over one another and through hoops and did various tricks just like a couple of dogs. Another black man entered the wolves den and chased them round while a gong was beaten and the men were shouting. I believe I have seen this representation of a wolf hunt before. This same black also went into the cage containing the two Nubian lions. The lions took great springs up and down the cage as the man rushed quickly about. There was evidently some danger in this performance and the lions growled a great deal at the man after he'd got out.

7   Johnson's Circus.

I had meant to have gone in here on Saturday night but the show was always on when I got up to it.

8   Wallace the Untameable Lion.[123]

This lion belonged I think to Day's but was here exhibited in a separate show at the charge of one penny. It was a fine bearded lion and the cage was entered by a man whom it was said to have attacked a week or two previously. I noticed this man put on, especially to enter the cage, a coat with a large tear in the back – an unnecessary risk I think. He rushed the lion about the cage for a few minutes but did not make it do any tricks. This lion, too, was very savage when its 'tamer' got out of the cage. These exhibitions seem to me to be quite [un]necessary and they are very risky. In a small compartment of the cage was a hyena which had for a companion a little dog.

The Fine Art Gallery I did not visit but I went into

10   to see the Fat Bullock.[124]

---

[123] The generic name for ferocious menagerie lions after George Wombwell's famous 'Wallace', an African lion supposedly bred in captivity in the 1850s.

[124] Perhaps Woolley's show, which visited the Goose Fair the following year. See p. 82.

Figure 11(a). Princess Dot and General Mite in their pony and trap outside the show, c. 1900

Figure 11(b). Clark's Ghost Show interior, 1890

It was about six feet high, I should think, at the haunches and of a proportionate length. It was a monster beast and its skin, for everybody felt it in the orthodox manner, seemed stretched like a banjo parchment. It stood on a good heap of straw to give it a taller appearance than it really had and visitors passed right round it, at the end going over some boxes from which they could view its back.

11 and 12 I did not visit. Nor did I go into the two Diver's Shows. These last did not seem well patronised. There were large tanks in these shows with glass fronts and I suppose the Divers displayed in them their manner of working. One of the shows had a large engine working on the outside, supposed to be supplying air to the Diver.

14   Count Orloff.[125] I visited the 'Count' (I suspect he was a Yankee) and found him to be a great monstrosity. His head was of ordinary size and his face looked very intelligent, but he had a very small body, his arms were shrivelled up into an ugly shape, and his legs were tiny ones, almost circular in fashion. The book I bought shows the shape of the arms and legs, but does not give any likeness of the man's face. In one part of the leg, the flesh is so transparent that we could see a stick pass between it and a strong light, but the transparency did not at all resemble the highly coloured pictures there have been about. The Count sat in a large chair and had an apron over his legs so that when we went in we could not tell that he was deformed in any way. The showman was a gentlemanly looking man and he turned the chair round by means of a pivot. The book pretends to give a history of the man's life and states that he was born in Hungary but the huge number of medical and other references in America show I think that he is a native of that republic.

15   Pauline Nana, the Second Sight lady.
I went in here last year so did not do so again. This time the second sight girl had her face painted a light brown and she wore a white wig which completely altered her looks. One of the pretty girls is here again but the other (the prettier one) is gone. They have another girl, a young one, in her place. The girls do nothing but show themselves on the front and press the people in.

Radford and Chappells have the same old company. I did not go in and for a wonder I did not hear them sing on the outside.

18   Randall Williams Trance and second sight exhibition was the same that I saw last year. One visit was enough.

19   The midget show.
Went in here. The two Midgets were in a little carriage drawn by a pony and driven by a small boy in livery and when the show was full they got out into the sawdust ring. The man was a little lame old fellow, not quite three feet high perhaps, bow-legged and with hooky nose. His face was inclined to be purple and would seem to indicate that he had been fond of a glass though there was now a serious look,

---

[125] Ivannow Wladislaus von Dziarski-Orloff, born Hungary 1864, suffered from a complex lack of bone density, muscular atrophy and transparent skin. Known originally as the 'Living Ossified and Transparent Man', by 1896 he owned his own show, reputedly combating the constant pain he suffered by smoking an opium pipe. He died in 1904. For the reproduction of handbills for Count Orloff and Madame Hartley, the Armless Lady (below), see Richard Iliffe and Wilfred Baguley, *Victorian Nottingham. A Story in Pictures Vol. 4. Goose Fair* (Nottingham, 1972).

promising better ways. He was a good age, perhaps forty, I should think. The lady, said to be his wife, was a little taller; my walking stick, which is 3' 6" in length, came up to about her shoulder. She was younger also, appearing about twenty two or three, but with an oldish look with her, indicating her to be the boss of the track. She was in a somewhat faded plush red dress cut short at the neck the arms bare and when she went through a performance of lifting a heavy dumb bell we could see her muscles standing out prominently. After the proprietor had given a true (or otherwise) history of the couple, the lady went round shaking hands with such of the audience as were willing and collecting dues for herself and partners' private purse and the dumb bell performance over the couple said goodnight and retired into the somewhat confined area of their private 'brougham.'[126]

19   The Flying Ship and Aerial Machine.
I had quite intended going in here, but missed it. On Saturday I said I would leave it until I had had a spell at the Mechanics' to enable me to recover from the crushing of the crowd but on getting back into the Fair from that place I never thought of it again.

20   Burdett's Military Academy
This is one of the best patronised shows in the Fair and it is a treat to hear the Professor, sword in hand and silk hat on head, haranguing the crowd on his exhibition of the 'manly and noble art of self defence' and the feats of swordsmanship to be witnessed in his show. The interior of the show contains no elaborate fittings. There is simply a corded off sawdusted ring, at one end of which is a long seat whereon the performers sit while waiting their turns to exhibit with, in a corner, a retiring tent for the men. All the performers who exhibited with swords etc were former Army men and they were referred to as Private this or Trooper that.
        First two men who were attired in thick jackets and wearing wire headguards had a bout with swords; then the new bayonet drill was performed by a former Guardsman, followed by the lance and sword exercises by two others. The one who did the last was a Dragoon man, and he also cut a potato in two first on a girls hand and then on her bare throat. This was a ticklish feat but the girl went through it without wincing and the man was as cool as a cucumber. A stout broomstick was also suspended in two loops of thin paper held on two sharp razors and broken in half by the same performer without the paper being damaged in any way. The performance concluded with three separate displays of boxing by two young boys, two youths and two young men. The bout of the youths was rather a fraud, one of them being more given to dodging than hitting, but the men set to in fine style. This boxing though, is not much in my line, and I sigh for the time when the performance was a more military one and many of the men wore the uniform of their old regiments and a full dressed Highlander guarded the doors. Now most of them wear white singlets, white cloth trousers and top boots while the bugler on the front is not in a distinctive dress at all.

23   The Armless Lady.
Went in here. The old public house is divided in the front into two rooms connected by a door.[127] The part where this Armless Lady was shown was very dirty and it would certainly have been conducive to cleanliness had the showman done as he

---

[126] A routine 'midget' show, even down to the dumbbell performance.
[127] The site was one of the properties caught up in the continuing improvement of the Market Place area, and typical of the temporary venues used by showmen for exhibition purposes.

promised to do when someone said that the place was too small for him to see – to wit, remove the wallpaper. The showman was a fellow got up in evening dress with no teeth, an 'imperial'[128] and a great mop of hair. There was a coloured cloth in the window of a conjurer performing and I imagine that this was his profession. In the window also was a bill announcing the appearance of the Armless Lady with a number of other curiosities and performers in a building in Whitechapel, London. The object for which we each paid a penny to see was seated in a chair on a low platform. A small and dirty piece of curtain concealed her from view until the room was full. The Lady appeared to be some three feet in height, but she had a full-sized head with very common features. In the book I bought – it gives a good likeness of her – she is called Madam Hartley and so signs the account she is supposed to have written. There is a lot of rot in this account about her having been born in Sierra Leone and being the daughter of an English officer. I would say she was sooner born in the neighbourhood of the 'suburb' of London above mentioned than in any part of <u>South </u>Africa. She had no arms, her shoulders being peculiarly misformed, but she was able to use her toes, we were told, just as an ordinary person uses his fingers. She cut little bits of paper, like the one given me, into patterns, and so I was told by someone who went at another time, drank from a glass held by her feet before the audience. Owing to the crowd we could not see her properly and we were played out without having the chance to get up to her. She answered one or two questions of the showman as though she were in great fear of him and at his request stood upon her feet to show herself to the Company.

The bills given away outside stated that her 'beautiful baby' was also on view but we were told on the evening I was in that it had then been put to bed. I asked a commissionaire who was taking money at the door, how big it was. He told me it was full size, but said he with a grin, 'I don't think the kid's her own.'

22

The shop next door was occupied during the Fair for a trance exhibition. Having no fondness for trance displays I did not go in but one day I met a wagonette carrying a full-sized black "coffin" going up Derby Road. It was surrounded by some Gordon Home boys[129] and the Gordon Home bugle band was on the front. This was a great shame, I think. A man who was attracting the people rather amused me. Referring to the man in the trance he said, 'He arrived at 9.30 yesterday morning and was conveyed here in this special 'earse.' 'Thousands,' he went on to say, 'were at the station to see the ...' (a slight hesitation) '...er... er ... coffin.' A pair of cross eyes and a 'beery' face added to the piquancy of his description.

The same shop was occupied by the same people to exhibit a 'Fat Woman' the following week and I went in on the Monday night and had my first experience of the particular class of this kind of exhibition.[130] When I got there a company of fifteen or sixteen, chiefly men, but including several women, were watching a man with long

---

[128] Imperial: a tuft of hair on the lower lip.

[129] Gordon Boys' Home, Peel Street, was founded in memory of General Gordon, 'the friend of poor and destitute boys'. There were 2 bands – bugle and mixed. (*City Sketches,* October 1898).

[130] Another shop show and another human oddity, this time a 'fat woman', one of the most common to be exhibited. The overt sexuality and intended titillation does not escape Race: fat women were frequently infantilised in their entitlements ('Baby Ruth', 'The Giant Schoolgirl'), but also displayed as sexualised objects by, for example, wearing 'infant' costumes which revealed bare arms, chest and legs. See Ann Featherstone, 'Showing the freak: photographic images of the extraordinary body', in *Visual Delights. Essays on the Popular and Projected Image in the 19th Century* ed. by Simon Popple and Vanessa Toulmin (Trowbridge, 2000), pp. 135–142.

hair and very shabby garments doing a somewhat clever feat. He had a long rope fastened at one end and he was sending a curl along it up to a girl who was standing with a pipe in her mouth and this curl he made to wrap itself around the pipe. He also lassoed the girl's head in the same manner and afterward her feet as she jumped quickly up. Then the 'jolly fat girl' was announced and straightway walked out with much unconcern, an enormous piece of flesh of some twenty summers, wearing an ornamental dress reaching to the top of some theatrical looking boots. She had her dress cut short both in front and behind, showing a very plump pair of shoulders, and her arms were bare. After one or two explanatory items the man announced that the girl would take a collection and afterwards 'show her leg' and the more money she got 'the more leg she would show.' The girl walked round, again with much unconcern, but I did not notice anyone give her anything. The man then invited 'all single men to look another way' and the girl going some distance away coolly lifted one leg onto a low box and raised her skirts some three or four inches above the top of her boots, displaying thereby a portion of green stocking enveloping (it may be imagined) a leg of considerable circumference. 'You see.' said the showman, 'you have not given much or you would have seen much more. That's the kind of girl …' After which indelicate suggestion the barrel organ played and we trooped out with various expressions on our faces. A sorry exhibition.[131]

In the Market Place, which was the only space this year at liberty for exhibitions, were the following roundabouts:

> Galloping horses (two)
> Rocking boats [Sea on dry land]
> Children's roundabout
> Switchback rocking horses [two]
> Tunnel railway
> Switchback cars
> Switching back-rocking pagodas of superior construction (two)
> Roley-poley
> Switchback cars or gondolas of superior construction (two)
> and a long line of swings as usual.

Most of these roundabouts were lighted by electricity as in previous years but there was nothing novel or new in their construction and they had all been here before. This time they only charged a penny each ride with the exception of Saturday night when two or three of them doubled their prices. At a busy time when I was watching one it only went round three times. Another close by took passengers two more journeys for a penny.

In Sneinton Market this Fair there were no shows but there was a large collection of roundabouts etc counted up by me as follows:

> *8 sets of swings (four boats to a swing)
> *An apparatus arranged this way [sketch included] with boats at the four corners.
> *One childs roundabout
> *Ditto driven by a pony. I have noticed this before, I think The pony runs on a peat track and its master strokes it when he wishes it to slacken down.

---

[131] A similar description of a 'fat girl' show can be found in Tom Norman's memoirs. See Tom Norman, *The Penny Showman* above.

*One roundabout of bicycles driven by steam. The treadles of the bicycles worked themselves but some of the stronger boys who went on it managed to keep their feet on them.
*Two switchback horses
*One rocking boat

Two large boats rocked by steam. The ends of these were covered in with strong wire netting which was necessary because the boats nearly went almost perpendicular as they swung quickly up and down.[132]

Thursday October 1st
Had as I have mentioned a holiday this afternoon so went down into the fair. There was one long line of stalls from the Wine Shop at Chapel Bar corner to Skinner and Rooks at Clumber Street. Many of these were nut and gingerbread stalls; then there were book stalls bearing also cheaply framed pictures and pot stalls. At Boots' at Mount Street another line of stalls commenced and went down Angel Row to St James Street corner. Here were to be found sellers of braces[133] and nougat (a kind of toffy) and refreshment and photographic stalls. On the last named were photos of well known politicians and writers, most of them capital likenesses. But the greater part of the stalls was taken up with photographs of sporting characters in attitudes exhibiting the noble art of self defence, etc and pictures of theatrical beauties in various stages of dress and undress with a few children without any dress on at all. The men who keep these stalls have, however, more profitable wares than those they exhibit in a large stock of indecent photographs which they keep concealed either in their pockets or in a box on the stall. If a man stays a while to examine the displayed goods they will ask him, in a subdued tone, if 'he wants any.' With Countrymen especially they do a good trade in this way and it is evident that as there is only a poor demand for the other class of thing they sell, they must dispose of a lot of these photographs.[134]

Another line of stalls commenced about opposite Foster and Cooper's shop and [is] contained, on both sides, and in the form of a triangle, down to Wombwell's show. Here were chiefly to be found fried fish and potato, 'smoking hot peas' and refreshment stalls. The refreshment stalls exhibited piles of loaves cut up into slices or made into ham sandwiches with a row of cups on the front for tea and coffee drinkers.

Here also were to be found those devices for the extracting of money from the skilful and unskilful (chiefly the latter) by feats of throwing. One of these had a cloth marked out in little squares and for a penny were given three round pieces of metal each of which just fitted inside a square. The lucky one who did the almost impossible feat of landing one of the metal pieces inside a square so that in no direction it touched a line was promised a 3/9d clock or a fine silk handkerchief. Another apparently simple but very difficult feat was this: on a board was a large coloured spot about eight inches across. With five (I think the number was) large round pieces of tin, somewhere about 5 or 6 inches in diameter, this spot had to be completely covered. The men who held the stall could do this easily and quickly but for any one

---

[132] Once again Race notes the increasing dominance of rides. See Scrivens and Smith above, and also the National Fairground Archive website (http://www.nfa.dept.shef.ac.uk) for a fascinating gallery of photographs showing the build-up of Harry Lee's Steam Yachts.
[133] Unclear. Possibly a local term, as yet untraced, for a kind of fair-time sweetmeat or 'fairing' (see p. 52).
[134] See Simon Popple, 'Photography, Vice and the moral dilemma in Victorian Britain,' *Early Popular Visual Culture* (3:2) (2005): 113–133.

else the feat, though it looked ridiculously easy, was extremely difficult. There was nearly always a tiny spot of red showing when the tins were all down and if there wasn't and the person who was doing the trick looked soft the men would pretend the thing had not been done properly or in the course of an argument edge a bit of a tin off. I heard of this being done with a girl who had spent many pennies in the endeavour to do the trick.

At another stall I saw a round wooden box placed with the back tilted up. The feat here was to get a marble, thrown at a distance of several paces into the box and to make it stay there. The men who possessed the stall threw the marble to the top of the box whence it fell downwards but others tried to drop it down into the bottom and from there is invariably bounced up and out. A fourth and easier trick though the prizes were not so good was to break one of the glass windows, which were an inch or two in height, in a board painted to represent the front of a house.[135]

There was a further row of stalls from Beecrofts at the corner of the Exchange to the Black Head Inn at High Street corner and also a row in front of the Exchange itself. Stalls and roundabouts (a small one for children by the Prudential Buildings excepted) were not allowed in King and Queen Streets, but a photographers booth and shooting gallery were wedged into a space just before the new Post Office. Business however would not be very brisk with them there.

The 'fun of the Fair' this year was the 'Dudart'[136] a tubular roll of paper which was projected out by blowing and drawn in again by the same means. It would go out in this way to a length of about twelve inches and there was a feather at the end which jumped up and down by the action of propelling the thing out. Paper 'confetti' was also for sale but was not thrown in any great quantity.

Of course there was endless number of hawkers about with toy watches, moustachios, eye glasses, false noses, etc.

In one or two dark corners I saw men exhibiting a couple of small wooden dolls which danced about and fought in a realistic fashion. I bought a pair and found them made of clothes pegs, the ends having been sawn off and then fastened on loose with nails and the top painted to represent a head. The figures were on a string, one end of which was fastened to a box and the other jerked by the man. Owing to the darkness it was not possible to see this thread and the man worked the figures much more realistically than I was able to do when I got them home.

Goose Fair (continued)
Friday October 2nd
This evening is the 'town's evening' the special feature of which is the crush on Beastmarket Hill. The crush is maintained by strings of young people (whose ambition it is to belong to the genus 'toff') who go up and down in two rows, occasionally colliding and frequently getting up a rush which culminates in a sudden stop and consequent knot of heads and bodies. Three or four policemen stride up and down the Hill and land any particularly energetic gentleman out into the outer darkness with a roughness which amuses everybody but the party principally concerned.

The proprietor of Days Menagerie must take the palm for 'big tales' in their newspaper advertisements. They have nowhere near twenty carriages (ten would be about the mark) or the same number of lions. Nor have they 500 specimens of birds,

---

[135] Games on the fairground are not widely covered, but see Geoff Weedon, *Fairground Art: the Art Forms of Travelling Fairs, Carousels and Carnival Midways* (London, 1981).
[136] The modern equivalent is a 'party blower'.

beasts, and reptiles, as they allege. The coloured poster of this same establishment is a treat as per the following extract:

> Special attention is requested to the Cleanliness & Politeness of the Employees & its dazzling brilliancy when illuminated at dusk. And anything that is at all offensive or obnoxious is strictly avoided & under the Personal superintendence of the Proprietors & an Efficient Staff of experienced Keepers so that nothing is deficient to render the collection an Agreeable Lounge & Promenade & prove Enjoyable, Amusing & Instructive to all classes of Society.

Saturday [October 3ʳᵈ]
Went down early in the evening and perambulated the Fair till about ten. The shows filled as fast as they could empty and there was no need for songs or display on the outside. There were many trippers in as could be plainly perceived in dresses and faces. Beastmarket Hill had become rather rough and the regular crushing impossible.

Sunday [October 4ᵗʰ]
Went down this afternoon to find only the following shows remaining: Walls, Deppo Diver, Johnsons, Radford and Chappells and the Flying Machine. Most of these were partly packed for departure. All the stalls were gone and so also, which was surprising for they took two days to erect, had the roundabouts. The whole of the Market Place had been swept beautifully clean.

On Johnson's Show 'Jimmy' Dupe was holding his harvest festival. A company of ten or twelve, all men (of the 'Methody' order) save a single lady, sat on the platform listening to 'Jimmy' speaking when I arrived. Afterwards they sang 'God be with you till we meet again' and had considerable difficulty in starting as they could not pitch on the right tune and a drunken man in the small crowd was endeavouring to upset them by singing a tune of his own composition. When they had finished this Mr Dupe led off a long line of verses on Elijah and then they finished up with the Doxology. When the service was over they gave away small plum cakes to all the needy ones who went up to ask for them. I saw several men of the navvy stamp, who were wearing their working clothes, and some who looked like tramps fetch these gifts and some seemed very glad of them. They all put them in their pockets, I noticed too, without wrapping them in anything and they did the deed quickly. I saw none eat them on the ground. To one or two old women these good souls also give little packets of sugar and tea.

I crossed the Market Place again in the evening with W. and found the service going on as before. The front of the show was not decorated, as I have seen it, with corn etc. but there were two large bunches of flowers hanging from an upright.

At the bottom of King Street the old Fair Evangelist whom I heard here some years ago was holding a service but the young folks who were crowding the Row seemed quite oblivious to his efforts and he could only get a very thin ring round him.

Saturday October 17ᵗʰ
This evening when walking with W. down town he told me that Walls show was in Sneinton Market – a fact which he had discovered that morning. As I had promised to go with him to an entertainment in St Georges Hall I was unable, to my great regret, to go off immediately to it…

Got to Sneinton Market when the company were on the front engaged in the last song and dance. It was a very different Walls from that which had been seen at Goose Fair a fortnight previously. The gorgeous front had been replaced by quite a plain one and the costly appointment of the interior had given place to commoner but more serviceable ones. Mr Wall himself too had exchanged his fine costume, a triumph of the tailor's art, for one more calculated not to spoil by contact with the Sneintonites and his honoured head no long bore the shining tall hat but was covered by a useful square 'bowler.' The play I saw had some relation to the story of Faust but the presence of the ghost glass prevented us from hearing well and consequently from following the action of the piece. The only important things I have carried away with me were the appearance of young Wall made up as a terrible representative of Mephistopheles all in flaming red and the extraordinary way in which he rolled down and down before our sight in the glass finally disappearing, as it were, to the regions below. I stood by one of the lady dancers on the outside at the Fair – the light haired one whom I have seen there so long inside the show – and found her a little bit 'wappy' to use a vulgar expression. She is Miss Wall it seems. The show was leaving on Tuesday for Ripley and so I did not get a chance of seeing it again. For Monday *Maria Martin* [sic] *or the Murder in the Red Barn* was announced, a gruesome tragedy, the delight of the habitues of Sneinton Market, which I have no desire to see again. This evening the performance I got in at did not commence till about a quarter past nine so I could only spare twenty minutes for witnessing it. [137]

1897

Saturday January 30th

Caldwells have been showing the 'Living Pictures' in their shop on the Long Row for some time past now and tonight I went there to see them. This marvellous invention which only appeared last year is, I take it, a development of Edison's Kinetoscope. In each case, I believe, an enormous number of photographs, taken consecutively, are whirled with speed of lighting, before your eyes. In this case the pictures are thrown onto a screen by a magic lantern. The screen at Caldwells was placed between us and the operator and when all the lights had been put out the pictures were thrown on it, in size about five feet by three or four I should think. The following were among the views I saw:

Place of the Opera, Paris with numerous buses, cabs and passengers continually passing.

Some children skipping with a gentleman or two playing about with others, a boy watering the garden with a hose, and at the rear the traffic of a street seen through the railings.

Two gentlemen playing cards in a Restaurant. One accuses the other of cheating and after an argument they fight, the table, etc., at the finish being cleared off by a grinning waiter.

The sea washing over the promenade and some watering place. The photograph did not bring out the waves very clearly, but we could see them dashing up and down and at times leaping the promenade.

Three girls in a skirt dance. These showed up well.

Fire engines turning out of the Fire station.

---

[137] Mr Wall's change of attire is of a piece with the now plain frontage of the show and the more serviceable interior, both of which are concessions to the non-fairtime venue and audience.

Two men wrestling.

A scene, apparently at an Exhibition; a fountain in the centre and a circular train coming in and discharging its passengers.

The Czar in Paris. This was very good. We first saw the road lined on each side with mounted soldiers. At his side was a row of Cuirassiers and it was very strange to see a horse shake its head while the men sat quite motionlessly. The effect of standing figures making a sudden movement was the most curious of all in the pictures. Down this road pressed by the military came the procession; squadrons of cavalry, carriages, a troupe of Arabs (easily distinguished by their dress and manner of riding), more carriages and more cavalry and then the Czar and Czarina and their escort. The cavalry rode in bunches and you could almost hear them trotting so lifelike was their manner, and it was curious to notice officers, every now and then, forging ahead of their troops.

A railway station. A porter and one or two officials came bustling along and then the train came slowly in. Passengers got out and hurried off and others got in and after an interval the train moved off, some in the carriages put their heads out of the windows as it did so. It was funny to see a door open and a lady and gentleman jump out, apparently from a flat surface containing nothing.

There were other scenes which I do not remember and the affair was distinctly novel and wonderful. The pictures lasted about a minute and unlike the Kinetoscope did not seem to disappear almost as soon as they appeared. You had time to take in the scene fully and there was a leisurely air about it though you know that the operator was working as fast as his machine would allow him.[138]

Saturday February 13th

The last evening of the Circus at the Victoria Hall so I go in at half time to see the old-fashioned drama of *Dick Turpin*.[139] Three or four gay fellows are drinking round a table when enter a country bumpkin and his wife riding together on one horse. One of the drinkers – a fine looking fellow in a green jacket, white trousers and top boots with long flowing hair and a heavy moustache – gets up and gallantly assists the lady to dismount. Then while the countryman betrays his innocence he makes love to the lady and finally possesses himself of a heavy box they are carrying. The foolish couple presently find their loss and depart with the protestations in their ears of the lady of the inn that she and the people in her house are most honest. Next enters the renowned Dick on Bonny Black Bess and he agrees with the gentleman in the green coat – by name Tom King – to crack a certain house. The two afterwards enter the house – represented on a canvas thrust out of one of the entrances – and are surprised by a Beadle and his satellites. These representatives of the law had opened the drama

---

[138] An important and detailed early description of the cinematograph show from the point of view of the spectator. See Vanessa Toulmin, 'The Cinematograph at the Nottingham Goose Fair' (above) for further discussion and a list of the dates of the films Race mentions. See also John Barnes, *The Beginnings of the Cinema in England 1894–1901; Vol. 2, 1897* (Exeter, 1996). For a handbill of Caldwell's show (dated 1897) see Richard Iliffe and Wilfred Baguley, *Victorian Nottingham. A Story in Pictures.* Vol. 3 (Nottingham, 1971), p. 47.

[139] *Dick Turpin and the Death of Bonny Black Bess* was a drama frequently performed in the circus, allowing for demonstrations of equestrian skill and clowning. The death of Black Bess was a key moment, requiring the horse to 'play dead' and be carried out of the ring. For earlier accounts of a performance, see Jacky Bratton and Ann Featherstone, *The Victorian Clown* (Cambridge, 2006), pp. 53–4, 64–7.

by reading a warrant for the apprehension of Dick Turpin to applause from the drinking gentlemen. At the end of every sentence the Beadle would say to his son – a middle aged gentleman whose usual occupation was clowning but who had now to play a comic part in short trousers and a big hat – 'Ring the bell, Sam.u.el.' Sam.u.el would answer 'Yes Pa' and make a great pretence of heavy work in producing the required sounds.

In the melee that now ensues Tom King is shot dead by misadventure by his friend Turpin and dies uttering at some length his parting farewell. Dick then starts on his celebrated ride and when he next appears in the ring his horse is daubed with white paint to represent foam. The Beadle with Samuel and four or five other gentlemen of the law follow after him and manage to create much amusement by their comical appearance. When Dick comes to a toll gate his horse leaps it but the other cavalcade have to rouse the old man up which – for he is a knowing beggar – is a long job and when he is awakened it is some time before they can agree on terms. At an Inn he comes to Dick calls for a glass of wine which he empties into a bucket and gives to his mare to drink. It was comical to see her ears pricked forward as the bucket was placed over her nose. When she has finished Dick finishes the wine from the bucket himself to the astonishment of the ostler. Finally Bonny Black Bess can go no further and lies down to die. Dick utters a panegyric over her and the two are borne round the ring on a big stretcher carried by some twenty men. The mare stood this fairly well but could not forbear raising her head once or twice and as she was not carried out but released in the ring the illusion was somewhat spoiled.

The circus was packed as I believe it has been nearly every night in the five month season. This would not be regrettable but for the fact that the promenade[140] which is nearly all taken up by men smoking, is largely resorted to by women of unfortunate character whose conduct is not always as modest and quiet as it should be in a place supplying this class of entertainment.

Thursday June 10th
This dinner time saw the procession of Sanger's Circus which has been exhibiting in Meadow Lane since last Monday, it was as follows:

> Band in carriage drawn by 8 horses
> 8 led horses with grooms
> Two clowns in carriage drawn by 2 horses
> A black man riding
> About 24 men riding in single file
> Two black men riding
> Three more horsemen
> 6 elephants (one really a monster in size and another nearly as big)
> 4 camels + 2 dromedaries
> Reed band of ten men (mounted)
> 7 men riding
> 9 ladies on horseback
> 13 small ponies and two horses drawing carriage containing clown and driver
> 4 horses drawing car on which was mounted black man
> ditto but a mounted Red Indian

---

[140] The circus promenade, like the theatre's, attracted a perambulatory audience, and was often frequented by 'swell' gentlemen and prostitutes. It was the only area in the circus where smoking was allowed.

ditto Black man

4 black horses drawing car on which stood a milk white horse with its rider, a
    black man

Car containing 2 ostriches drawn by 6 horses (3 x)

ditto   3   ditto

Large ornamented car drawn by 9 horses

Ditto 9 white and brown spotted horses with 5 men in striped black & white
    dresses standing at the corners

Carriage (open victoria) containing 2 gentlemen in walking costume, a
    blackman and a lady drawn by 6 milk white ponies

Thursday June 15th

I am afraid my interest in shows must be a good deal on the wane for there have been
a good number in Pelham Street lately, in the shop opposite Thurland Street formerly
occupied by a tobacco manufacturer, which I have omitted to chronicle. There was for
instance a waxwork exhibition into which I went and that was followed by a juggler,
an Electric lady, a strong man, a peep show, two fat ladies and one or two other
exhibitions into which I could not muster up courage to go. Last Easter there was a
combined strong man and performing lion show in the Market Place and this
Whitsuntide we have had three separate shows – the Cinematographe,[141] an exhibition
of models and Radford and Chappell's Ghost.

    … coming back through the Market Place went and saw the Cinematographe
after 11pm. It was a dirty canvas tent with the sheet arranged by the entrance and the
apparatus stuck on an old box or two opposite it where it was worked by a grimly
looking individual as black as a stoker. Some of the scenes were very good. We saw
soldiers marching (a picture I had seen before), a Serpentine dance, an American
Cattle fair, carpenters at work, waves at Battery Point, USA, and a scene called 'The
Nightmare.' The last was exceedingly clever. A man lay in bed to the foot of which
comes a female. Up he jumps to embrace her and catches hold of a nigger who dances
on his body and completely upsets the bed. Then a Pierrot dances in and jumps off
over a balcony while a big moon appears at the back and grins a very broad grin.
Finally – though I do not give the thing in its entirety – the three intruders come
dancing in arm in arm.

    But the scene which some of the audience were on the lookout for, though of
which, when we entered, we had not the slightest knowledge, was called 'The
Model's Bath'. A woman – we could detect a large smile on her face – divested
herself of her skirt and other outer objects of clothing and appeared in her white
drawers and chemise and when the picture expired was just dancing a jig. Dose
number two: the girl was in a large white night dress which had fallen down from the
breast disclosing a well developed 'frontage' and was in search of a 'flea'. After one
or two dives she appeared to catch and squeeze it in her fingers and then she flopped
into a bath. Here an attendant came up and pulled off the white thing while the lady
displayed a fine pair of calves in black stockings and darkness – in time to hide
greater disclosures – opportunely covered the screen. It was a dirty and suggestive
exhibition though we really saw no indecency.

    I notice on the bills of this and Radford and Chappell's show some scenes –
including one called 'The Bride's Dilemma' – which show to what base uses the

---

[141] The first occasion on which Race uses the term. His erratic spelling ('cinematograph' and
'cinematographe') perhaps signals its novelty.

Cinematographe can be put [by those] who possess one and shady characters will need very close surveillance to keep them from public 'mischief.' I am glad it was late at night when we saw the thing and that no lady was with me.

On Wednesday I went into Radford and Chappell's show and after a feeble ghost illusion on the usual comic lines saw some more Cinemateographic figures on the following subjects:

A train discharging passengers, Carpenters at work, boxers, a Fire with rescue of inmates from burning building, a Serpentine dancer, a French garden scene with nurses and soldiers, and a 'ghost' illusion where half a dozen figures in winding sheets and some in armour frighten a visitor to an ancient chamber and some others.

P. S. I find that with the exception of the bath scene I have put the wrong pictures to the shows. Radford and Chappell's had the smaller and inferior display.[142]

October 7th, 8th, 9th
Goose Fair
The shows this year were:

1 Wombwells
2 Wall's Ghost and Cinematographe facing Long Row
3 Lawrence's Marionettes etc
  "
from Long Row to South Parade:
4 Wadbrook's Cinematographe
5 Sedgwick's Menagerie
6 Payne's Fine art
7 Divers
8 Wallace's untameable lion
9 Williams's Fine Art
10 Coxwain Terry's crocodiles[143]
11 The Heifer with 5 legs
12 William's Cinematographe (looking up Wheeler Gate)
from Friar Lane, Beastmarket Hill to St James's Street ditto
13 Strong Man and Woman
14 Unzie the Bushman
15 Count Orloff, the transparent man
16 Amyes' Mechnical Exhibition
17 Radford and Chappell's Cinematographe
18 Buckley's performing hares, rabbits, etc
19 Powell's Fine art [Gallery]
20 Burnett's Military Academy
From St James' Street to Market Street:
21 A 'French' peep show
22 The largest Bull ever seen[144]
23 'The Castle of Content,' a peep show

---

[142] The films listed by Race are taken from the Lumière Cinematograph shows, first exhibited in December 1895 in Paris. For discussion of the 'dirty and suggestive' films, see Simon Brown, 'Early Cinema in Britain and the Smoking Concert Film', *Early Popular Visual Culture* 3:2 (2005), 165–178.
[143] The *Era* notes that Terry also had a python (*Era*, 16 October 1897).
[144] Probably Woolley's show with the mammoth ox and the three-legged heifer.

I counted the following roundabouts etc in the Great Market Place: 2 sets of jumping horses; 'sea-on-dry-land;' a row of swings; children's miniature roundabout; the railway; 2 sets of switchback cars and one of switchback cars, horses and ostriches; one set of switchback and rocking horses and one of rocking switchback pagodas; a roundabout of bicycles, the wheels of which you could work though they revolved by themselves; and a 'rolley polley.'

The land at rear of the Prudential Buildings (facing Parliament Street) was occupied by a round about, several sets of steam swing boats, and a great collection of shooting galleries, cocoa-nut 'throws' and the like. Here also were two shows – a swimming exhibition and a fine art gallery.

I had a look round Sneinton Market at Saturday dinner time and found the usual great gathering of roundabouts, cocoa nut 'throws,' sweet stalls and the like. Day's Menagerie occupied a prominent place in the market and by it were a Fine Art Gallery[145] and what was apparently a fat woman show. The last was of a very dubious character if the signs that it displayed were any index of what was shown within: 'The Egyptian dancers,' 'That naughty little girl', 'All sorts of positions', 'The oriental dancers from the harem', 'The girl with two,' 'The man with three' (whatever they may mean) and has a significant warning: 'No ladies admitted unless accompanied by gentlemen.'

[page missing]

… In Williams' and Wadbrooks shows I saw some views of the Jubilee procession – three shown by the latter, to the accompaniment of a drum and fife (playing 'The Soldiers of the Queen'), being particularly good. In Williams' I saw a picture said to have been taken during the Greek and Turkish war – but I much doubt it. It represented the interior of the house into which soldiers came running in great haste to begin firing out of windows. There was much smoke knocking about, then fire and the place began to fall to pieces. Several soldiers fell down apparently dead and (what made us doubt the truthfulness of the picture) one immediately had his head enveloped in a bandage by some unseen and extraordinarily quick agency. A nurse came running in and commenced to attend her work with unusual celerity and calmness and altogether there was a great sense of confusion when the picture vanished. To heighten the reality of the picture a boy, whose principal work was to attend to the barrel organ, fired several shots from a pistol – which startled the ladies into real fear.[146]

I visited three other shows, in the first I saw the cow with five legs. The extra one was growing out of its right flank. It was quite as long and nearly as solid as those it stood on, but the hoof at the end had grown claw shaped and could be knocked about in a loose fashion. It gave the animal no pain to touch its fifth leg; for the cow went on calmly eating the hay at her head while the people in the show were extending it no particularly gentle usage.

In another show I saw 'Unzie the Bushman'[147] who had an immense head of long and silky white hair. It covered his face like a mop, but it was so fine that he could gather it all together and place it inside a tall hat, when he looked just like any ordinary individual. 'Unzie the Bushman' was an albano [albino] and his hair was white also as I have said. His exhibition consisted solely in the display of his hair and the gathering of it into his hat.

---

[145] A tableaux vivants or poses plastiques exhibition. See p. 22.

[146] An example of an 'actualité postiches', literally a phoney newsreel by Georges Méliès.

[147] Probably an imitator of Unzie the Albino Aborigine. Photographs show him in formal dress with a wild abundance of white hair.

I also went into the strong man show and saw him lift some very heavy weights both standing and when reclining on the ground. A young fellow in the same show swallowing several tin swords of various lengths – which feat makes a very uncomfortable impression on one. They were rather a dirty lot – the people in this show.

I have hardly seen so much of Goose Fair this year as on previous occasions, partly because I had no half holiday and partly because, through my mother being in bed, I was not able to get down town on Thursday and Friday nights until nine o'clock. On Saturday I went to see Sir Henry Irving play[148] and we had to be at the Theatre by 5 o'clock. I did not get into the Market Place until half past ten when Will and I strolled twice round the Fair.

December 18th
Walk back to Mansfield Woodhouse [from Pleasley] and arrive in Mansfield again – the train being very late – about half past eight. F. goes on to Nottingham but I get out having seen the bills of a Pavilion Theatre which I had resolved to visit. The Theatre is in the White Hart Croft[149] again but I have some difficulty in finding it till a country man – whom I had asked if he knew of the whereabouts of a 'show' – said 'did I mean the Royal Thay-ater?' The description seem to apply so I acquiesced and on reaching the wooden building there sure enough, was a lighted signpost or lamp on which appeared the words 'Theatre Royal.' I took a seat in the pit and found the play – whose name I forget – to be an Irish one apparently of the date of the first Home Rule bill for there was a lots of conversation concerning eviction.[150] I do not remember that there was anything striking in the play. In one scene a striking finale for the curtain was produced by the villain descending a well down which he imagined the hero to have gone. But the virtuous one has escaped and when the villain is hauled up again by the rope, lo and behold there are half a dozen rifles pointed at him – several held by ladies of a militant disposition – and to our great delight and enthusiastic appreciation the wicked man has to throw his hands up and declare himself beaten.

One of the best characters on the stage was the wealthy owner of a great castle who resembled certain portraits of Charles Dickens. He had Dickens' spare, pointed beard and a fine bald head; displayed a large amount of white linen and wore top boots of cowboy character. Another good looking figure was his wife – a lady in a yellow dress, eyeglasses and a white powdered high wig. She looked a good Lady Teazle and certainly did not betray her aristocratic birth by vulgar speech. A pert girl with a pretty face was a servant maid but she was a little too noisy in action. The leading lady in the Company – Mrs Leybourne, wife of the proprietor – was a country girl of spotless character doomed to suffer much trouble. She wore her hair down her back and had on a pink dress of juvenile dimensions but as she was stout and unmistakably married seemed hardly well cast for the character. Her 'father' was a lean looking individual who appeared to have gone through hard times both on and off the stage. Of course there were the usual two comic characters who appear before a footcloth and plot to waylay the heroine while the scene behind is being shifted. One had a really funny appearance with a turned up nose – ingeniously blackened - and a wide silk hat of ancient build.

---

[148] See p. 111.
[149] See Jennings's show in Mansfield in 1896, pp 57–58. This is George Leybourne's portable theatre.
[150] First Home Rule Bill 1886.

Before leaving I enquired at the doorway for a bill and was invited to go with the party I had addressed for one. My guide led me round to the back, up the narrow stairs which the artists ascend, and onto the stage where I observed the play going on and at the same time stood among the artistes who were waiting their cue. Behind the scenes was a more curious place than I imagined. There was only the space of three or four feet between the end of the side scenes (their technical name I forget for the minute) and the wooden sides of the show and the performers were seated about on boxes and various other articles which afforded a seat. Some were following the play from manuscript books, others (these were gentlemen, of course) were talking and one or two were smoking. The aristocratic owner of the mansion and his lady looked much less imposing on a near view for they were heavily made up – which was a point. The properties were lying about anywhere – some in a heap in a corner where they were thickly covered with dust. Mr Leybourne, the manager, was on the stage when I got in but he afterwards came up and shook hands and I offered him a cigarette which he took. His wife sat near and we chatted together on various little matters. The Company were at Newark last summer and were staying here all the winter. They never perform the same piece twice in one town and have hundreds of plays in their repertoire. Half an hour's rehearsal each day serves to prepare the evening's fare. Unfortunately I could not stay very long having my train to catch but Mr Leybourne invited me to 'go behind' any time I was in the town which I promised to do and so we parted with mutual regrets.[151]

1898

October 6ᵗʰ, 7ᵗʰ, 8ᵗʰ
Goose Fair
I have not the patience to describe the Fair fully, but these were the shows:

> Bostocks menagerie
> Wall's Ghost (opposite Market Street)
> Lawrence's Cinematograph (facing Spaldings)
> Wadbrooke's Cinematographe (commencing the avenue from Binghams to Lambs)
> Day's Menagerie
> ? Cinematographe
> Wallace the Untameable Lion
> A second sight woman
> Coxswain Terry's Crocodiles
> Randall Williams's Cinematograph (looking down Wheeler Gate)
> Count Orloff, the transparent man
> The bear-faced woman
> A child-dwarf
> Ayme's Mechanical Exhibition
> Radford and Chappell's Marionettes (late Ghost)

---

[151] This final paragraph offers a rare glimpse of the 'world behind the scenes' of the portable – the cramped wings, the wooden 'shutters' which formed the sides of the building, and the manuscript copies of the play (rather than printed ones here) which the performers 'con' before their entrance.

Buckley's Performing dogs etc.
A swimming exhibition
Prof Burnett's Military Exhibition
(opp Wombwell's) Baby incubator and midgets

I am not sure that this is a correct list as I cannot find the particulars I took down at the Fair, if indeed I did take any. But it is substantially correct.

I saw the child-dwarf. She was a poor little thing, the size of a baby a few weeks old, but said to have been born three years ago. She sat in a little chair and was lifted up by her mother for us to see her; but it was a poor exhibition and the child was not 'all there.'

I went in most of the cinematograph shows and saw some really good pictures. Most of them showed a bull-fight – views of the real thing – and very savage did the bull show himself. We did not see the actual death, but we saw several poor horses knocked down and dragged out of the arena lifeless. Randall Williams had a capital picture taken at Lords on Dr Grace's Jubilee day, taken as the two elevens were making a ceremonial parade of the ground.[152] The Doctor came first and raised his hat most affably, as he got up to us. Walking with him was Arthur Shrewsbury whom it was quite easy to recognise, and the great Gunn came a little way behind, and also W. Dixon, the Notts Captain.

Walls showed two coloured pictures – the first I have seen – and also a view of the Gladstone Funeral procession.[153] This last was a very good picture. The Commons came first, marching four abreast, then there was a little interval and the Lord Chancellor wobbled across preceded by his mace bearer. After him came the Archbishop of York, walking alone, some of the temporal peers in fours, a group of bishops, and another set of peers. Last came the mourners, before whom walked the Bishop of London and then the body. The pall bearers who walked beside the hearse were quite recognisable – of Lord Salisbury we had a particularly good view and the Prince of Wales and the Duke of York we could see at the end. Among the mourners were some little boys who hardly seemed to comprehend the ceremony and at the rear walked the Revd. Gladstone by himself. Any faces one knew were easily picked out. Sir Mathew White Ridley and other Front bench men who headed the Commons I quickly recognised.

Another capital picture shown here was taken in front of a train as it dashed through the country. The hedges, signal posts and telephone wires all went quickly by and the bridge which we could see ahead grew larger and larger as we approached until we had passed under it. Then we rushed by a station and could see the people walking up and down its platform and rapidly drew near a tunnel ahead. We saw the training entering it, then the sheet went black as we were [*pages missing*]

The roundabouts I did not count this time, but the only novelty among them was one on which large (wooden) ostriches were placed, the animals taking gigantic strides as the machine went round. There were three seats on the beasts, the first one so narrow that the person on it had to cling to the ostrich's neck to keep on at all, and the rear one so small that it was necessary to clasp your partner round the waist or you

---

[152] This took place in July 1898, was shown here in Nottingham in October 1898, Randall Williams dying of typhoid fever in Grimsby a month later. Showmen began to commission special films, often on local subjects, from around this time. See Vanessa Toulmin, *Electric Edwardians. The Story of the Mitchell and Kenyon Collection* (London, 2006).

[153] Prime Minister W. E. Gladstone died in May 1898, and was buried in Westminster Abbey.

were in constant danger of falling off. This roundabout was much affected by 'spooney' couples.

In one thing the Fair, I think, was remarkable this year – there was a tremendous amount of kissing on the roundabouts. And it was going on vigorously at an early hour of the evening too.

I had a look in Sneinton Market on Saturday and found three shows there – one cinematograph, another a strong man show, and the third labelling with a dubious title indicating the Parisian beauties were to be seen within. The Parisian beauties turned out to be stereoscopic ones – coloured – representing the various 'ladies' in compromising attitudes of rising from their beds or taking a bath. I looked into the cinematographic show and saw the tail end of the performance which wound up with a picture mentioned as seeing at Day's, but here the lady did not quite complete her disrobing.

The following Saturday evening I came into the Market again and found Wall's here. The gorgeous front and the dozen musicians had gone, and a very different audience filled the inside. The performance had been on some time when I got in, but I saw a portion of the drama in which one villain killed another, the two being in love with the same fair damsel, and also a comic interlude by two very small men. During the Fair, this portion of the entertainment did not last ten minutes, but here it occupied over half an hour, being regulated obviously by the patronage. Afterwards came the inevitable living pictures and it was curious to note how these which in the other market had been nothing but proper were here exceedingly improper. At least this was the case with two or three of them. One represented a dance by two couples in fantastic dress, of whom the two ladies in long flowing skirts were exceedingly lively. They not only touched the gentlemen's noses with their toes, but displayed the whole extent of their lingerie and in other respects were the reverse of modest. And to conclude, we had another Bride picture, this time a coloured one, the parties being represented as mulattos. The gentleman as before made himself very anxious behind a little screen but the lady was not so immodest as in the other picture. Here, when she had nearly completed her undressing, she made an arch nod towards the expected bridegroom (who was standing on a chair looking over the screen), and so vanished.

In this show I saw a curious picture representing a medieval execution. The scene was a scaffold, the block and other objects in the front. There were several figures walking about and presently in walks a man, bound and supported by two Sisters of Mercy. The man was laid full length on the scaffold with this head over the block and then the executioner with a shining axe did the deed of decapitation, afterwards holding the bleeding head to view while the body fell backwards into a basket.

It was not difficult to see how the trick was done. When the prisoner came on he was arranged on the block by the executioner – an individual wearing wide flowing robes – and while temporarily hidden from our view, a false head was tacked onto his living one and this was what was struck off by the axe. Still the picture was an ugly one and ought never to be allowed on exhibition for children to see.

There was another of these mechanical pictures on view in the Fair, but a cleverer one and without the nasty suggestion of the last. Here a box stood on a chair. A little boy came on and dropped into it; and then the box was shown empty! Again it was closed and two boys exactly like the first were brought out. Next their heads were knocked together and nothing was left in the conjuror's hands but a few bits of rubber which immediately turned into two great flags. A little later one of the boys had been produced again by some means, he was split in two by an axe and lo! there were two boys. And so the game went on with puzzling celerity.

There were others like these in the Fair – one an Astrologer, another a representation of a statue which came to life and went back to marble accordingly as the ardour of the individual who owned it waxed or grew cold – and it is evident that there are some firms – foreign ones I should say – who make a speciality of mystical pictures.[154]

1900[155]

October 4th, 5th, 6th
Goose Fair
Owing to the alterations for the new trams, the Market Place was wholly re-arranged for this Fair, and not, I think, to advantage. Two rows of shows were placed back to back by the Exchange, Wombwells were placed down Beastmarket Hill with their front looking towards Wheeler Gate and the rest of the Market Place was given over to roundabouts, the swings and fish stalls being abolished. Under this new arrangement, there was plenty of room to get about but I do not think the shows had anywhere near the same financial results as they were away from the great avenues of access to the Market Place. As this was probably the last year in which the Fair will remain on the old spot it seems a pity to have disturbed its arrangement. Walls, for instance, which has stood at the bottom of Market Street for 15 years at least was hidden in the middle of the second row, and Beastmarket Hill, formerly the feature of the Fair with its long line of shows looked dark and dismal. I think the old order might have been left for the wind up, which as it was rather a dull one for, whether owing to the weather or some other cause, there did not seem nearly the number of people in the Fair that one has before found there. As a recompense, the crushing and horseplay on Beastmarket Hill was greater than ever, the way 'whips' were used being enough to give one the creeps. But I was not able to take part in the sport owing to a great event which is impending,[156] and on the whole the Fair proved rather a dull one to me.

The shows:

Facing the Exchange (from Long Row to the Parade)
  Cinematograph and 'Wild Indians'
  Wadbrooks Cinematography [sic]
  Lawrences   "
  Burnett's Military Academy
Back to back to above, starting from Long Row
  Twigdons Cinematograph
  Paynes   "

---

[154] The foregoing is a fascinating description of early trick films, and Race is quite correct in identifying some of them as 'foreign ones'. These were undoubtedly made by either Georges Méliès or the Pathé brothers (Société Pathé Frères). See Toulmin, 'The Cinematograph at the Goose Fair'.

[155] Race's journal entries for the Goose Fair for 1899 cannot be traced. The brevity of this entry for 1900 is a clear indication that Race was losing interest in documenting the popular entertainments of Nottingham. Inadvertently, however, he reveals the changes which had taken place, both in the orientation of the fair, and in the dominance of the cinematograph amongst the shows.

[156] There is no indication of what this might have been. Perhaps the marriage of one of his older sisters?

Walls   "
Bucklaws Circus
Between above, facing South Parade
     A 'fine art' exhibition of doubtful character
     Count Orloff the Transparent man
     The Living Doll
And near Wombwells
     Wallace, the untameable lion
     Williams Fine Art
     and another   "

Figure 12. Theatre Royal, Nottingham, c.1900

2

'The life of the good playgoer is a life of experience'

Sydney Race at the theatre

Between his notes on Nottinghamshire churches, on local exhibitions and sales of work, and amateur performances of Bardell versus Pickwick *at the Debating Society, Sydney Race recorded his impressions of playgoing in Nottingham.*[157] *He was selective in the performances he chose to record, and although they do not necessarily represent the entirety of his theatrical experience between 1892 and 1900, they do isolate moments in his – and the reader's – understanding of late nineteenth-century theatre.*

When he writes about the theatre, Race reveals a maturing style and attitude. The early writing – he is an immature seventeen-year old on his very first visit to the theatre (see p. 93) – is self-conscious and imitates the reviews he read in the Mechanics' Institute newspaper room, a style that Henry Morley likened to 'great lakes of milk and honey'.[158] *Used to the 'drama Queens' that he had seen in portable theatres, he is mildly shocked by the display of theatrical 'lingerie' to which he is exposed, but on the whole his first visit is a pleasant one, and perhaps not what he had been led to expect. 'The amusement was of a most innocent character,' he writes, 'and I have not felt any of the ill effects said to follow a visit to the Theatre.' His reporting style discloses a keen eye for visual detail, particularly in costume and scenery, and provides for the reader a vivid encounter with the spectacular lavishness of late nineteenth-century productions. Describing the setting of each scene, for which he certainly consulted his programme, he details the minutiae of colour, style and even the fabric of the costumes. Telling details, such as Miss Fortescue's unattractively red nostrils and Wilson Barrett's 'seedy' appearance off-stage, enliven the descriptions. The description of the first scene in* Olivia *contains some of Race's clearest expressions of enjoyment and amazement at the scenic art. It 'gladdens the eye', he says.*

But whilst he is fascinated by spectacle, Race also understands the popular trend for elaborate staging, and how provincial audiences had come to regard Shakespeare's plays in particular as displays of 'stage scenery and fine action' rather than 'poems or dramas'. Even at twenty-one years of age, he has a sense of how theatre and theatre-going had changed and although this is often tinged with an immature pomposity, Race shows that he is aware of the issues, both artistic and economic, which had transformed theatre and performance over the last fifty years. Though he was too young to have experienced them, he longs, he says, for the days when Shakespeare was a 'regular' feature on a programme, and when the evening ended with 'a hornpipe and a rollicking farce'. Such sentiment is exchanged for more insightful observation as he matures and develops his writing skills. From descriptions of how Wilson Barrett as Marcus Superbus in The Sign of the Cross *'flopped about' the stage and Marie Lloyd in* The ABC Girl *as 'a stout, ugly, common*

---

[157] His accounts of seeing *The Belle of New York* at the Shaftesbury Theatre and the ballet at the Alhambra, both in London in 1898, appear on pp. 150–152.
[158] Henry Morley, *The Journal of a London Playgoer* 2nd. ed. reprinted (Leicester, 1974) p. 12.

creature,' he reflects not only on his own feelings – 'After Olivia,*' he says, 'one feels better' – but also the responses of the people around him. His comments on the provincial audience, and particularly on sitting in the gallery, are pen-pictures of the moment – the discomforts of gallery-going, the heat, the smell, the large hats of the ladies, his fear of a 'panic' and of being unable to get out of the theatre safely. Wilson Barrett's* Claudian *is amusingly mediated by the 'beery looking party' who sat behind him and who was continually sending his wife (his 'old woman') out 'for three pennyworth of whisky while his foul breath blew on me the whole evening'.*

The economic condition of Nottingham's theatres at the turn of the century was not unhealthy, despite the competing pressure of the Empire Variety Theatre, built by Oswald Stoll in 1898, and which actually adjoined the Theatre Royal in an architectural quadrant, the more refined performances at the Albert Hall and the Mechanics' Institute, and the handful of pub music halls in the city.[159] *Touring companies of some note, as Race reveals, performed at the Theatre Royal, and the Grand Theatre, two miles away at Hyson Green, accommodated the shows with a broader popular appeal. Race's observations on Sir Henry Irving, Ellen Terry, Frank Benson and Wilson Barrett reveal a local entertainment industry which relied heavily upon established national touring companies to attract full houses with a programme of classical as well as popular dramas, and if Shakespeare was not performed as often as Race would have liked, at least he was able to witness F. R. Benson's open air production of* As You Like It *and Clare Howard's melodramatic rendition of* Hamlet, *with its new scene.*[160]

Race's comments on the process and practice of late nineteenth-century provincial theatre usefully re-focus existing retrospectives. He is aware, for example, of the reliance upon an elderly repertoire – Olivia, The Bells, A Scrap of Paper *– and the dynastic touring companies which dominated. He is curious about the emerging trend for 'toga plays' but not altogether convinced about their quality or dramatic depth. He enjoys the pantomimes, although he is aware they are 'second-hand' (noting that scenery and costumes seem 'tired' and worn) and, unlike fifty years before, were imported complete from London. In all, Race seems aware, young as he is, that he is living through the death throes of a 'golden age,' and is already looking back to theatrical moments which he regards as pinnacles but which, of course, he was too young to experience: the longing for Sadlers Wells, and the 'hush' which fell upon the audience, and the 'actors of the old school' such as G. V. Brooke – those who were suitably histrionic both on and off the stage. To this end, his accounts of Frank Benson, Ellen Terry and the Kendals are described with an uncomplicated reverence, whilst his description of seeing Sir Henry Irving for the first time is already tinged with nostalgia.*

---

[159] Jeffrey Richards, *Sir Henry Irving. A Victorian Actor and His World* (Hambledon and London, 2005) provides a scholarly and insightful location of Irving within the context of the Victorian stage; Viv Gardner, 'Provincial stages, 1900–1934: touring and early repertory theatre,' in *The Cambridge History of British Theatre. Volume 3. Since 1895.* ed. by Baz Kershaw (Cambridge, 2004), pp. 60–85 gives an overview of the provincial theatre at the end of this period.
[160] See pp. 102–103 and 131–134.

1893

[*April*]

At night Belle takes me to the Theatre Royal to see Horace Lingard's Company in *Pepita*[161]. This was my first visit to a Theatre. Ones first visit must always be a noteworthy one. To me, at home, the Theatre has always been denounced as a wicked thing and I was surprised to find nothing to object to at all in it. Firstly then I was struck with the smallness of the place, i.e. in length and breadth for there were 4 or 5 galleries round. I had imagined a place like the Albert Hall here but the reality was much better, of course, for both seeing and hearing. The pit was quite full but in the other parts there were only a few handfuls of people, probably owing to the weather being so hot. The audience was a very respectable one, much of the usual concert stamps, at which also I was surprised as I had been told that the audience at the Theatre was the worst thing there.

Now to the performance. Of the plot of the piece I only obtained the outline but it seemed that 2 inn keepers had lately married. Unfortunately their wives disappeared in a day or two and only returned one day each fortnight. The husbands learn that they are at a neighbouring Court so depart there and get in the Household Cadets. Here they are surprised to see their wives appear as French Vivandières.[162] It seems that they are the Kings Daughters and have assumed this disguise because his Prime Minister, Palaques, has sent 2 spies dressed as above to look into matters. Later Pepita persuades her husband Pedrillo to fight as Bull because if he kills it she gets the crown. He however runs away at the critical moment, so Pepita surrenders her rights and Inez and her husband Inigo step into the former couples places.

Scene 1 was the interior of an Inn. Here Inigo and Pedrillo are merry making attended by a crowd of fair damsels. Some of the latter are in short skirts and low bodices and some are in male costume with tights. Some of them are good looking and some are not. Some are old and some are young. Some have shapely legs and some have not. All without exception are much rouged with big dark lines round the eyes to make them shine. Generally this is very apparent without any aid to eyesight, thro the opera glasses it can plainly be seen. Now appear the principal ladies Pepita and Inez. Both are good looking and not 'made up' extravagantly. Pepita looks charming, had a pretty turned up nose, with a 'bang' on her forehead and wears a captivating smile. She sings splendidly. Here a scene illustrates the ladies characteristics. Inigo and Pedrillo agree to ask their wives the cause of their frequent absences. Inigo asks the question but Inez waxes him into a good humour and finally shuts him up with a kiss. Pedrillo does likewise and Pepita makes him fetch a chair, then to sit on it and not stir till he has her permission, and tells him then *she* is boss and that she will *not* give him the information he seeks. Then the scene concludes with a general song of happiness and Pepita and Inez do a castinet dance on a small scale [?] at the end whereof Inez displays about two inches of her drawers. Inez

---

[161] Race's first visit to a theatre occurred probably at the Theatre Royal, Stockport, whilst he was visiting relatives: the entry is incomplete (the preceding part of the notebook is missing) and there is no record of the show at Nottingham's Theatre Royal. *Pepita* was a comic opera, by Charles Lecoq, and the touring property of Horace Lingard and his company.

For theatrical biography, see *The Green Room Book* (London, 1906 and 1907), and the *Oxford Dictionary of National Biography* (2007 and online updates (http://www.oxforddnb.com).

[162] A female attendant in a regiment, who sells spirits, etc.

generally wears shorter skirts than Pepita who shows no 'lingerie' on any occasion, but this was the only time there was anything the most particular could comment on.

Scene 2 shows us the Interior of the Palace and a company of Lady Cadets in a brown costume with tights, breast plates and swords go through some military evolutions singing the while. Also appears now an enormous figure – a guard who walks after the fashion of a wooden doll and who comes across Inigo and Pedrillo searching for their wives. However as they have the password it is all right. These two gentlemen join the other soldiers later on. They are dressed in most peculiar fashion, a mixture of fans, bucket lids, boots half on, coats in wrong position, etc. Palaques finds them also and there is a witty war. Palaques tells them he is a general. Pedrillo says he hardly looks like one and asks where his umbrella is. There was a roar at this hit, and also at several other smart sayings which were dropped. The two Vivandières interview Palaques and affect to be French. Their broken talk with the General was most amusing. Also there was a most amusing duet between Palaques, who is a small man of peculiar appearance, with a cracked voice, and Bombardos. The scene concludes with Pepita coming in dressed as Queen, standing with two Halberdieres, crossing their bills over her head and the other soldiers ranging themselves round and in a well sung song she explains her position as heiress to the throne.

Scene 3 was the liveliest of all. I was beginning to think the performance was rather poor stuff but this scene changes that opinion. The drop went up and disclosed a gaily lit and well painted market place. The chorus stood round singing. They had changed their dresses and now wore ones of a brighter looking character. So then comes in a dancer – Miss Connie Rossall – who gives us a solo. She has on a long clinging black robe with a big red sash wrapped round her waist and hanging down to the ground and tights of a like colour. Her dance consists chiefly of putting herself in various postures and I am not much struck with the performance. However it must have been hard work as just as she finishes she falls down in a dead faint and is pulled off – not to appear again that evening. Inigo and Pedrillo also appear, the former as a seller of drink and the latter with chestnuts, each of them carrying their goods in a can arrangement. They sing a topical song in which some of the popular and unpopular acts of eminent people are referred to. Mr Gladstone wants to give us Local Veto and Home Rule[163] etc, Chorus

> But it's cold it's cold
> Very cold

which was received with great applause. Later flower girls appear in a very pretty costume and sang us a song. Pepita and Inez also come on and don several pretty dresses. The former looks very pretty in one of green trimmed with black and as a Spanish Toreador – the only male costume she wore – is very taking. While wearing this she describes the Bull fight before mentioned. Then comes in Palaques and says she must renounce the throne. This she willingly does to Inez. Bombardos explains all and so the ladies having donned fresh costumes and taken possession of their husbands the curtains falls amid the hurrahs of the stage crowd and the cheers of the audience.

I was greatly pleased with the performance. The amusement was of a most innocent character and I have not felt any of the ill effects said to follow a visit to the Theatre.

---

[163] The Home Rule bill (for increased self-governance in Ireland) 1893 was defeated in the House of Lords; a local veto bill restricting the sale of alcohol was abandoned in the Commons.

Horace Lingard (Inigo) a big stout man, was very comical in his part as was Palaques (Mr Charles Usher). The Pedrillo of Mr W. H. Rawlins was also good. Miss Rita Presano as Pepita scored heavily. She has a splendid voice, is a good actress and looks very pretty. Miss Olga Schuberth, the Inez, has not so many opportunities but possesses the former lady's last named virtue.

1895[164]

December 1895
Aladdin at the Theatre Royal[165]
… [*Pages missing*] There was a large crowd outside the early doors so we decided to go for the upper circle which cost 2/-. We got on the front row just at the side and had a capital view of the stage and also heard well. The pit and circle were more than filled with the early doors and by [the time the] performance commenced there was not a vacant seat anywhere and crowds were standing. In the dress circle there were many ladies in ordinary evening dress without bonnets though none had low cut or evening dresses proper. The boxes all had occupants some without bonnets etc. as the others, the gentlemen in several cases being in evening dress.

Of course I was very anxious to view the mysteries of pantomime. I do not think I was so eager when I saw *Pepita*. My recollections of that visit having become rather dim so I had all the sensations this evening of a first visit to the Theatre. I must confess that there was just a slight tinge of disappointment after the affair was over. The panto seemed just like what I had seen elsewhere whereas I must have expected something entirely different and greater. The first scene represented a Market Square in Pekin (I should have said that the panto is entitled *Aladdin, or Harlequin, The Scamp, the Lamp and the Mighty Magician*.) Round the back of the stage were houses approached by steps and up and down these gaily dressed Chinese (chiefly girls) were coming and going. After a chorus some of the principal characters are introduced to us. There are two chief comedians Widow Twankey (George Walton) and Abanazar (Fred Manning), the Emperor (Mr Bert Haslem). A very fine looking man in a superb Chinese costume, his daughter the Princess and Aladdin him (or rather her) self. Aladdin was played by Miss Emmeline Oxford, a very vivacious young lady, possessed of good looks and a tidy singer. She was dressed (very modestly) in the usual tights and gave a charming representation of the character. Miss Rosie Nott was the Princess. She was much older than Aladdin about 32 or 33 I should think, very

---

[164] If Race visited the 'legitimate' theatre in 1894, he did not record it. All of his theatrical experiences were in the circus or the portable theatre. See 'Nottingham' section.

[165] Nottingham's Theatre Royal was built in 1865 by the Lambert brothers, factory owners in the local lace industry. With a capacity of 2,200, it stood at the head of the newly-made Market Street (its intended name was Theatre Street), a grand and imposing building. See Figure 12 and R. Benyon (ed.) *The Theatre Royal Nottingham, 1865-1978. A Theatrical and Architectural History* (Nottingham, 1978). For early pantomime see David Mayer, *Harlequin in his Element:the English pantomime 1806–1836* (Cambridge, Mass: 1969). A new and scholarly overview of the pantomime is long overdue, A. E. Wilson's *Pantomime Pageant. A Procession of Harlequins, Clowns, Comedians, Principal Boys, Pantomime-writers, Producers and Playgoers* (London, 1946) and *The Story of Pantomime* (London, 1949) still offer a thorough, if dated, account of the genre from the late Victorian up to the 1940s. Gerald Frow, *'Oh yes it is!': a history of pantomime* (London, 1985) is a more popular view up to the 1980s. Jill Sullivan's doctoral thesis ('The business of pantomime: regional productions 1865 to 1892' unpublished PhD, University of Nottingham, 2005) deals with the economics of the regional pantomime in nineteenth century Nottingham.

attractive looking but having one of those faces which show that they are up to a thing or two. She was in a light-blue dress, very smartly made, that reached nearly to her ankles and she wore a charming 'picture' hat. Fred Walton here brings on three or four dummy soldiers as the Emperor's body guard. They are an exact copy of the toy Grenadiers children play with and he himself is got up just like one. He has on white trousers, red coat and a wooden busby and over his face he wears a flexible mask which allows him to wink his eyes and open his mouth and gives him a most curious appearance. With his soldiers he goes through some funny 'evolutions', casting them about from place to place, saluting them each time in a comical fashion and walking himself in an automatic way.

Scene 2 was a front cloth representing the Exterior of the Magic Cave and when it was taken up we were introduced to the 'Interior of the Jewelled Cavern'. This scene went back a great distance. It showed the walls all covered with curious animals, some of them having eyes shining by the Electric Lights. Here Mr Jean Stanley made up like a demon, did a fantastical dance. Round his wrists were 'bracelets' which opened out in wide folds and he also had one right down over his head onto his breast. This he could make to take various shapes so that at one time he looked like an Indian Chief and at another like a beefeater. The stage was in darkness while he danced (sometimes he took great leaps) and he was followed about with the limelight. Here also there was a general ballet and a *pas de seul* was danced by the principal danseuse. She was in the regulation short full white skirts and was very intricate in her postures. Several times she came along on the tips of her toes, a feat in which I can see no beauty. Four girls also appeared dressed in Mephisto costumes and did a more exciting dance, in which their legs were given free play.

Scene 4 was 'The Widows Home.' It was a picture of an ordinary kitchen with bamboo work about. Here there was such fun from the comedians and Miss Louie Freear (who I saw when she was with the Midget Minstrels) appeared got up as a slip shod maid of all work. She is only small in height and as she wore old clothes and had her face blacked etc. She looked the character properly. The dummy Soldier also came on and did some curious feats, including the washing of a couple of rabbits (not real ones of course) in a wash tub and the hanging of them up to dry on a clothes line. Aladdin also appears and there is a feast. When the things are set on the cloth Fred Walton pulls the cloth off by a jerk leaving the other things on the table. The characters made their exit by Walton turning the table upside down, putting (wooden) plates to it to form the wheels and an old top boot to represent an engine funnel, in which he lights some stuff, seating himself as the engine driver and then drawing off (the apparatus was really pulled by a rope worked from off the stage) a chair in which Aladdin is seated.

Scene 5 was the reception room in the Emperor's Palace. I may here describe some of the many ladies in the cast. There were eight or ten principals, some rather good looking. Most of them appeared in tights but all of them (but one or two) were very modest in their dress. Only a few of the girls in the entire company had their dresses cut low in the front though some were not so modest as regards their backs. Miss Hyson was one of the principal lady characters and Miss Madge Lucas (who is I understand one of the Waltons' wife) looked very fine in the character. W. admired most a young lady in a yellow dress who certainly was not at all stagey in her manner. I thought a girl in dark green one of the best on. There was Electra, Slave of the Magic Lamp, who made a very good looking Fairy with little to say, and also Hymen, Slave of the Magic Ring, a dark girl of a Jewish cast of features dressed in a deep red who had a splendid voice and sang a song in which nobody seemed interested.

Scene 6 was the Grand Hall of the Palace and a very fine one too. Here there was a grand procession of nations. Girls came on, one after the other, in dresses of the national colours bearing each the national flag. They were escorted by a little girl and boy dressed in their typical costumes of the country. Ireland was greatly cheered and so was Scotland who wore a Highlanders busby. As they came on the principals who were formed in a semi-circle stepped out in turn to say a few lines. When Russia came on some enthusiastic person tried (in view of the sentiments lately expressed) to get up applause but there was very little clapping. The same when France appeared. Germany was soundly hissed and then when Britannia arrived escorted by a miniature John Bull there was terrific cheering and a few bars of 'Rule Britannia' [were] sung on the stage followed by 'God save the Queen' (the audience all standing). However the war fever has died away a bit and so the singing was not very hearty. This was followed by a Song called 'Sons of Britain' written by the proprietor's wife. It is fearful bosh but the sentiments and not the words are what we care for.

Scene 7 showed 'The Aviary'. There was a 'Coon' dance[166] from the quartette who appeared before and then Fred Walton did a most amusing act with two of his toy soldiers. He stuck a medal on the breast of one of them to which he pretended that the other objected. Then in dumb pantomime he carried on a long conversation with them the purport of which was quite plain to [see] as thro' his actions in listening, nodding, approving and remonstrating with his head and arms. To settle the matter he had a toss up and the medal finally was transferred from the first holder to the other. This was exceedingly clever. Afterwards the Emperor sang a song 'Trilby will be true',[167] Trilby being the young lady whom it is the fashion to be enraptured with. Then there was a most amusing burlesque of Trilbyism by Geo. Walton and Manning the two comedians as respectively, Trilby and Svengali. The latter pretended to mesmerise Trilby who had enormous bare feet and to make her sing. Svengali was a Jew and the representation of the character by the comedian was very clever. This was one of the best things in the Panto. Afterwards Miss Louie Freear got up in gentleman's evening dress and sang a song called 'I'm a foreigner' describing the adventures of a Frenchman who only knows a few words of our language in England. It was very droll.

Scene 8 was a front cloth of 'Outside Aladdin's Palace' and this quickly gave way to a Scene 9 view of 'The Spa at Scarboro' on a Summer's Day'. The scene showed, to the left, one of the row of buildings just past the Band Stand with the broad promenade to the right, the boundary wall. In the distance was a realistic view of Scarborough with the Grand Hotel looming large. Here was a very gay scene. First some children dance 'a life boat ballet' in which they pretended to pull oars and these were followed a ballet of bathers, in pretty bathing costumes. Then four girls (the quartette I have before mentioned) came on. They were in light coloured dresses with broad black bands round the bottom, and wore Toreador hats and had each a long fur boa on. These danced what was termed a Parisienne Quadrille in which they kicked very high and displayed a cloud of white skirts. They also introduced several times a

---

[166] Simply a dance 'typico' performed by African-Americans, but here probably referring to the 'cakewalk' or similar, a parody of formal European dances performed by slaves in the southern USA. It was accompanied by ragtime music.

[167] 'Trilby Will Be True' (1895) written and composed by Leslie Stuart. *Trilby*, by Paul Potter (after George du Maurier's novel of the same title) was first performed at the Haymarket Theatre, 30 October 1895, the female Trilby's bare feet and the hypnotic Svengali characterising the fashion for 'Trilbyism'. See Edward L. Purcell, 'Trilby and Trilby-Mania, the Beginnings of the Best-seller System', *Journal of Popular Culture* 11:1 (1977): 62–76 and George Taylor, 'Svengali, mesmerist and aesthete' in *British Theatre in the 1890s* ed. by Richard Foulkes (Cambridge, 1992).

little trick of hitching their dresses up behind. Though they gambolled to a lively tune and were very energetic in their movements this dance did not at all carry me away and I gazed at it with a very cool eye. Afterwards Aladdin led on about a dozen girls all in military costume, in which they looked very smart with their little round caps on their heads and their canes in their hands. These gave us a military song and chorus. Most of the other characters came on here, some in a change of costume. The Emperor was now an up to date swell as was also one of the girls, with a cigarette in her mouth. The soldier, Walton, had exchanged his military dress for that of a very outré sea-side swell and he cut a most comical figure. The curtain descended on a general rally and chorus.

The transformation scene was a representation of two china plates the full size of the auditorium. They represented the old fashioned blue kind with figures, bridges, etc. In this case some of the figures were girls in Chinese costume. The second plate rose through the floor and then slowly opened out like a fan.

Last of all came the Harlequinade which was not a Harlequinade at all. The scene showed a Toy Bazaar with all kinds of toys scattered about and some boys and girls dressed like toys among them. Enter a little French clown who in pantomime proposes to the toys to have a dance. The toys agree and then get up and dance, generally in couples. Several little dots went through this capitally, doing the splits and 'high kicking' with great energy. Lastly a very big toy, Miss Nellie Beryl, in heliotrope dress, rises and does some elaborate steps and laboured poses. I thought it rather poor but people who 'knew' said it was good. Perhaps my judgement was somewhat biased owing to my knowing Miss B., through having seen her in the streets, to be a sickly looking girl with an unattractive face. All this time the fingers of a large clock which stands in a prominent place in the bazaar have been moving on and when they reach the hour at which Pierrot first came in the clock strikes and all the dolls return to their places and become inanimate again.

1896

Wednesday April 8ᵗʰ
This evening went to the Theatre Royal (by myself as Will in York) to see Miss Fortescue[168] in *Romeo and Juliet*. As the *Argus* has printed my critique[169] of the performance I need not say so much here.

This time I went in the Pit and by getting to the Theatre at 6.50 I managed to get a good seat (about 8 rows down) without going in at the early door. The pit was filled and there were some standing up round it, but only two or three of the boxes had occupants and there were not many in the dress circle. The stalls were full, the rest of the house I could not see, so that my remarks in the *Argus* on the 'house' are based largely on imagination.[170] I like the pit; I had an excellent view of the stage and could hear well.

---

[168] Born 1862 – Race is correct in his estimation of her age – she formed her own company in 1886, touring America as well as the United Kingdom.
[169] Race's notice appeared in the *Nottingham Argus,* 18 April 1896.
[170] 'The play was staged on Wednesday and Saturday nights, and though the boxes and stalls might have been better patronised, the fallacy of the statement that Shakespeare spells ruin was demonstrated by good audiences on both occasions'. (Ibid)

I did not much admire Miss Fortescue's beauty chiefly because (a curious detail) her nostrils were red (probably by rouge) while the rest of her nose was white. She had a soft way of speaking too, which was not Shakespearian. In the potion taking scene she went, as it were, hysterical and some of the people in the pit began to laugh. Several pittites too endeavoured to raise a smile at other serious portions of the tragedy.

I should think Miss F. is between 30 or 40 years of age though of course she is made up younger. The best scenes she had were those with the Nurse (Miss Kate Hodson) who was a dear old creature.

Romeo was played by Mr Julius Knight who certainly acted well. If I examine myself though I should perhaps have to acknowledge that I look for a better Romeo – a more romantic interpretation than Mr Knight gave.

Mercutio (Mr Gerald Maxwell) was very good though he had not much at all to say that Shakespeare wrote. When he was slain by Tybalt it was fine to see the way he leaned on Benvolio and a citizen and gasped out his dying words. The servant Peter was played by an older actor than the others, Mr Basil Dyne. When he came in, backward, fanning the Nurse, everybody had to laugh.

The dresses were grand and so was the scenery. The ballroom in Capulet's house was set very fine with a lot of 'supers' (including several lady dittos) seated about. Here a graceful minuet was danced. Romeo came to the ball in a monks dress which I was nearly pointing out in the *Argus* was incorrect. Certainly he ought to have carried a torch, according to the play, whereas he held in his hand a "painted bow of lath." The garden scene was very good, the back of the stage being one mass of leaves.

Before I went to see the play I had read it carefully through (in the four or five preceding days) so as to thoroughly understand the various scenes.

Saturday October 24
W. and I to the Theatre Royal to see Mr F. R. Benson[171] and Company in *Richard III*. Went into the Pit by the early door and so got onto the very first row thence we had a capital view of the stage. There was a very select audience. Every seat in the stalls was occupied, the dress circle was fairly well filled, and the pit was crowded. There were however only two ladies in the boxes; the rest of the house we could not of course see but I should imagine both the upper circle and the gallery would be crowded. The part around us in the pit was chiefly engaged by School Board and other teachers who seemed to have turn up to see 'Shakespeare.'

Looking back on the play after the lapse of a week or two I find that I was thoroughly pleased with it. A short interval is a good test of the quality of a piece because one often persuades oneself that it has been an enjoyable play when reflection tells otherwise. The acting was of all round excellence and if Mr Benson was not a great or clever Richard III he made a careful and conscientious attempt to portray the character. Mr Benson is tall and slim and I think the King would best be represented by a short, somewhat thick set man. Of course he went about with a limp and he had a humped shoulder. He was best in his delivery of the tragic lines: in the love scene with Queen Anne I did not think him wily enough nor did he affect to be filled with that passion which – though false – brought the erstwhile enraged Anne to her knees. Mr Benson has a hooked nose and is slimly built. He spoke his lines with great

---

[171] Frank Benson (1858–1939), whose company toured the provinces performing Shakespeare from 1886 until the end of the First World War, visited Nottingham a number of times (see below pp. 102–103). See J. C. Trewin, *Benson and the Bensonians* (London, 1960).

Figure 13. Mr F. R. Benson, promotional postcard c.1900

clearness and could knash [sic] his teeth and roll his eye with great ease. Mrs Benson also is tall; she has nice looks (not at all stageyfied and not even spoilt by a large nose) and spoke like an educated person as indeed did each member of the Company. When the curtain had fallen he and Mrs B came to the front to bow their acknowledgement and she looked very nice in her walking dress and hat.

Mr Frank Rodney as Clarence went through the Dream scene with much effect but I think more might be made out of it with a little more study. This scene I knew by heart; indeed I have a fancy to perform it myself. Mr E. Lyall Swete was a handsome Richmond and spoke his lines, which were not many as the play had been cut down in parts, with a very pleasing effect. He and Richmond had a terrible combat lasting many minutes. The 'gods' cheered a lot over this. Mr Oscar Asche (Buckingham) is almost a Mulatto in appearances and the actor who took the part of Sir William Brackenbury (he was styled Mr Grimwood on the programme but he also took another character, which I forget, under another name) had a fine Roman nose. Mr G. Fitzgerald who was Stanley is an old actor of handsome presence, helped by a tall figure and a stately demeanour. The two Murderers were capital. One – the fearful one – was stout and well fed but the other – the one who did the deed – was a lean and wicked looking beggar. Mr G. R. Weir, the celebrated exponent of Falstaff, only came on for a minute or two as the Mayor of London, and then he had his back to us nearly all the time and so I should not know him again. He is a Falstaff, I should say, in size without any aid from padded clothes. The Prince of Wales and the Duke of York were represented by two young girls, almost exactly alike on the stage. They were dressed in a short black frock with black tights and had a profusion of gold hair. They spoke nicely too and altogether they were a regular treat. Lady Anne was played by Miss Frances Wetherall with, I think, a little bit too much energy. When Richard was paying his addresses to her she raved in a terrible manner but somehow we were not convinced that she meant it. This was just the impression Miss Fortescue gave me in tragedy. There must surely be a way of convincing an audience and leaving them with an idea of the reality of the words uttered but neither of these ladies obtained this ideal though, I admit, Miss Weatherall accomplished it more than the representative of Juliet. Miss Alice Denvile the Duchess of York was a splendid old woman. The way in which she blessed Richard was a complete exhibition of irony.

The dresses were good but not of any especial brilliance and the same remarks apply to the scenery. There was a fairly large stage crowd and two of the scenes looked well. The State Room in the Tower was best with the young Prince on the throne surrounded by the Court and heralds and men in armour grouped all over. There were twelve or fourteen men in armour and in this scene they wore doublets (?) worked with the royal arms. In the London street some young urchins did a little dance. For the scene on Bosworth Field Richard lay on his bed and a curtain at the back opened and then in turn appeared Henry, Clarence and the two Princes. They seemed to be a great distance off and as a green lime light was thrown on them the effect was very ghostly. The other visitants of the play did not appear as their deaths had not been referred to and as Richmond was not shown in his tent the words to him had to be omitted. During this scene Mr Benson's teeth were chattering as though he was possessed with an awful agony. The rival leaders each gave their addresses to their armies and were answered by a great shout from the invisible men. The Battle of Bosworth Field consisted in about twenty or thirty men getting together in a great bunch and so working their way from one side of the stage to the other, the while knocking their swords and halberds together overhead and raising a great shout.

1897

Saturday July 17

This evening W. and I went to the open air performance [of *As You Like It*] by Benson's[172] company in the grounds of Forest House, Mansfield Rd. I have described the surroundings in a short account of the performance inserted in the *Mansfield Advertiser*. Unfortunately I could not criticize the acting as I was afraid of making the article too long.

Mrs Benson was a good Rosalind, though hardly a great one. But she wore the doublet and hose well; had a very winning way; and looked charming. Celia (Miss C. Robertson) was a pretty creature with winsome ways. The costume of the Forester suited some of the ladies to perfection; they looked quite dainty in the green and buff. One of them was carried on a stretcher in the hunting party I have mentioned and in crossing the uneven ground was nearly upset. Mrs Benson went to her assistance with a laughing face and there was an interesting scene for a few moments. The young rogue on the stretcher was all smiles and some of us would have liked to have seen her upset for the fun of the thing.

Mr Oscar Asche made a stately Banished Duke; I liked his manly delivery of his lines. Jacques (Mr Rodney) I have commended for the speaking of blank verse. He was the only member of the company whose lines I could count but I think he should have made more of the 'Seven Ages' speech. He spoke it sitting with little animation and I remember that in *Richard III* he disappointed me with Clarence's 'Dream'.[173]

Mr Weir was a laughable Touchstone and Miss Wetherall (Audrey) was not afraid to be a real country wench. Mr Weir could, I have no doubt, play Falstaff 'without stuffing' as was Stephen Kemble's boast.[174] He has much dry humour but should I think take his lines a little slower. I should say that the rich dialogue with Corin on country life ('then thou art damned') was spoke too hastily; the words ought to be rolled, so that we may swallow them, as it were.

Mr Benson was a good but not a convincing Orlando; his self seems to cling to him in all his plays. I should for instance, have picked him out by the tones of his voice if I could not have seen him, for it was just the same as he had had in *Richard III*. He has a dreamy way with him which would I think make a good Romeo, but he lacks fire and, unless he excels in characters I have not seen, I should also say he wants genius. But he is a conscientious player and his company is a good all round one. The provincial stage would be much the poorer without his presence and though I do not hold any extravagant idea of the representations he gives of Shakespeare … I should always praise it carefully in any critique.

I might note here that Mrs Benson has an ugly way of stepping when in a long costume with train which I have noticed twice.

I should have said that some performers – the program says it was a lady but I feel sure it was a gentleman – sang some glees with pretty effect; and the chorus

---

[172] Benson's outdoor performances of Shakespeare, often abridged, were given, during the spring and summer months, in parks and in the grounds of houses such as Forest House (owned by T. J. Birkin, Esq. JP).

[173] Race is doubtless referring to the performance he saw by Benson's Company at the Theatre Royal the previous year (see pp. 99–101 above).

[174] Stephen Kemble (1758–1822), the son of Roger, boasted that, given his physical size, he could play Falstaff 'without padding'. Presumably Mr Weir was of similar proportions.

singing was very pleasing. I have not overstated in the *Advertiser* the pleasure the performance gave me; I think I enjoyed it more than any theatrical representation I have yet witnessed...

September 13
Miss Ada Rehan[175] in Nottingham
Last Monday the Theatre Royal opened, after a thorough renovation extending over four months, with a performance by W. Augustin Daly's Company,[176] whose chief member is Miss Ada Rehan of *The Taming of the Shrew*. During the time that the house has been closed, the interior has been almost entirely re-constructed.[177] New boxes – two on each side – circles, and gallery have been erected, and the floor, which is now divided into orchestra stalls, pit stalls, and pit, has been lowered to give a better view of the stage. The upholstery is in red plush and the proscenium curtains of the same materials; the decorations are in white and gold; and the electric light has been installed throughout the building.

Altogether the house presents a handsome appearance, and in its new state is a most agreeable change from its former condition; but though the painter and decorator has done nearly all his work excellently, we have to find fault with the names he has inscribed on the ceiling, names presumably of the greatest ornaments of the British Drama. There are ten in all – Shakespeare, Milton, Spenser, Chaucer, Johnson, Goldsmith, Sheridan, Garrick, Macready and Sullivan. Now of these, five – Shakespeare, Goldsmith, Sheridan, Garrick, and Macready – have an incontestable right to their position; but to the rest some exception must be taken. Milton the Puritan though he wrote *Comus* – it was last performed we believe at Drury Lane in 1865 and never has been a frequently acted play – would hardly be cause for his name to adorn a playhouse; and great and good Doctor Johnson, the author of an unsuccessful tragedy, whose connection with the stage, even as a spectator, was not a great one, would not look down with much favour on, for instance, the gambols of Little Tich in *Lord Tom Noddy* which is to occupy the stage of the Royal next week. Spenser and Chaucer, great names in English literature, never aspired to be dramatists, and therefore must be struck out; but why should Barry Sullivan appear in the list when his betters are excluded? Where is the name of Kean, the greatest of our actors after Garrick, whose Sir Giles Overreach sent Byron into a fit? And we know of no reason why Mrs Siddons, the most brilliant of tragediennes, before whom a long series of great critics were spell bound, should not take her place with Garrick and Kean. Phelps, who produced the plays of Shakespeare as no man before him had done, and no man since, would be worthy of his place in such a company; and Kemble, a giant of an earlier period, has surely a claim to stand with Macready. Kemble the ideal Coriolanus, and Macready, the creator of Richlieu and Virginius, stand or fall together, for they were players of the same school. We would plead for one more name. It is not the name of a dramatist, nor the name of an actor; but the name of a man who has preserved the art of both for posterity – the name of the greatest of

---

[175] Ada Rehan (1860–1916), American actress and member of Daly's company.
[176] Augustin Daly (1836–1899). Daly's American career – as critic, dramatist, manager – also allowed him to bring his stock company, which played melodrama and comedy as well as Shakespeare, on successful European tours. In 1893 he opened Daly's Theatre on Cranbourne Street, off Leicester Square., Ada Rehan (q.v.) having laid the foundation stone two years earlier. See D. Forbes-Winslow, *Daly's.The Biography of a Theatre* (London, 1944).
[177] Architect Frank Matcham reconstructed the earlier auditorium of C. J. Phipps. See *The Theatres Trust Guide to British Theatres 1750–1950. A Gazetteer*. ed. by John Earl and Michael Sell (London, 2000).

critics, the writer who has painted the glories of Mrs Siddons and Kean and Kemble in words that can never fade – the name of William Hazlitt.

During their stay in Nottingham, the Daly Company have appeared in five plays: three of Shakespeare, *The Taming of the Shrew, As You Like It* and *Twelfth Night*; Sheridan's *School for Scandal*, and *The Last Word,*[178] a German adaptation. Of the first named play, which occupied the most prominent part in the repertoire – Miss Rehan has been termed by one critic 'an ideal Katherine' – we shall shortly speak at length. *As You Like It* was pronounced a fine performance by the critics, but the *Twelfth Night* scored the greatest success of all. The play, that is, which is the pleasantest to follow and which produces the most laughter, attracts the biggest audience and obtains the most applause. And we do not wonder at it. Conscientious efforts on the part of proprietors and actors to educate the tastes of their patrons, to elevate the Drama into an art and not debase into a money making pastime, are so rarely made nowadays that the people who go to the Theatre for intellectual edification are comparatively few in number. Limited liability companies are ruining the constitutions of play-goers; and have worked so much havoc in Nottingham that we are afraid that the Daly Company have gone away disappointed with the reception they have received. Their program was not happily selected to secure good houses on a first appearance in this city. The Americans may have a great reputation in London, but they are little known outside of it, and the only Company which can draw good audiences in Nottingham with Shakespeare's plays is the Benson one. The Bensons are to the provinces what Phelps[179] was to Sadlers Wells; and for their earnest propagation of the highest art, and for the intelligent and painstaking manner in which they play Shakespeare a deep debt of gratitude is owing them. But though the well known Benson Company draws large audiences, it does not follow that the Daly Company, whose merits have not been learned, will; and to expect to fill the Theatre three times over with *The Taming of the Shrew* was a mistake. It would take a much larger town than Nottingham to find six thousand students of Shakespeare, or appreciators of this particular comedy. Audiences of the present day judge the plays of Shakespeare not on their intrinsic merits as poems or dramas, but on the amount of stage scenery and fine action they give. Actors too often turn the play into a farce or an intense melodrama, and much that is valuable from a literary point of view in the 'book' is cut out because it affords no scope for 'business.' The players who loved to mouth long speeches have long since disappeared from the stage; and with them has gone, in a great measure, the art of intelligibly reciting blank verse. We sigh for a return of the times when a Shakespearian play was a regular item with an intelligent stock company; when the scenery and the accessories were subordinate to the words, and when – for we are not ashamed to allow that it is good to send an audience home with a good laugh – the play was followed by a hornpipe and a rollicking farce. And oh! for the return of the Sadlers Wells times when a hush stole over the listeners not after, but just before, the most telling parts of a great play.

Returning to *The Taming of the Shrew*, I must confess that the acting, after the extravagant opinions formed on report and the increased prices, was rather disappointing. Leaving out Miss Rehan, the Company possesses no one of great brilliance, and is unable to provide the satisfactory performance that the Benson Company, for instance, gives. The Induction was the best performed part of the piece

---

[178] Written by Augustin Daly (1890).
[179] Samuel Phelps (1804–1878), manager of Sadler's Wells from 1844 until 1862, presenting a programme Shakespeare and other Elizabethan and Jacobean plays, and creating perhaps what Race implies here – a loyal local following.

and here the excellence of the 'make-up' of the actors was very apparent. Several players here gave us an impression of good things to come that were not fulfilled, and we have to thank one of them for a momentary picture of the great Dramatist. Having a sparse beard and moustache, and dressed in green, he looked as he leant against a pillar like Shakespeare himself. The rest of the play, when Miss Rehan was absent, was not well done; in the hands of the Daly Company it was no longer a comedy but had become a rollicking farce and might just as well have been supplied by Mr French of the Strand[180] as William Shakespeare, Gentleman, of the Globe Theatre. Mr George Clarke, the Petruchio, was a swaggering, whip cracking slave driver, and when he was not endeavouring to be tender, had the manners and voice of an Adelphi villain. Grumio, as played with much humour by W. Wilfrid Clarke, was a satisfactory performance; and of the Bianca of sweet looking Miss Marie St John, though she had a trick of speaking softly, we should be loth to say anything hard. The rest of the performers did not surpass, perhaps were not equal to average Shakespearean actors of native growth.

We have left Miss Rehan to be considered in a paragraph to herself. She is emphatically a great actress – a truth that reflection impresses more deeply on our mind. Oh! the dignity of her demeanour, the sweeping majesty of her walk, her haughty bearing, her fierce denunciations, her wrath, her uncontrolled passion. In the first part of the play Miss Rehan was much finer than in the humbler scenes towards the end where timidity and humbleness are required. She cannot be weak; she excels in strong parts. We would like to see her in some great play where she could evoke the power of the gods and hurl their defiance on the head of injustice. We would like to see her Queen Katherine in *Henry VIII* – how she would excel in this part – and we would like to see her as Lady Macbeth, when she could follow after the footsteps of Mrs Siddons. She has a *voice*. Not a woman's voice, for it is neither shrill nor weak; nor yet a man's voice, for there is no harshness in it but a voice that speaks powerfully the genius of its owner. Miss Rehan, too, has a stage presence. As she entered with short imperious steps and stood in the middle of the stage, arms folded and the long train of her red brocaded dress spread round her, we knew this was no woman of common ability, no puffed up stage beauty unpossessed of art, but an actress of power, one who had brought her intellect to bear on her profession and who was about to exhibit the fruits of her studies mingled with the genius with which she had been gifted. And we were not deceived, though it was not so much in Katherine that we beheld her greatness as in the triumph that we knew should be hers when she had forsaken comedy for tragedy. How can she, a mistress of stage craft and art, bow before a Petruchio – and above all before such a Petruchio as Mr George Clarke. She was tamed, the shrew was tamed; though she avoided the hysterical cries, the shrieks of common Katherines, she could not stoop to her master, she could not humour him, she could not coax her sisters – it was unaffected softness – she was made for tragedy.

The piece was well mounted. Some of the dresses indeed were so good that we must take exception to them and denounce again Mr Daly's taste and his selection of the supports to Miss Rehan. There was the tailor for instance. He came in dressed like a French clown and carrying his clothes in a basket identically similar to the one the dogs – the little terriers of the circus ring – delight to roll in when they are required to play at see-saw or to walk on their hind legs or do any other trick rather than that particular one. There were other examples too – Petruchio looked like a waxwork

---

[180] Samuel French, theatrical publisher of 89, The Strand, London (to 1900). French acquired the publishing and performance rights of many plays performed during the nineteenth century. This included the 'comedy' and 'rollicking farce' to which Race alludes.

King in Madame Tussaud's exhibition; and for an example of what stage management ought not to be, commend us to the eight or ten female figures that stood crowded together at the banquet in a row behind a gauze curtain. We felt a wicked impulse to shie at them so as to obtain the cocoa nut that would surely be given for each one knocked down.

With the rest of the Daly Company's plays we do not propose to deal, save to notice that *The School for Scandal* had been rearranged by Mr Daly, a proceeding which seems totally unnecessary. The audiences during the week have not been very large, except in the gallery, for the prices were practically all doubled and under the new arrangement the pit accommodation has been reduced to make room for a second price set of stalls. The prices of admission have been again changed this week, during the engagement of the Independent Theatre Company and Mr and Mrs Kendal,[181] making three different arrangements in a fortnight. This is not likely to be a lucrative policy, for playgoers are always a little unsettled under a new management; and in this case we are sure that a more moderate scale of admission would have paid the proprietor much better, besides opening his tenancy of the renovated house with greater eclat.

October 4th–9th
First impressions of Sir Henry Irving[182]
Nottingham Theatre Royal
I have during the past week made my first acquaintance with Sir Henry Irving, Miss Ellen Terry and the Lyceum Company, at our Theatre Royal. Needless to say, the audiences have been large ones, and those who went into the popular parts of the house have been very grateful for the introduction of the 'queue' system by which the terrible crushes that always take place when a popular player is appearing have been avoided. I think I may take some credit for the adoption of the plan, for though I believe that it has been very generally adopted during the present tour of the Lyceum Company, it had never been tried in Nottingham, and knowing this, and anticipating the great crowds there would be, I had written to the *Guardian* last Saturday, proposing that it should be introduced. The Theatre authorities had a good staff of policemen on, by whom the people were arranged in twos right down Sherwood St., with a little laughter and embarrassment on the part of the persons operated on, whom darkness fortunately quickly concealed. Prices of admission went up this week with a bound. Stalls were 5/-, Upper Circle 3/6, Stalls 2/6d. Pit 2/- and Gallery 1/- , and for the last three at any rate it was necessary to go early doors, which was another sixpence. The Upper Circle on Saturday night had only a row or two of occupants, to my surprise, but everywhere else was packed. I am not ashamed to confess that I patronized the gallery, and very select were its regal occupants on both occasions. It is a very good gallery – this of the Theatre Royal – the seats are arranged well above one another, and if one is in the first or second row – though for seeing the stage I prefer the fourth or fifth myself – one has also a good view of the dress circle and the occupants of the boxes and stalls. On Saturday evening, I was on the second row – behind W. K. who had got on the first – and I had a good view of the fair ladies whose beauty ornamented the house, not to mention the diamonds which ornamented the fair

[181] Madge Kendal (Margaret Robertson) (1848–1935) and William Hunter Kendal (1843–1917) who were touring the provinces. Race sees them three years later in *The Elder Miss Blossom* (see p. 138).
[182] This was the week of Nottingham's annual Goose Fair, which saw a huge influx of people from town and country. Theatres and music halls took advantage of this and offered attractive programmes. See Richards, *Sir Henry Irving* (above) and Joy Melville, *Ellen Terry* (London, 2006).

shoulders of the ladies. Most of the ladies in the dress circles and boxes were in evening dress, of which I have seen very little on my former visits to this house.

The programme for the week comprised five plays – *Madame Sans-Gêne* (which I saw on Tuesday) being played the first three evenings, *Journeys End in Lovers Meeting* and *The Bells* on Thursday, *The Merchant of Venice* (also played at Saturday matinees) on Friday, and *A Story of Waterloo* and *The Bells* again on Saturday evening.[183]

Madame Sans-Gêne is not a great play but it gives Miss Ellen Terry a delightful part, and I must confess that before Tuesday evening was half over, I had fallen a complete victim to that lady's charms. If I was, when the week had gone, still undecided about Sir Henry Irving's claim to greatness, there was no doubt in my mind that Miss Terry was a Mistress of Comedy and the most fascinating of actresses. I have never before seen such a charming woman of the stage.

The Prologue, where the scene represented the interior of a laundry, was the most interesting part of Madame Sans-Gêne. Here Miss Terry appeared and began the duties of a blanchisseuse,[184] taking the hot irons from the stoves, spitting on them, and then going through the usual process of ironing. The back of the laundry was a long window, opening onto the street and along this street crowds of excited men and women on their way to the Tuileries were continually passing. And here the perfection of Sir Henry's scenic art was fully shown. I have never seen such a perfect stage crowd before. Odd groups of excited revolutionists first went by and then came a yelling crowd of red capped men and frantic women, mixed up with which were soldiers of the National Guard a party of whom dragged a great cannon along. When this rabble had past more of the National Guard – no doubt the ones we had previously seen but they conducted themselves differently – came by, marching in military order with long swinging steps and a drummer at their head. The uniform of these soldiers – blue coat with lapels and epaulettes, white cross belts, and white trousers and long gaiters – made them look very picturesque. After the crowd has gone, Sans Gêne clears out her girls, puts her shutters to, and is about to go herself when a wounded man comes tumbling into the room. She has hardly time to speak to him before a sound of knocking is heard at the street door. It is the Sergeant Lefèbre, her lover! If he sees the wounded man – who is the Count de Neippery, an adherent of the Royalist party – he will have him made a prisoner, so Catherine for a minute cannot think where to hide the man who has thrown himself on her mercy. In haste, she bundles him into her bedroom, and then lets in the Sergeant with two or three of his fellow soldiers. They have taken the Tuileries and are in good spirits about it and all goes well until Lefèbre thinks he would like a wash which he proposes to get in Madame's room. This will never do, so we behold some wonderful coaxing on the part of Miss Terry but strange as it seems Lefèbre will be neither hugged nor kissed into washing his dirty face elsewhere. Then the lady tries another plan and fills her beautiful eyes with tears which excites the Sergeant the more. After a struggle he takes the key from her by force. He goes into the room and Madame Sans-Gêne gives all up for lost. Lefèbre, though, is made of honest stuff and finding the wounded man there he understands all that the woman has done and will not betray her. He comes out of the room tells his companions who had helped him to obtain the key, that there

---

[183] *Madame Sans-Gêne* by J. W. C. Carr (1897) from Victorien Sardou; *Journey's End in Lovers Meeting* by J. O. Hobbes (1894); *The Bells* by L. D. Lewis (1871); *A Story of Waterloo* by Sir A. C. Doyle (1894).
[184] Fr.: washer-woman.

was nothing in it, and when they have gone kisses Catherine, telling her that she was a silly woman not to have let him into her secret at once.

This ends the Prologue which like the rest of the play is a little faulty in design. Lefèbre's companions would not have been likely to have stood idly by while the quarrel with Catherine went on and after the scene that was necessary to obtain the key, without doubt they would have gone into the room with him to search for its secret. Here they went on eating and drinking, which was absurd; but really the playwright need not have introduced them into the scene at all. It is, too, only fair to suppose that Catherine would have had enough tact not to have aroused Lefèbre's suspicions. I should mention that in this scene occurred one of those double entendres – albeit most in the play were of as innocent a nature as a double entendre can be – of which we heard several during the evening. 'Give me the key of your room,' says Lefèbre. 'You shan't have it,' says Catherine with a stamp of her foot and then, with a delightful, tearful face and voice, 'You shall go into that room when you are my husband and –' this with an indignant nod that made the house roar – 'not till.'

When the curtain rolls up on Act 1, twenty years have past and the former Sergeant of the Guard is now a Duke under an Emperor, and the washerwoman, Catherine is his wife, the Duchess. The scene – the interior of the Palace – was a gorgeous one, the walls of white being picked out with gold, and the furniture in the light and graceful style of the Empire lending additional dignity to the scene. It is morning and the Duchess – still with the fine and easy manners of a washerwoman – is about to receive the costumier, a bootmaker and her master of deportment, a professor of dancing. She enters in very loose and apparently scanty attire, slips off her dressing gown - and we get a very liberal view of Miss Terry's shoulders and bare arms. Then she tries the thing on, in all kinds of ways, striking various attitudes and pulling her pretty face into many shapes and generally acting like a clown – only a most delightful clown. The bootmaker follows and a very life like bootmaker he was; Mr Archer might have served his time to the trade so well did he act the short part. Monsieur le Professor de deportment takes his turn next and we have another amusing time. Madame must do so, he says, striking a very graceful attitude. She does; but her legs go one way – two I mean – her arms flap like the sails of a windmill, and her body coils itself into a most awkward shape. Then she grins and jokes [with] the Professor and they try again, with worse effect. It was most amusing to see Miss Terry manipulating a long riding dress, with a green jacket on, two or three sizes too large for her, and a white felt hat cocked onto her nose, but it was not the Duchess de Dantzig nor the clever washerwoman of the Revolutionary days. Then Lefèbre, the Duke, comes in and remonstrates with her for her ridiculous ways. 'And you ought not to expose your person, before all these men as you do,' he says. 'La, it's nothing to what you'll see when I'm dressed for the Ball,' is the reply of his good lady. The Ball is one thing and her apartments another to the Duke and he proceeds to tell her that the Emperor has commanded him to divorce her, and marry some insipid thing, whose name I forget for the minute. Madame laughs in his face, expresses her great contempt for the party named, jeers at his want of courage at not refusing to obey the Emperor, and then breaks down and begins to sob her heart out. Through the tears she tells with what vigour she would have treated Napoleon if he had given her similar commands. Lefèbre draws her near him to comfort her. Why has she not, he asks, inquired what answer he gave the Emperor. And now came a wonderful bit of facial play from Miss Terry. She holds him at arm's length. Fear first on her face; then doubt, then confidence; then joy; and then a big hug which we should have all liked to have received and a big laugh which we all heard and understood. He has told the

Emperor he can't part with her! Of course he has, and off he sends her to get ready for the ball.

The ball scene was the finest I have seen on the stage. Gorgeous lackeys preceded each set of visitors and it was a treat to see with what grace and dignity the guests glided into the room. Last came the Queen of Naples and the Princess of Piombino, sisters of Napoleon, but the Duchess is not there to receive them. When she comes bustling in she commences to talk in a loud manner and her actions are the freest. The sisters of Napoleon, with whom she is very familiar, want to get her to tell them a little anecdote she is fond of so that they may tell tales to the Emperor. It is about a little sweep who stole some of her jewellery and who was stripped in her presence; and she is just on with it, having easily fallen into the trap, when Fouché, her friend, who has given her previous warning, stops her by the sign arranged – which is the tapping of his snuff box. Fouché (Mr Mackintosh) was the best actor on the stage this evening and of his performance I shall have more to say before I conclude. When he starts tapping, Madame at first pays no heed to him; it grows louder and she is forced to hear. Then there is a clever pantomime for a minute or two and the tale comes to an abrupt termination. The princesses are enraged at being baffled and they burst out with hard words; Madame Sans-Gêne replies with interest: and there is a pretty scene until the ball breaks up in confusion. The ladies dresses in this scene were lovely; and as for the gentlemen – well for once our better halves were beaten on their own ground. Some of the men were in cavalry uniform and carried their gorgeous headgear under their arms, with their swords trailing on the ground, others were in the particularly graceful civil dress of the Empire period. But the dress was not all; every man <u>looked</u> his part and his bearing was that of the beginning, not the end of this century. Some of the older men might have been the veritable gallants they represented, so perfect was their demeanour. This says a great deal for Sir Henry's stage management.

The 2nd and 3rd acts took place in the Emperor's room, which was a fine specimen of stage art, the built-up book cases giving an air of great truth to the scene and the good workmanship of the furniture making the room look like a real palace. On the curtain rising I had my first view of Irving. He was seated writing at an escritoire, the shaded lamp throwing a light on to his bent down face. Of course there was much applause and when it had continued some time the actor rose – and still holding his face bowed – still the real Napoleon – stood with bent figure until it ceased. Then the play continued. Sir Henry's makeup was very good. He wore the familiar green coat – buttoned tightly up – and white breeches and though he is, I believe, rather slim in stature, yet by increasing the width of his body, he prevented this from being noticed.[185] I had heard of the contrivance by which the trousers were held out, but it was not discernible in the contour of the figure; and the stage Napoleon appeared to have a very well shaped leg. Sir Henry's voice is naturally thick and it was easy for him to be gruff and sharp, thus indicating the traditional manners of the Emperor; and he always kept his head bent well onto his chest.

The Princesses – who by the way were poor actresses – were the first to appear on the scene to lay their grievances before the Emperor. Presently they begin to quarrel one with the other, and Napoleon who has risen from his writing desk and is standing by the fire place, takes up the tongs to separate them. They exit in

---

[185] 'His huge costume and fleshings were thickly lined to make him seem short and fat. His desk was huge to make him seem small, and all the men surrounding him on stage were above his height, and even the stage set had oversize pillars.' Madeleine Bingham, *Henry Irving. The Greatest Victorian Actor* (London, 1978), p. 279.

disgrace; and Napoleon sends for the Duchess. He is very angry with her at first but Madame gradually works round him and they have a pleasant time together. She knows she was a washerwoman; and a lieutenant of his old regiment still owes her a bill. Ah, says Napoleon, and when she produces it, and says she would like payment, opens it and finds it is one of his own old scores. (I omitted to mention that in the Prologue, Sans Gêne sends off some clothes to a young lieutenant in the Blues, Napoleon Bonaparte by name, of whom the girl is not to ask for payment as he is very poor – which serves to introduce the future Emperor, of whom Madame and Fouché also talk). Then Napoleon becomes still more pleasant and smacks the Duchess several times on the bare shoulders. The *News* [reporter] says this sent a shiver through him, and it certainly makes one recollect that the two must be on very familiar terms after playing together so long. They sit together on the sofa and the Emperor would like to take more liberties. He examines her necklace with great interest, possibly because it allows him to touch her neck. They revive old memories; and Sans Gêne tells him that she has fought for him and actually received a wound in his service. He asks where it is; and the Duchess pulls her sleeve up and shows him a mark on her arm, which the Emperor reverently kisses. He thinks this a sign that he may proceed further and is feeling happy when Madame gets up and making him a very low curtsey exclaims, 'Monsieur I have no more wounds for you to search for.'

The rest of the play revolves round an intrigue between the Empress Marie Louise and the Count de Neipperg, whom Sans Gêne saved in the old days. It does not seem clear why the affair should be introduced at all, and it creates but a mild interest, for the circumstances are not made very clear. It is not certain, for instance, whether Neipperg was really guilty or not; Napoleon sends a letter, apparently from the Comte, to the Empress whom we see in bed in a dim light through folding doors, and the reply that he gets is innocent enough. However, the Emperor has the Comte arrested and orders him to be shot and then the Duchess and Fouché plot to save him. Fouché has fallen into disgrace and there is a new Minister of Police who gives instructions for the command of the Emperor to be obeyed. When this has been done, the Emperor rushes in and wants the order cancelled. The Minister says 'impossible' at which Napoleon exclaims in a temper, 'Damn it all, if Fouché had been here this would not have happened.' On which Fouché turns up to say the Comte is still alive, thanks to himself. This cleverness on the part of Fouché restores him to the office and the supplanting Minister is dismissed in disgrace. All this takes place in the last act (the 3rd) and has very little interest for us as Madame Sans Gêne is not concerned prominently in it, except in some passages with Fouché, in which Mr Mackintosh appeared to great advantage.

Madame Sans-Gêne is Miss Ellen Terry's play; take her out and not even Sir Henry Irving's name would make it draw. It is only the charm of Miss Terry's acting and the mounting of the clever stage management which have made the piece a success. Of these, I have already spoken and were I to write much more I should fail to tell all the delight that Miss Terry's acting gave me. Miss Terry a grandmother, and yet a paragon comedienne! Miss Terry fifty, and yet doing the foolish things of twenty five! Miss Terry is pretty, as agile as if she were a young girl making her debut! Miss Terry, our greatest actress, using naughty expressions and being smacked on her bare shoulders by the first actor-knight, the head of his profession!

Let us pass to Mr Mackintosh. Had I been a newspaper critic, and been deputed to write of the performance, I should [have] awarded him the highest praise among the gentlemen – Sir Henry himself did not make a better Napoleon than Mr Mackintosh a Fouché. He was the cool, calculating Minister of Police to the life, and though he was not required by the dramatist to make Fouché an evil-minded person, yet by insinuation he clearly gave us to understand that he was a plotting, self-seeking individual. Mr Mackintosh's enunciation is clear and he can made good use of his features. Above all he acts with his head. I like Mr Mackintosh; for he is of the old school; and a careful player to boot.

Sir Henry Irving was as good a Napoleon as his part allowed him to be; but a player with a much inferior reputation could have given an equally clever representation. In some respects Irving is suited by temperament for the character, for his voice is naturally thick and it is easy for him, I imagine, to adopt a sharp, irritable manner and tone of voice.

For the rest, the Lyceum Company, at any rate as it appeared this evening, is a very inferior body of performers. Excepting the Master of the Ballet (Mr Norman Forbes), the costumier (Mr W. Farren jnr) and the Bootmaker (Mr Asche), who all had small parts, none of them shined with anything but the average merit; indeed many of them, to tell the truth, appeared to have hardly a grain of dramatic genius. I suppose Sir Henry picks his Company to show up Miss Terry and himself to great advantage. If so, he accomplishes his object. Mr Frank Cooper, of whom I have heard much, was a very commonplace actor to my thinking; and the ladies were a very inferior lot. It is a rather hackneyed thing to say – at any rate in Nottingham – but omitting Miss Terry, Irving and Mr Mackintosh, the Benson company are certainly a more capable set of actors than the Lyceum one.

On Saturday evening I went to see *A Story of Waterloo* and *The Bells*.[186] This was Sir Henry's opportunity for Miss Terry had no part which was to be regretted, and it must be doubted whether the two plays are a good combination. Both are tragic; and both of the characters which Sir Henry takes are cast in the same mould, one mournfully pathetic, the other terribly serious. As a relief then to the audience, *A Story of Waterloo* and *The Bells* should be alternated with some lighter piece, which would make one realise Sir Henry's creations better and prevent the thought that the Mathias, old and haggard, is that ancient veteran Corporal Brewster, late of the Blues, grown young, with his innocence changed into harrowing remorse.

Irving's Corporal Brewster is a marvellous sketch, worthy I would be bold to say, of Garrick himself. He is an old man of 80 to the life. The voice is there, the tottering legs, the bony hands and the mannerisms and more wonderful than all these in the extraordinary play of the face. I examined it most carefully through the glass and underneath the paint and powder which had given him his pallor, one could see that the actor had become, for the while, a veritable old man. His thought was feeble and his memory poor. His very mental faculties were those of a worn out, unlearned soldier of 80.

When Corporal Brewster gets down to his old rooms on this particular morning in 1881, he finds a sprightly good looking lass there who is busying herself in getting his breakfast ready. 'And who may thee be?' he says. 'Why don't you know me, I'm your niece, uncle.' 'What brother Jarge's lass,' says the old man shaking with

---

[186] As a pair, *Madame Sans-Gêne* and *A Story of Waterloo* were vehicles which allowed Terry and Irving to shine in their separate spheres, whilst *The Bells* and *Waterloo* present, as Race notes, a rather heavy dramatic meal.

Two fascinating studies of these plays are W. D. King, *Henry Irving's Waterloo. Theatrical Engagements with Arthur Conan Doyle, George Bernard Shaw, Ellen Terry, Late-Victorian Culture, Assorted Ghosts, Old Men, War and History* (Berkeley, 1993), and *Henry Irving and* The Bells. Irving's personal script of the play by Leopold Lewis, edited and introduced by David Mayer (Manchester, 1980).

pleasure, 'and how is thee fayther.' 'Fayther's been dead twenty years now, uncle; have you forgotten?' The old man takes no notice but goes on, 'And how's that pup that I sold him before I took the shilling; it was a fine pup, it was.' He goes on a little while in this strain and then sits down to his breakfast, which Irving, true to nature, eats with all the ravenousness of an old man, drinking his tea with a loud sipping noise and spilling a good part of it onto the clean, white table cloth. A tap comes at the door and there enters a dapper sergeant who has come from his mess mates yonder to enquire how the Corporal is. He is on the way to the butts and has his musket in his arms. The old man takes it up and it appears to break in two at the nozzle. He looks up at the sergeant in astonishment (and fine Irving's face was as he sat astonished), who explains that this how a rifle is nowadays. 'Lordy, Lordy,' says the old man, 'it wouldna' have done for the Dook' – and there are several other things that he finds during the evening that would not have done for the Dook. The Sergeant, though on an errand of mercy in regard to the old man, finds that the niece is a very attractive young lady and he is chatting to her with good humour when the old man begins to cry like a child. They rush to him and beg him to tell them what the matter is. He has broken his old clay pipe!

This was a fine bit of acting; and for all the world we might have been looking at a man 'in his second childhood.' The Sergeant easily consoles the veteran by producing a fine new pipe together with a good pouch of tobacco which pleases the Corporal immensely. The Sergeant departs, after he had made a little more love to the niece who throws the window up to see him down the road. 'Oh look Uncle,' she cries, 'here are some soldiers,' and sure enough as the old man totters to the window, we can hear a band in the distance. It comes nearer and nearer and when the music is underneath the window, the old man, in a mechanical way, raises his stick to attention and with the old military look in his eyes begins to mark time. This was a touch that brought the house down; and finer acting I cannot wish to see. But the effort is almost too much for the Corporal and he sinks exhausted into a chair where the lays gasping for a few minutes. His niece would like to read to him and suggests a little bit from the Bible. 'Th' parson,' says the old man, 'reads to me but he allus wants to read from New Testament, but give me Joshua says I, give me Joshua, them was battles as Joshua fought.' Then he goes on to tell the girl that the parson has told him that there will be a last final battle – Arma – Arma – and he hesitates, 'Armageddon uncle,' says the niece. 'Hi that's it,' the old soldier feebly murmurs, 'and I'm thinking that the Dook'ull be there – the Dook'ull have a word to say, he will.' Now a gentleman enters – a fine straight man, with a single eyeglass, and glove and a light cane in his hand – who has come to see how the Corporal is, and the two help him back to his chair near the fire. The gentleman would like to hear about the Battle of Waterloo, so Brewster shows him how the forces were arranged by placing his match box, his medicine bottle, and several other little things on the table which is covered by an old fashioned red and blue striped table cloth. This was an occupation over which the Corporal could wax eloquent and thoroughly enjoy himself. 'And here,' he says, 'where I place my new pipe with the amber mouthpiece were the Prussians.' Then the gentleman asks him what he chiefly remembers of the Battle and the Corporal replies that that morning he lent Jim somebody, his rear flank man, two half crowns which were to be repaid next day. Jim was killed in the fight, 'and I'm afeard, I'm afeard,' says the old man, 'that them two half crowns is as good as lost.' The gentleman must now be going. He hopes the Corporal is fairly comfortable. 'You know, I am rather anxious about you,' he says, 'for I am the Colonel of your old Regiment.' The old man jumps up as though he were shot, bringing his hand to his forehead, and vainly endeavouring to make the other salute.

This was a marvellous piece of realism and the house thundered. It nearly did for the old man, though, and the Colonel and the niece have to make haste to settle him in the chair again. When the old man has come round a bit, the Colonel pulls out two or three bank notes which he wishes him to have. 'And don't thank me, corporal,' he says 'for I'm not giving you them, we subscribed for them at mess the other day.' The Officer (Mr Ben Webster) was a capital representation, and in every look the actor was perfect and in all his [*word missing*] looks just what a gentleman in this position would be. The old soldier tries hard to utter his thanks and the Colonel goes out with a sob in his voice, hoping that the old man will soon be better.

Now the Sergeant appears again. He is on his way back from the butts and has invented a pretty excuse to see the Corporal's niece again. The two stand by the window talking like lovers when a slight sound is heard from the old man. He is leaning back in his chair and talking to himself, his eyes are closed and his face seems unusually pale. Suddenly he rises with all his old strength, and waving his stick in the air, shouts in a voice of thunder 'The Guards want powder! The Guards want powder and by God they shall have it!" (I am not quite sure of the words, as one could hardly catch them in the excitement, but think they are right.) Then he drops down again and the girl tries to rouse him. 'Uncle! Uncle!' she says, 'do tell me what is the matter.' The Sergeant gently kneeling at the old man's feet, reverently removes his cap, and in a low voice says, 'I think the roll call of the Scots Guards is completed now.'

There can be no doubt that this sketch of Sir Henry Irving's is a masterpiece. I have endeavoured to give some idea of the play and the actor's performance in it; but a cleverer pen than mine is at present needed to describe the whole details of the acting. Its greatness is apparent; and if Sir Henry has been assisted – as indeed he has – by the cleverness of Dr Conan Doyle's tale, he has made the thing a wonderful reality and created a living Corporal Brewster, a real old man, with all an old soldier's idiosyncrasies. The effect on the audience was magical and I should think that everybody felt a lump in their throat at one period of the play or another. At the end, the cheering was loud and prolonged and Sir Henry had to bow his acknowledgements three or four times.

I have already praised Mr Webster's Colonel. Putting aside Sir Henry's more difficult performance this was the best piece of acting I have yet seen on the stage, but then the actor was only impersonating himself – a gentleman. Sir Henry had to be somebody else entirely. The Sergeant (Mr Mellish) was very good, if anything almost too much like a real sergeant instead of being an idealised one. I did not like the niece (I now see by glancing at my programme a grand niece; I had been puzzled before how she who was so young, could represent Brewster's niece) but she did not spoil the picture.

The scene representing the interior of the Corporal's lodgings was a very realistic set. Over the mantel piece was a picture of the Corporal in his regimentals and by the side of it a rack filled with his old white and blue china crockery. In one corner was a shelf of books and an old grandfather's clock ticked slowly along. I have already referred to the table cloth, which was of the real old fashioned pattern; and the fire was practicable one, for the niece fried some bacon over it. The room in fact was an exact replica of what an old man's room would be and the only bit of anachronism about the play was that the military band was too obviously that of the Theatre Royal for we could hear the strings plainly. I thought that we should have heard the tramp of the soldiers and perhaps a cheer that they would give the old Corporal. After they had passed, Brewster began to laugh. He had only just found out what was wrong with them. They had no stocks, he said. 'It wouldna have done for the Dook,' was his comment, 'the Dook would have had a word to say, he would.'

After a short interval the curtain drew up on *The Bells*, the play in which Irving made his first 'hit' for which reason I had wished to see it.[187] As I have said, it was perhaps a pity that this should follow *A Story of Waterloo* for one would prefer not to have to compare Corporal Brewster with another of Sir Henry's great tragic parts, but the fact that Irving – who has nothing if he has not a nice discrimination of the tastes of playgoers – should link *The Bells* with *A Story* and play the two successfully is an indication of his strength. I do not propose to describe this second piece in full but let me say that the actor was particularly good where he counted up his gold, in the scene in which Hans gives his theory of the murder, in the 'trial' scene and in the last few minutes of the play where he rushes onto the stage a maniac. As he sat at his desk with his money bags in his hands and the gold pieces in a heap before which – for a second or two – he runs his trembling fingers, endeavouring to count up his hoard and then has to thrust the gold hastily away again, one got a very good notion of his powers. So too when Hans says he thinks the murdered man must have been placed in the lime kilns and under the vast expanse of forehead, Irving's eyes are seen, furtively gazing with a terrified glare.

The trial or dream scene is, I imagine, Irving's great opportunity in this play. He disappears to bed through a curtain in the side of the stage and then we behold his dream. The background of the picture on the stage vanishes in a complete darkness and we see in a misty light the red gowns fur lined of four judges, one of whose voice is heard examining Mathias. Irving stands in the centre of the stage, the limelight thrown on his face which looks terribly wild as he answers the questions put to him. He is not guilty, he cannot be guilty, and then as he makes the profession, he half turns and his hands fall on the body of the murdered man. Then the mesmerist approaches and with earnest heartrending voice Mathias entreats him not to operate on him. But the mesmerist does and when the judges have heard his confession and he is sentenced to death, the stage is again hidden in darkness, the old background appears, and Irving rushes from the side a raving lunatic. Hans and the people of the Inn have just battered down the door; but they can only see Mathias when he is no longer fit to be seen. 'The rope – the rope – take away the rope,' he exclaims, struggling with an imaginary cord round the neck and in this terrible scene, the curtain falls as the spirit of Mathias leaves him for another world.

A powerful play truly but not one that I should much care to see twice; and I do not know that some 'one-play actor' of indifferent reputation could not make as impressive a Mathias as Irving. I should like to have written an article on Irving and to have compared him with the great names of the English stage but having only seen these three plays – which do not lend themselves for comparison with those in which other actors have appeared – I refrained, and wisely, I have not the least doubt, from attempting to write anything for publication on the subject. I had recently read the lives of Kemble and Macready for the sake of this comparison and certainly Irving can lay no claim to stand beside them as a Shakespearian actor.[188] From 1878, when

---

[187] The reputation of Irving as Mathias in *The Bells*, as Race implies, was an attraction for many audiences. Irving first performed it at the Lyceum in November 1871, and it remained in his repertoire until his death.

[188] Race had probably read James Boaden, *Memoirs of the life of John Philip Kemble, esq: including a history of the stage, from the time of Garrick to the present period* (London, 1825) and William Archer's *William Charles Macready* (London, 1890).

he undertook the management of the Lyceum Theatre to 1893, fifteen years after (I have not the exact particulars to the present date) he has staged 9 different plays whereas Mr Archer says that Macready during his first season of 211 nights at Covent Garden, produced eleven of Shakespeare's plays. And I do not know that Irving has created many parts which will hereafter be ranked with Macready's Richlelieu, Virginius or Werner. Irving has never attempted any of the Roman characters in the plays and in other ways must be reckoned an inferior artist to Kemble; and I have never heard that anyone equally great has said of Irving's Shylock what Byron said of Kean's, 'This is the Jew that Shakespeare drew.'[189] I should however give Irving every credit for the efforts which have placed the Stage in the present honourable position that it holds in most people's estimation. On the whole, I do not regret having not published anything on this subject, for my knowledge of theatrical matters is steadily increasing and I can well afford to wait a while before rushing into print.

To return to *The Bells*, Miss Ethel Barrymore, who has not yet lost her girlish figure and voice, made a very pleasant Annette, and the other two ladies in the play were good. Mr Cooper, the Hans, was again too ordinary I thought; old Sam Johnson made an excellent gossiping Hans, a good stout burgher, and was ably seconded by a brother wit Walter (Mr Wm. Farren jnr). The rest of the company acted their insignificant parts in a fairly satisfactory way.

The sombre stage pictures that decorate the play were well set, and of course the accessories and dresses were very good. Of the scenes, the best was the second; here the burgomaster, after Annette has kissed him good bye, draws the curtains and we look through the latticed windows onto the villagers who go by in little groups of twos and three. They tread noiselessly along, for snow is covering the ground, and we hear, as they pass, the tinkling of the bell that is summoning them to church. This was a very pretty scene. Another good effect was produced when the merrymakers at the Inn had a dance together and afterwards when hidden from view they sang a sweet glee as Mathias occupied the stage by himself.

The Bells is a German play and not very pleasant. One seems to need a good laugh after seeing it to shake off the dismal feelings it has given. In the first scene we behold a full size picture – a dream again – of the murdered Jew on his sleigh, with snow falling in thick flakes; this was somewhat like one of the most miserable of Hamilton's pictures[190] and in other ways the critic finds faults, I have no doubt, with the play.

When the curtain fell on Mathias's death struggles, there was of course tremendous – no that is perhaps too expressive a word for it is rather too optimistic of Nottingham's welcome to our chief actors – hearty cheering and after a little time we got Sir Henry to make a short speech. I need not write it down here for it is given in full in the *Express*; but I must say that it is suspiciously like all the other speeches which Sir Henry has delivered during this tour and which I have read in the *Era* and one or two other papers. There is always the thanks to the gentlemen of the press for their eloquent and generous tribute to our work and a reference to the 'more than cordial and enthusiastic welcome' that he has received, and in one paper – the Sheffield one I think it was – I even read that the manager of another Theatre was possessed of 'merry men' which [statement] ought to have been confined, I think to the home of Robin Hood.[191] One speech that I read in the *Era* was almost word for

---

[189] The couplet is usually attributed to Alexander Pope on seeing Charles Macklin's portrayal in 1741.

[190] Hamilton's diorama.

[191] In his address to the audience at the Grand Theatre, Hull, Irving thanked the Manager Mr Hart, 'and his merry men for what they have done so spontaneously' (*Era*, 6 November 1897).

word the same as that which we cheered so vigorously, thinking we were hearing something original. Sir Henry is not an eloquent speaker and has to help his words out with his hand. My friend W. was rather surprised at this.

I noticed that both Miss Terry and Sir Henry Irving said *aunt* (ant), not *arnt* as Nottingham people are fond of pronouncing it, and also *France*; and in several other words they used the short *a*. I was not able to catch many of Sir Henry's affectations but I noticed *Landon, honesteee, poshon* (portion), *re-fur* (refer) and *juke* (Duke). (I am not now referring to the Corporal Brewster impersonation.)

The Nottingham Pantomimes 1897

Five weeks after the date, I sit down to write an account of the Grand[192] pantomime *Aladdin* which I visited on the last night of the old year. This was my first visit to the Grand, if a look inside it many years ago at a political meeting be excepted, and I anticipated, perhaps, a prettier house than I saw. There are only two tiers – the dress circle and the gallery – and the latter is much more open than the Royal one. The floor is divided into pit – bare forms, – pit stalls, and orchestra stalls, there being one row of the latter only. The dress circle is divided, the side seats being called the side circle, and priced 1/6 only, the circle proper being 2/6. We sat on the side circle, on seats next to the dress circle, and had an excellent view of the stage. The back of the dress circle is also let off in cheaper seats. There was not a good house on the occasion of our visit which would have been surprising had the pantomime been a better one for it had only been running five nights.

I think Mr Mulholland's choice of *Aladdin* for his pantomime was an unfortunate one for it was produced here only two or three years ago when it was one of W. Beryl's greatest successes, with Miss Louie Freear in a prominent part. The company on this occasion could not be considered at all equal to the one that performed at the Royal. The hero was impersonated by Miss Marie Wright, a very vivacious young lady, petite in build, but a common creature. Miss Marie Terry was the Princess. She was a prettier girl that the other, but she could not sing or act, and would not take the piece seriously. One or two of her songs went well however particularly one in which she gave a little dance, culminating in a display of 'lingerie' and a red garter as the big drum gave a fearful smack. But her other dancing was weak and one – a kind of clog dance – was more suited to the intelligence of the gods than the inhabitants of the dress circle. Had I been the manager I should have given her less to say and more to dance; and then she would have done better. The rest of the ladies were a very poor lot, particularly the young damsel with closely cropped and curled hair who looked like a public house amateur. The chorus was a local one, and contained some queer characters. Among them I beheld to my surprise Miss Dot Stevens, whom I knew by sight. Her father is in the Post Office and I believe she has had a situation in one of the Branch offices; but though she and her two sisters are reputed to be 'fast' girls I had thought that a post in the 'Grand' chorus would have been a little below her dignity.[193]

The comedians were a better lot; and I was rather surprised not to see them carry off more honours. With other ladies to back them up they would have put more life into the piece. The Widow Twankey (Mr Chas. Gardner), Wishee Washee (Mr Chas. Clark) and Abanazar (Mr Arthur Watts) were all clever artists and worthy of a

---

[192] The Grand Theatre, Hyson Green was built in 1884, accommodating around 3,000 people. Situated in a predominantly working-class suburb of Nottingham, it had a reputation of presenting old-fashioned melodramas and sensational dramas. See Iliffe and Baguley, *Victorian Nottingham. Vol. Three.*

[193] Race's only barely suppressed prudish streak!

good performance. Two of the comedians though – Messrs Clifton and Gibson who were dressed as policemen and described as 'knockabouts' – were very common in their antics and they had a pronounced Cockney accent which made them the more repulsive.

The scenery had been used at Camberwell the previous Christmas and was by no means brilliant. In the first scene a large Sphinx occupied the greater part of the stage and from it Electra sprang after the usual chorus in the darkness, but as we could see the two doors and their hinges through which she made her appearance, there was little charm in the illusion.

The cave was the best of the evening; and some really striking effects were produced in it by the thunder and the lightning. The 'Lamp' reposed in a cave guarded by a moving dragon which was really a very formidable looking monster.

There was nothing very striking in the business, but I saw for the first time those very long and giraffe looking animals which are produced by elevating a handle [?] in a pole[194] covering it and the man who bears it with a black cloth.

The costumes were but moderately pretty; and even the Princess made only one change. Some little boys who appeared in one of the scenes wore blue suits picked out with white; and these are the only dresses which now strike my memory … I have omitted to mention the Phasey troupe of four lady dancers. They were very clever in their art but did not display themselves to any advantage at all – except it be in that their costumes were exceedingly scanty, which is a mistake, I think, for a good many rakes would sooner see petticoats than bare limbs. They met with very little appreciation from the audience.

The harlequinade was, I rejoice, to add a good one; and the Cockneys who have little to say made an excellent clown and pantaloon. Some of their work here was capital; the harlequinade was a good one; and Columbine looked a really charming creature and certainly danced well.

The corridors of the Grand are hung with some very interesting engravings of members of the profession and with some old play bills in frames.

1898

January 19th
Theatre Royal Pantomime – *Cinderella*
[Pieces of pages missing]
…. This pantomime was extremely pretty and I have not yet seen such fine scenery and pretty dresses on the stage. Of the scenes, the second – 'In the Merry Wildwoods' was wonderfully pretty. There was a running waterfall (of 'real water') in the background and it was crossed by a rustic bridge on which some country children grouped themselves during the greater part of the scene. Previously they had performed a country dance, which by reason of the innocency [sic] of its performers, and its general appearances of the fresh air, and the delightful figures the children worked themselves into, had brought down the house. Some of the chorus men in this scene wore English hunting costume, and a hunting song and chorus were sung.
The kitchen was a very realistic set with the old fire place, but the Fairy Boudoir where electricity was profusely introduced was of course much finer. The gem of the lot however was the Ball Room – perhaps it put into shadow the more naturalistic

---

[194] A phrase which is impossible to decipher.

woodland scene – where Cinderella arrived in her coach and took her seat under a wonderful canopy of glittering silver lights. Cinderella's coach by-the-by was drawn by 4 black ponies which hardly seemed to harmonize with the scene and moreover they were very stubborn ponies and had to be pulled along instead of trotting like the ordinary animal. The harmony in colours of the dresses worn by the chorus was really magnificent – a fine shade of yellow giving a very rich appearance. The ballet in this scene was a fine one, some of the girls dancing in 18th century costumes and looking most graceful. In this pantomime Mr Arthur seems to have dispensed with the half dozen showy figures of the 'London ballet' and to have introduced local people with more liberality. Perhaps some of the girls were not such fine specimens of the female kind as those we saw last year, and if the costumes were generally more scanty than before there was not such a liberal display of bosom as *Dick Whittington* had given – all of which tended of course to the more desirable standard.

Of the company the best and most delightful performer was Miss Lily Morris, the Cinderella. She was only young and had not mastered all the stage tricks, but she had a happy smiling face, and a winning manner, and she acted without the slightest trace of vulgarity. In the kitchen scene she sang 'Creep Mouse', a pretty song, at the end of each verse of which came a little dance. Now this dance was executed without the faintest glimpse of 'lingerie' and with no high kicking, and though I must confess that with me the flesh is weak as regards dancing, I have never before had so much pleasure in seeing a dance. She was an educated girl too and spoke well, and it positively did my heart good to see her pleasant face behind the footlights. Miss Julia Kent now, who was the Prince's valet, was a different kind of girl, or rather woman, altogether. She too was petite, but she had a very 'knowing' expression on her face, wore an eyeglass and smoked a cigarette without looking in the least abashed. She was the regular music hall 'boy' and one of her songs sung as by an empty headed masher called 'Dear Boys, [?]' was a very common thing. On the other hand she sang 'Somebody got to bear the brunt', a patriotic song, with rather touching words, with much feeling. The Prince Peerless (Miss Clara Bernard) was not a very good impersonation. She was a tall, finely built person, but she could only act and sing moderately well. The other ladies were a fair lot, but not noteworthy, either in appearance or ability.

Honours among the gents were easily borne off by the Darnley Bros, who as the two Ugly Sisters were constantly making the house roar. In one scene they gave an exceedingly humorous and life like representation of a dialogue between two actors in a penny gaff. One of them was the villain and the other a tender heroine, aged about 40 and stout in proportion to her years. The former had long hair and a loose cloak, and a moustache, which last was constantly coming off. He was Harold and spoke in a very gruff voice; she knelt at his feet imploring him to give her that paltry million pounds he owed her, and when he threw her off roughly, a little toy engine came along and ran over her prostrate body!

To back them up they had the wicked Baron (Mr Willie Scott) and in the Ball Room Scene (exterior) these three created a great amusement. Arm in arm they approached the flunkey at the door and were contemptuously thrust aside. Then they went through any number of tricks (unsuccessfully) to get inside, and afterwards when someone came along and told the flunkey to pass them in nothing would induce them to enter. Arm in arm they made for the door saying 'now we are going in', and then they would make a turn, go round a post, and come back with 'now we are coming out' on their lips. It was most comical. A clever thing they did was to give an imitation of the cinemateographe. The stage was darkened, and they flopped about like the figures which appear on the screens, and light – white and dark alternately – was thrown on them from the wings. The illusion was excellent particularly as we heard the usual grind of the instrument which gradually slowed down as the performers got to the end of the dance.[195] The first Broker's man (Mr W. Downes) was a very comical man. He was dressed like the great figure who appears to advertise Quaker Oats and in the last scene but one joined with his comrade in singing an (apparently) impromptu song which took immensely.

The pantomime closed without the usual 'rally', the curtain being brought down rather suddenly after the scene at the Ball by the principal characters appearing before a front cloth to recite a few lines of tag, and finally making their exit with Mr Albert Darnley at the rear beating a big drum.

The old fashioned harlequinade was dispensed with as usual, this year three 'tableaux de marbre'[196] taking its place. These consisted of groups of classical figures formed by a large number of persons – said to be thirty – grouped on a revolving platform in the middle turning in the opposite direction. The stage was darkened but a strong light was thrown on the figurants, who all wore white tights (with a middle cloth) and white curly wigs (classical fashion), and had their faces whitened. There were both men and women in the tableaux and they all looked perfectly modest. The three groups were entitled 'L'Ideal,' 'Les Hercules' and 'Le Massacre', most of the performers in each were forming some classical figure, having bow, spear or hatchet in their hands. At the sound of a gong, the positions were changed, and in a second or two the figures were perfectly still again. In the last tableau, a monster horse was occupying the greater part of the platform. These scenes were very cleverly done, and from the cleverness with which those who appeared in them posed and the stillness with which they kept their positions, I imagine that must have been specially trained for the performance.

An excellent pantomime, this of *Cinderella* and I only regret that I have postponed writing this account of it until my recollections of many of its details has been somewhat dimmed.

Easter Tuesday April 5ᵗʰ
This evening to see Miss Marie Lloyd in *The ABC Girl*.[197] The ABC girl is an Aerated Bread Company's waitress, and the first scene shows the interior of an ABC shop – the usual restaurant, counter at rear, door and pay office on the right, and round tables with cane chairs at which the visitors are seated over the rest of the shop. The play of course was nothing and everybody went to see Miss Marie Lloyd, who by the way, must be coming down the theatrical ladder when she can leave a first class London hall to appear in the Nottingham Grand Theatre. We were all three very disappointed. I had expected to see a clever actress, and found – a stout, ugly, common creature who spoke like a Cockney and used such lady-like phases as "blithering" and "kisser."

---

[195] A fascinating observation on the new cinematograph entertainment in which the process and the performance are reduced to their comedic essentials. Compare with Race's descriptions of the cinematograph shows at the Goose Fair, e.g. p. 86.

[196] Tableaux vivants.

[197] *The ABC Girl*, written by H. Chance Newton with composer George le Brunn, was not a success. Marie was uncomfortable as Flossie the Frivolous, the 'ABC Girl', and the show never reached its anticipated London heights, closing at the Metropole and Stratford East Theatres in May 1898. W. Macqueen-Pope, *Marie Lloyd: Queen of the Music Halls* (London, 1947), p. 115.

In the first scene she was positively repulsive in manners and in dress was the reverse of attractive – she had on a black velvet dress, cut to a little below the knees and showing a pair of worked stockings, and her hair – of a reddish colour – was heaped in a great mop round her head. Over the velvet dress, she wore a white pinafore and as she is by no means youthful and as too her figure is more than inclined to be stout the combination was by no means successful. Her other dresses were however much more becoming; and when she appeared in green 'bloomers' with her 'bike' as she called it, she certainly looked far from ugly. Of course she sang many songs, but they were surprisingly free from that suggestiveness for which she is, I believe, notorious. Then too she danced, but with much moderation; but of her style – the clog dance variety, of which she gave us several examples – I am no admirer. In one scene she and Mr W. L. Thompson joined in a Coster duet. In the end Mr Thompson was requested to put his arm round her – which he did with evident shyness. 'Nah, (the pronunciation was not affected) don't you know your business?' says Marie. Whereat they kissed and William who is an authority on these matters was careful to inform me that it was a genuine one – which had been apparent for they had quite flattened one another's noses.

In another duet with the same performer she appeared as a little child, and the result was amusing, not to say ludicrous in its fidelity. One little scene in which Miss Lloyd called on a stockbroker was apparently introduced to allow her to sit on a chair and lift one foot over the other. We were too far back to see properly but the people in the stalls must have had a good view as the dress ascended.

Of the rest of the piece there is not much to tell. Mr Thompson was a clever lift boy in the first act, and a good coster in the second. Miss Marie Wright (the Aladdin of the 'Grand' pantomime) was a very humorous slavey girl, from the country, and a good deal more successful than as a boy in the pantomime. She and Mr Thompson as a couple of dolls sang a capital duet. Miss Margaret Warren was a graceful 'Lenore Mayville' and she sang and acted with some taste. One of the few gems of the evening was a song sung by a girl in white of 'A Big, Big Man' and it went with the more force because she was small and had to stand on tip toe when she wished to impress on us how tall her big, big, man was. She and two other girls did the dancing which was of a very advanced order. My friend who has witnessed more of this kind of thing than I says that he has not seen anything to equal it. But we were well behind.

Saturday May 20th

To see at 'half time' this evening Miss Kate Vaughan in *The Country Girl*. [198] Got an excellent seat in the pit, which is now nearly entirely under the dress circle, but I could see all over the stage, though not to the full height of the scenery. *The Country Girl* is in 4 acts, of which I saw three. In the first of these Miss Vaughan appeared disguised as a boy. She is petite in figure, and also very young in spirits. As a boy she wore a slate coloured suit, in which she looked delightful. In the next two scenes she was a girl again beloved by a young lover but under the toils of her old guardian who wished to pass off as her husband. In these scenes she acted a 'romp' part in a mild

---

[198] Kate Vaughan (?1852–1903) was one of the original 'Gaiety Girls' and famous as a skirt-dancer in the 1870s. Her 'skirt' dances exploited 'the mystery of the petticoat', the antithesis of the much more revealing ballet costumes. See W. MacQueen-Pope, *Gaiety: Theatre of Enchantment* (London, 1949), pp. 177–178 and Clement Scott, *Drama of Yesterday and Today,* II (London, 1899), pp. 244–245. *The Country Girl* (not to be confused with *A Country Girl* (1902) by Lionel Monckton and James T. Tanner) was an adaptation of William Wycherley's bawdy Restoration comedy, *The Country Wife*.

way, being fond of sitting on a table and dangling her legs therefrom. Also she had to write a letter to the young lover, at the dictation of the old guardian, which she did with many grimaces. This was good fun.

After *The Country Girl* she came on in evening dress – low cut bodice – to recite a monologue called 'How It Happened' – the 'It' being a proposal. Miss Vaughan in this monologue very cleverly imitated the drawl of a swell to whom she was giving a lesson in waltzing - and then she danced. Her dancing was sedate, sinuous and very pretty – ordinary waltzing with various poses. Miss Vaughan was very clever and very delightful in what she did but I suppose that had I to write seriously as a critic that I should say she was not a great, or even moderately great, actress. Pleasant is the better term.

The rest of the company were passable, most promise being shown by Mr C. T. Collings. A veteran, Mr Philip Gordon, made a good old man, and did a drunken scene without giving any offence.

Postscript: Miss Vaughan must be getting on in years[199] for she has been on the stage since the early seventies, and it is more than fifteen years since she was a leading light at the 'Gaiety.' Like many another member of the 'light' branch of the profession she has, after basking in the glorious times of popularity, fallen on evil days, and a few years ago she was I believe in a very bad way. So to earn a living she turned herself into an old English Comedy actress. As with Miss Fortescue, the transition is not in every aspect satisfactory; and one has a half suspicion that she does not really understand the art of acting. But she is very pleasant on the stage, and as she is trying hard to work the 'legitimate' business she certainly deserves every encouragement. In figure she is, as I have said petite and indeed when she was in her pretty boy's suit she looked very small. She has small features and her face makes up so well that under the footlights one would take her to be not more than twenty two or three. She is very active; and has a highly infectious, light hearted way with her; but I have seen other actresses play ingenue parts – kissing and hugging of refractory guardians and parents – better. *The Country Girl* is not a well constructed piece.

Regarding the rest of the company, I see that Mr Clement Scott[200] says they played *She Stoops to Conquer* though they were playing *opera-bouffe*. Perhaps this was true of them when I saw them, and certainly they reminded me of the performers I saw in *Pepita* more than the individuals I have drawn in my own brain as fit to play comedy. Another critic – the *Era* one – said some nasty things of W. Philip and I have half a suspicion that my judgement of him was tempered by the fact that he is a 'veteran.'

October 29th
Mr Wilson Barrett in *The Sign of the Cross*
Mr Wilson Barrett's program for the week only included three plays, *The Manxman, The Silver King* and *The Sign of the Cross*.[201] I should have much liked to have seen his *Othello* and wrote to the papers to say so, but the suggestion was not adopted though one or two correspondents and the *Guardian* critics supported it. So on the Saturday night went down to see *The Sign of the Cross*, partly with the intention of going into the gallery – an intention which would not have been carried out had I arrived on the scene half an hour earlier and was well repaid for my sloth and my

---

[199] Kate Vaughan was approaching 50 at this point.
[200] Clement Scott (1841–1904), theatre critic for the *Daily Telegraph* for almost thirty years.
[201] W. Barrett, *The Manxman* (1894) and *The Sign of the Cross* (1895). H. A. Jones and H. Herman, *The Silver King* (1884).

niggardliness. The doors had not been opened more than five minutes when I got to the Quadrant, and there were two long lines of people stretching right round to the *Guardian* offices in Sherwood Street! To go into the pit under such conditions was absurd, so with a few blushes I joined the 'queue' – when it had greatly diminished – to the gallery door, thinking that there at any rate I should get a comfortable seat. But when I got inside – at about 6.20 – I found every seat taken, and a good number of people standing up behind. There was over an hour to wait for the curtain to rise and with the prospect of seeing only part of the stage at the finish, but there was no help for it, so I held on. After all, the life of the good playgoer is a life of experience, and what a glorious experience this will be, say thirty years hence! The heat was stifling, the light too bad to read, and nothing more exciting than the frantic rush of an attendant to an individual who was smoking to pass the time along. There was not a scrap of the theatre to be seen beyond the stage, and to see that one was always dodging between people's heads, and there was the pleasant prospect before me of a fearful struggle should a panic start, a not unlikely event in such an overcrowded building.

But after enquiring whether it would be possible to get a seat elsewhere and receiving the reply that every seat was taken outside the dress circle and boxes, I settled myself near a doorway and prepared to watch the play. It is a blessed feeling to know one is having an experience, even if it is certain that the play itself is the last thing which can be appreciated.

The Sign of the Cross as produced by Wilson Barrett is remarkable for the luxuriousness of its scenery and the dresses. The first scene represented a street in Rome, with a house owning a practicable balcony on one side, and a distant view of the city and a glimpse of blue sky at the back. Here Marcus Superbus entertained some of his friends – fair women in deep red costumes and a curious old party (male) whose virtue was not temperance – and here Mercia – a beautiful looking girl whose dark hair hung down over her white robes and whose shoulders were covered by a heliotrope mantle – was set upon by the crowd. Of course Marcus' soldiers came to the rescue of the fair Mercia, and then she hurried home to the house of her aged father to whom she tells the tale of assault and rescue. Suddenly there is heavy knocking at the door. Mercia, in agitation, asks who is there. 'A friend, a friend' is the reply, and so she lets in a muffled figure with a long white beard. He has come to warn them that they must be careful for they are watched. 'But who are you?' enquires the old man suspiciously. 'I am the Prefect, Marcus Superbus,' replies the muffled figure as he undoes his mantle and throws away his false beard.

Scene III shows the interior of a prison where Stephanus – Mercia's brother – who has been captured by the Romans is being questioned. He must tell them, they says, where the Christians meet for prayer. He refuses, and so is carried away, with many unavailing cries, to the rack. We hear the cruel sounds, and the child's cries, and some of us in the gallery cannot help declaring our minds with much rude vigour. Stephanus is brought back. Will he tell now? No, he won't, and so is hauled off for another trial of torture. When he comes back again, this time unable to stand and writhing with pain, he gives the answers he is required to, and then enters Marcus who turns fiercely on the men who have ill-treated the boy.

The next scene represents 'A grove by the Castian Bridge.' On a rock stands a Patriarch, a long white-bearded Christian, with Mercia by his side, holding in her hand a rudely-shaped cross. At their feet are the kneeling figures of the Christians, some singly, others in twos and threes, from whom rises that pathetic – at least so it seems in the theatre – air 'Shepherd of Souls.'[202] When that is finished, one of them ascends to the side of the patriarch to recite some passages out of (I believe) the Epistle to the Romans, and has not finished before the soldiers are on them with sword and spear. Many have fallen and all are singing 'Shepherd of Souls' again when Marcus and his friendly men rush in to the rescue. And don't we galleryites cheer the rescuers?

Act III is divided into 3 scenes, the first of which represents the house of Berenis – 'friend' of Marcus - and the last the Prefect's own palace. Berenis' house was a magnificent set. The lady, too, was as brilliant as her surroundings. A ring – Marcus is coming! – so she settles herself on a couch in an inviting attitude, toys with a hand glass, and listens with dreamy eyes to the harp of her little handmaiden. But it isn't Marcus at all; it is Dacia with whom she pretends to be most friendly, and up she jumps in most modern fashion. Dacia has come to tell Berenis of Marcus' admiration for Mercia, and is particularly pleasant (after the manner of rivals) in doing so. When Marcus does appear, a little later on, moody and undetermined [?], he and Berenis have a passionate scene which ends with his determination to throw off the 'world.' The prefect's house had not such a gorgeous interior as the last. He sent for Mercia and the girl was standing wistfully in a corner while he lay on a couch darkly thinking on his resolves. She would return his love, but she would not forsake her Christianity – that was her message. Through a door which opened occasionally we had a glimpse of Marcus' friends – revelling in the old style in which he had joined, and presently in they came, fondling and tumbling. Let somebody sing and dance said Marcus; and so we had a song and a very free dance, at which Mercia would not look. Let every soul leave me but the girl, cried Marcus, and let all the lights be put out. When his orders have been obeyed, he turns to the girl. She must come to him, he will have her, he says, and he is laying his hands on her when there is a sudden flash, an illumination of Mercia's white robed figure, and the man falls down before it. 'It is a sign' - and she holds aloft a small cross – says Mercia: 'Thou canst not harm me.' And thus the curtain drops.

Act 4 opens with a view of Nero's Palace. Nero – a tottering, worn out old man, whose hand cannot keep its steadiness – sits on his throne, and before him appears Marcus to beg the life of Mercia who is condemned to death. He can't have her if she will become a Christian, says the Emperor. Marcus pleads his past services for a less unconditional promise, but the Nero – supported by his wife – will not move, so Marcus departs fiercely. Then there is a street scene and the curtain rises on 'a dungeon off the Amphitheatre.' The Christians are all there, singing 'Shepherd of Souls', and in the midst of them stands white robed Mercia over the lying figure of Stephanus. A door at the back is opened by two helmeted soldiers and the Christians are ordered out – still singing – into the arena. I think this was the most pathetic part in the whole play. One or two of the eldest led the way, after them came, more slowly, some of the younger ones; then others boldly pressed behind these, and lastly came two or three feeble old men who had to be helped along by their stronger friends, the very last of all being one middle-aged Christian who could not help casting back one look at the prison which he was leaving for a worse fate. And so they all disappeared to their death, 'Shepherd of Souls' dying away with them, leaving Mercia and the boy alone, it would be his turn next, and he did not feel that he could bear it. 'Think, Stephanus,' said Mercia, 'of that other world, more bright and beautiful, where sorrow

---

[202] Written by Edward Jones, the hymn became widely available as an instrumental piece and was sold in theatre foyers. See David Mayer, *Playing out the empire*: Ben Hur *and Other Toga Plays and Films, 1883–1908. A Critical Anthology*, (Oxford, 1994), pp. 109–110.

Figure 14. Wilson Barrett and Maud Jeffries in *The Sign of the Cross*, c.1895, promotional postcard

is not, nor persecution, nor suffering.' And when she had comforted him, the doors opened again with a bang and the two silent figures wait for the lad. So he starts off, gets inside the ring, and runs back with a shriek. Mercia hastens to him, and very shortly he makes another effort, crossing his arms on his breast; and finally, after a pause or two, rushing manfully forward while the heavy doors close on him. This again was done with a wonderful effect, the frightened air of the lad and the hesitancy of his steps being reproduced with great effect.

Mercia was now alone. Another side door opened and Marcus Superbus walked in. He had come to make one last appeal. 'Would she be his wife?' – and when he said 'wife' she asked with trembling anxiety did he really mean wife. Yes, he meant wife, and if she would be his, he would become great for her sake. 'See,' he said, 'I have friends; Nero is tottering; if you will marry me, they shall make me Emperor, and you shall be Empress.' 'Will you, will you Mercia, become my wife?' But Mercia could only hesitate a second; she sought a Heavenly, not an earthly crown. She cannot give up her faith, she will go to her death. 'Then,' says Marcus, dropping immediately all his kingly ambitions, 'I will go with you.' He takes her by the hand, and stands on the step leading to the arena. 'Thus hand in hand we go to our Bridal. Chrystos has triumphed. The light has come. Come my bride, come to the light beyond.' And as his hand points upward, and the two stand on the steps ready to go to the lions, the curtain slowly descends.

What was the impression *The Sign of the Cross* made on me? Not a great one certainly, for I was too far off the stage to see and hear in comfort, and had continually to be dodging between ladies' hats to follow the actors at all. But from a sentimental – or if you will – religious point of view the play did not strike me. It has not a line which breathes the real and genuine spirit of the Christian of its age, and speaking with all caution, the biblical part of it is not written as – let us say – a bishop would write it. The play does not impress, but many of the situations do, because the author was here resolving what he, and of course everybody else, knew to have been. Most pathetic of all was the scene where the Christians were entering the arena – the strong, and the infirm, the aged and the young – and where Stephanus, cheered by Mercia, goes manfully to his doom. Some of the others were not so impressive – the opening scene where the old men were assaulted in the street and one of them, asked whom he followed said 'I serve the Son of Man,' the torture scene which Miss Gertrude Hammond, the Stephanus did not make sufficiently realistic, or rather spoilt its realism by actors' tricks, such as jumping into the soldier's arms instead of allowing herself to be dragged there, and the Grove scene which was tawdry, because the Christians were butchered in stage fashion, and because the passages from Scripture sounded anything but scriptural – all these lacked something to make them quite impressive. The scene, too, where the lighting plays around Mercia – an insignificant little puff from the wings but followed by a brilliant lime light from above – was a little spoilt by the way in which Marcus flopped about before finally settling on his knee with an upward gaze. Considering the play from another aspect, if it was intended to have a religious influence the world part of it has been made too tempting. Half the people who see it must be as much attracted by the gay views of Rome as by its Christian element and herein perhaps lies much of the success of the play. Some of the scenes were really 'rich.' What with the bright dresses of the dancers, the armour of the soldiers, the hangings of the palaces, the marble (painted) columns and the red roses which strewed the ground, it needed little imagination to believe that it was the real Rome we were beholding.

Of the acting, there is not much to say. I should like to have analysed Wilson Barrett's art but in such a play, seen under the conditions I saw it, it is impossible. Very often he spoke too quickly, but at time he raised his voice and declaimed magnificently. His is a very powerful voice, when exerted, and he made us hear it even in our distant corner of the gallery when he wished. Wilson Barrett is obviously a 'robust' actor, and I should think, much resembled G. V. Brooke[203] in style. I think he could manage some of Kemble's parts well … and Kemble were he to come to life again would be my ideal of an actor. Blank verse Wilson Barrett ought to deliver with much stateliness.[204]

Miss Maud Jeffries[205] was an exceedingly sweet Mercia. Her face is so faithfully reproduced in her photographs that there is no need to transfer it to paper. She is, as a lady-descriptive writer would say, 'all goodness', but the critic would have his doubts whether she is any actress. This part, however, being a reproduction of herself under certain conditions, she manages very well. I do not think, however, that her Desdemona would be the same success.

The rest of the cast managed to get along fairly well, but none of their performances were startling. Miss Hammond, I imagine, does not make such a clever Stephanus as Miss Haidee Wright.

(P. S. I did not like the latter part of this account at all on re-reading, and have altered it considerably. Had it to appear in print, however, its form would need much further alteration.)

December 1st
Olivia.[206] Lyceum Company and Miss Ellen Terry.
The Lyceum Company have been here this week (Nov. 28 – Dec. 3), but without Sir Henry Irving who lies ill in Glasgow.[207] They have brought with them three principal plays: *Madame Sans-Gêne* which was produced on Monday and Tuesday, *The Merchant of Venice* (played on Wednesday and Saturday) and *Olivia* whose sole performance I saw on the Thursday. On Friday they had a medley bill: *The King and the Miller, Nance Oldfield* [208]and a scene each from *Madame Sans-Gêne* and *Olivia*. Friday's performance was the one I had intended to see, but found I could not get that night, so went on Thursday instead, and was rewarded by the pleasantest evening I have ever spent in a Theatre. I have never felt so much interest in a play before or been able to follow one so easily, and besides *Olivia* gives a healthy view of an old English home. It teaches a far finer lesson than *The Sign of the Cross*.

---

[203] G. V. Brooke: a tragedian of the 'old school'.

[204] His speech from the stage certainly reveals a distinct missionary zeal and sense of 'self': 'You have recognised from the first time that there was a motive underlying my plays. I want men and women to feel kinder to their fellows when they leave the theatre. If I have done that I have done something that is dear to my heart. Your presence in this theatre seems to be proof of that.' *Nottingham Daily Express*, 31 October 1898.

[205] Maud Jeffries (1869–1946) was the original Mercia in *The Sign of the Cross* and Kate in *The Manxman*, both with Wilson Barrett. Her portrait, as Race notes, was widely available as a photolithograph, and subsequently in postcard form (see Mayer, *Playing out the empire*, p. 110).

[206] *Olivia* (W. G. Wills, 1878).

[207] Irving fell ill from pneumonia in October 1898, the provincial tour continuing without him.

[208] A 'medley bill' which included favourite or popular scenes from longer pieces was not unusual. *Nance Oldfield* by C. Reade (1883); *The King and the Miller* may be *The King and the Miller of Mansfield* by Robert Dodsley (1737), having a local connection.

The Company have not done so well I fancy, as was expected. The absence of Sir Henry Irving accounts, of course, for the great part of the falling off, but the raising of the prices of admission – an old fault of the new management – must have kept many people away. The plays, too – *Madame Sans-Gêne* perhaps excepted – are ones with which Sir Henry's name is associated, and most individuals prefer to see Miss Ellen Terry in her 'great' parts play with her well known opposite. Further, the tendency of play-goers nowadays is to visit the theatre, not for the sake of the play, but for the sake of the 'star' actor, as in Nottingham Miss Terry's name, alone, is not a sufficient draw, and so the Lyceum Company has suffered. A third cause was that both *Madame Sans-Gêne* and *The Merchant of Venice* were seen here last year.[209] *Olivia* which was new to Nottingham attracted, said the paper, the largest audience of the week.

Pit for the Lyceum visit was 2/- early doors, gallery 1/-, so I elected to go into the gallery. I got down to the Theatre a quarter of an hour before the opening and found only some twenty or thirty people waiting to go into the 'gods' and a comparatively small 'queue' for the other doors. Inside I landed on the second row, but a party in front wished to sit with her friend behind and so invited me to change places. This was a capital move for me as it took me into the front row right in the very centre of the bend and gave me a view of the whole 'house' and an excellent sight of the stage. Both hearing and seeing are remarkably good in the front rows of the gallery, and if one were not proud I should never wish for a better place. There was a very respectable gathering in the gallery, but hardly so fashionable (!) a one as when Sir Henry was here. And unlike the occasion of his visit it did not fill up with the early doors. There were barely three rows full before 7 o'clock. The rest of the house showed no anxiety to fill up before the opening of the ordinary doors but most of the seats were taken when the curtain went up. Both the dress circle and orchestra stalls had then a brilliant array of evening dress.

Olivia being almost a classic will ever be easy of reference in print, and so I am saved the trouble of a detailed description. The stage scenes were lovely. The first represented the Vicarage garden. To the left was the old gable vicarage, with its porch and diamond-shaped windows and its walls covered with roses. In the centre was an apple tree surrounded by a rustic seat, and to the right was the remains of a haystack – I saw a man afterwards carting it away on his back – in front of which some poppies lay to give a little colouring to the picture. At the rear ran a hedge with a swinging gate in the centre and behind this was a view of sloping corn fields, the houses of the village in a hollow with a great wood above them, and behind the wood a flat landscape of fields and trees which apparently stretched away for miles. It was a perfect little picture of an old country home, and the sound of the cuckoo fell every now and then on the ear to add to its truthfulness. The Vicar, as the curtain rose, was about to celebrate his silver wedding. Presently the bells of the church began to chime out a merry tune, and then in came a tribe of the villagers, the youngsters who led the way with cheers, leaping over the gate to enter the field. After the Vicar had welcomed them, they all sang a glee under his windows, and when the Vicar had been prevailed upon to make a formal little speech off they trooped with more cheers, some of them old men (in smocks) who could hardly toddle having to be helped off by the Doctors friendly arm. The villagers gone the Squire Thornhill, a bouncing buck, came in and there was a little love scene between him and Olivia who as she was Miss Ellen Terry – a lady of goodly proportions – looked old enough to be his mother.

---

[209] See pp. 107–111.

Scene II showed the Vicarage Parlour. Here there was a very pretty scene at the piano. Sophia (Miss Dorothea Baird) sat at an old harpsichord, Moses, her brother (Mr W. Kendrick) played the flute, and her lover, Mr Burchell (Mr Fuller Mellish) sang, and the three joined in a trio 'Happy Morn.' This little scene is enough to make the success of the play; but on the present occasion it was a little spoilt to hypercritical ears from the fact that the singing came from the wings and not from Sophia and her lover. The former however was really playing on the harpsichord – and very quaint it sounded – and the latter, who had his back to us, was working his shoulders and head about as though he was joining in the singing. This was a good stroke of the actor's art.

Olivia in this scene is leaving home on the morrow having promised her father to go away with him to some situation he has found for her – the old Vicar having fallen on evil days – and he bids goodbye to all the family in very pathetic fashion. There were two children on the stage, Bill and Dick (T. and C. Dearden) in this act, and it was amusing to watch them waiting for their cue. Miss Baird had one on each side of her and was showing them a picture book – and very pretty and motherly she looked while she was doing it – and when it got near their turn they kept glancing up for the word. 'Olivia' was in tears as she wished 'goodbye' to them, making them promise to always remember 'Sister Livy' in their prayers, and there were a good many handkerchiefs at work in the gallery the while. To make an honest confession, I was much touched hereabouts myself.

Mr Burchell plays his part manfully all through this scene, and comes in for some misdirected abuse from the Vicar's wife. Miss Maud Milton, the Mrs Primrose, could do the ranting pretty well but she was too young and probably not well enough trained for the post. I have seen better 'old women' with both the Fortescue and the Benson companies.

At the end of the Act the Vicar has a great scene when he learns of the flight of his daughter with Squire Thornhill. In a moment, blind with rage, the old man climbs up the chimney piece for his pistols with which to follow and shoot the scamp; his wife and daughter rush to him with tears to soothe him; and then the grey-haired Vicar sinks down, almost helpless, astonished to think that he should have thought of such a deed. This was a fine bit of acting from Mr Norman Forbes. In the manner in which he depicted the rage and helplessness of the old man he reached the height of his art. Indeed, Mr Forbes' Dr Primrose was such an excellent one that I doubt if Sir Henry Irving's surpasses it.

Scene III shows the interior of the Dragon Inn where Olivia reposes in the luxury of feeling herself the Squire's bride. There is a short playful scene, and then the Squire (Mr Frank Cooper) tells her that she is not married to him at all. Mr Cooper managed his lines here well. Ordinarily I should say he is too modern for the Lyceum Company, but a young swaggering part suits him and so he played the heartless buck well, while Miss Terry went from smiles to indignation, and indignation to hysterics. And when the Squire has left her, she is found first by Mr Burchell and then by the Vicar who takes her to his heart – a most pathetic and natural bit of acting this – rejoicing over the lost sheep that he has found with a great joy. Before the curtain falls there is an encounter between Mr Burchell and the Squire who at first treats his [*word omitted*] as an inferior and a nuisance and who afterwards learns to his great surprise that he is his uncle, the wealthy Sir William. This scene relieved the tension of Olivia's deliverance but it was a little too melodramatic and much too reminiscent of dramas of not so high a tone as this (i.e. those I have seen in 'fit-ups!)

The fourth scene is the same as the 2nd – the interior of the Vicarage. Olivia and her father have arrived at home very late at night – it is Christmas Eve. Olivia makes her old father comfortable in a chair but he cannot sleep and presently the family begin to come downstairs. Sophia and the children rush to their sister, but her mother stands [aloof] with some hard words and the aged vicar has to make the peace with her. Then Mr Burchell arrives. The news that he is the wealthy Sir William has preceded him but he brings almost as important tidings with him – Olivia was after all married to the Squire and 'here' he says, 'is my nephew himself now thoroughly repentant.' Then the light begins to break through the windows, we hear the cuckoo again, and as the church bells ring out a merry peal, the villagers out in the snow singing 'Good King Wenceslas'. And so, while the revered old Vicar gives out a general benediction and everybody's heart is made glad on this Christmas morning. The curtain falls.

After *Olivia*, one feels better. There is no need to disguise the fact that *Olivia* teaches a serious lesson and moves many who hear it to tears. The Vicar, even as Mr Wills transferred him to the stage, is a beautiful character and we feel for him as if we ourselves were searching for a piece of silver that was lost. The glimpse of country life in the first act, the tender scene of parting in the second, the finding of the lost in the third, and homecoming in the fourth – all these affected us, and gave me at any rate more delight than all my theatre going experience has ever given.

To turn to the acting: there can be no doubt that Mr Norman Forbes made a splendid Dr Primrose. In figure he is very slender and though he has a big head he has most lean jaws – which personal characteristics made it easy for him to get up as an old man, and the rest he managed to the life. In the tender scenes, and where troubles have fallen heavily upon him, his skill came out particularly, but it was good for me to see his old hairs shake and to hear his joyous laugh when a little enjoyment was granted him.

The *Express* said that Miss Terry could never have acted Olivia better, but it was wrong.[210] All through she fell a little short of the very highest range, and I fancy that a cold which she had, and which occasionally made itself plain in her voice, must have affected her. The parting scene in Act 2, in one or two of the important passages which follow she manages, I am sure, better than we heard her do tonight – though I am not saying, let me emphasise, that she did them other than well then. Critically I am afraid that Miss Terry is getting a little too old for the part. Olivia is not much more than a girl, but the actress is over 50, and though she is exceedingly buoyant she cannot be a girl of 20. Her figure too – she wore a loose green dress with a flowing train – is that of a woman, and Sophia and her mother looked very youthful beside her. The roguery of Madame Sans Gêne if I remember rightly suited her better, and the tearful parts of that play were given with deeper feeling. Perhaps the actress felt just a little out of the vein, and may be she was unable to play up to Mr Forbes, a young man, as she does up to Sir Henry, who is an old one. But let me not put the performance on record as a bad one. It has left the best memories behind it, and only my critical conscience impels me to say that it was one which was not faultless.

---

[210] Race was probably critical of the following effusive praise: 'Who, seeing the actress yesterday, could believe, unless stern fact confronted him, that she assumed that same character two decades ago. Miss Terry, to whom the inestimable boon of perennial youth seems to have fallen, looked a fresh young girl who had only recently left a score of summers behind... Seldom, if ever, has she given a more winsome representation of any part than that of last night. We laughed when Olivia was joyous and we deeply sympathised with her, many of us even to tears, in her sorrow.' (*Nottingham Express*, 2 December 1898).

The other actors were not important. Mr Frank Cooper was Squire Thornhill, and though he did well his forte would be, I imagine, a modern, not an ancient beau. In fact he seems a little out of place in the Lyceum Company whose repertoire consists, almost wholly, of classical plays. He is the only actor I have seen who wears a moustache. It was shaved down, rather close, but was a real one nevertheless. Mr Fuller Mellish made a good Mr Burchell, of rather a saturnine disposition. A little more energy would have much improved his part. The Moses of Mr Kendrick was well done, and his playing of the flute in Act 2 gave a realistic touch to the scene. Mr Kendrick looked very handsome in a plum-coloured suit. Old Sam Johnson – the Farmer Flamborough – is the only other individual among the males who requires mention. He was the old, uncouth farmer to the life. Mr Mackintosh, I was sorry to find had not a part in this play. He is the best actor in the Lyceum Company.

Of the ladies, after Miss Maud Milton who as I have said was too young for old Mrs Primrose, the only one with an at all prominent part to play was Miss Dorothea Baird who was the Sophia. Miss Dorothea Baird is not great as an actress, but she is natural and very winning. Her Sophia was a fresh, innocent creature whom it was a pleasure to watch; and the motherly care with which she guarded the two children (Bill and Dick) quite interested me. Miss Baird, who is the wife of one of the young Irvings, has a very pleasant face, and looks as sweet off the stage as on. I know this because I waited to see her leave the Theatre.

And now having had nothing but praise for *Olivia* have I any right to say that I don't think it a good play, or at least as good a play as it ought to be? Yet I think so, and with the copy before me I think I could point out its defects. The conclusion – Squire Thornhill's repentance, and the declaration that after all the marriage was a real one – seemed very tame, and here the author ought either to have departed from Goldsmith's story or else to have prepared his audience for the denouement. The Vicar is excellently drawn; the rest of the characters are weak.

When the play was over, I went round to the stage door to see Miss Terry leave. She came out the last of all with Mr Frank Cooper, she in a long loose cloak, wearing a low, round fur-trimmed hat, and he in an Inverness with a cap on and eyeglasses. As they came down, a Parson on some errand or other rushed up the passage, and as he passed them raised his hat. Mr Cooper had just said that he did not know him, as they walked by us – we were a little lot of inquisitive enthusiasts standing in Sherwood Street – and her reply was 'Then it was one up to us, wasn't it?' It sounded a little slangy from 'our beloved Ellen', but Mr Cooper – is he her son? – seemed on very familiar terms with her. They walked round to the Clarendon Hotel. I had seen her out driving the previous day when she stopped the coachman in an excited way to pick up a gentleman, who I believe was this same Mr Cooper, and when he had joined her she was very particular in adjusting the wraps round him.[211] In the street, Miss Terry does not look her best, as her face is made up, and her (dyed) hair is of a rude auburn colour.

---

[211] Decidedly not her son. The 58-year-old Terry was infatuated with Frank Cooper, a 'brawny' younger actor, towards whom G. B. Shaw was reputedly (and perhaps understandably) hostile. See Bingham, *Henry Irving,* p. 280. Also Nina Auerbach, *Ellen Terry. Player in her Time* (London, 1987), pp. 387–388.

1899[212]

October 26th
A Female Hamlet
At 9 o'clock tonight[213] to the Grand Theatre to see Miss Clare Howard[214] in *Hamlet.*
The company appearing there this week is Mr George Daventry's and with the exception of this one performance they are playing melodrama – *The Indian Mutiny* and *Lost in Paris.*[215] In both these plays, I think – certainly in *The Indian Mutiny* – Miss Howard takes a female character which she plays with much vigour to the great delight of 'Grand' audiences. *Hamlet* seems to have been added to her repertoire some time ago, to judge from the photographs I have seen about, but I had never heard of her until she appeared here. The scenery and the dresses look as though they were the company's own, so they must be playing the tragedy elsewhere.

Miss Howard, who according to the *Express*, is Mr Daventry's wife, is tall and has clear cut features with a well shaped nose. In *Hamlet* she wore a rather tight fitting gown, somewhat resembling a cassock, through which very occasionally we caught a glimpse of a black stockinged leg. Above this gown was a loose robe of the shape of an M.A.'s, and towards the end of the play she wrapped round her a dark heliotrope coloured cloak.[216] At her waist was a dagger. The hair was worn loose over the shoulders.

Miss Howard has not very emotional features, and the only passion she can indicate is anger. She has a loud voice, obviously that of a queen of melodrama, but as it is by no means a feminine one, it is not unsuited to the role.

When I got to the theatre, a nicely spoken, and evidently well-educated, girl was reciting the last speech of the player queen. The close of this scene, Miss Howard too, I thought, in a much too hysterical fashion. From her place by Ophelia, she grovelled across the stage to the King and then yelled her words into his face. This was very unnatural. Miss Howard did the business with the pipe,[217] which Mr Benson,

---

[212] The following accounts of Race's theatre visits are written in a separate notebook (DD921/3/3), each account clearly headed up, and the whole giving the impression of a critical essay. Race was no doubt honing his critical talents, given his small successes in having his work published in the local newspapers.

[213] Race is still adopting that rather archaic practice of 'dropping in' to a performance mid-way through.

[214] Clare Howard (Mrs George Daventry) was the leading lady at the Pavilion Theatre, Whitechapel, specialising in adventuresses, vamps and heroines, her husband equally popular as a melodramatic villain. Her 'reading' of Hamlet, therefore, was inclined to the melodramatic and, according to H. Chance Newton was 'acted and spoken "through" sundry bars of pizzicato, agitato, and other such strains of music. At this or that situation there was heard a melodramatic "chord" or "crash" and so on.' (H. Chance Newton, *Cues and Curtain Calls* (London, 1927) p. 216). Whilst Race does not note any musical accompaniment, he is certainly aware of the melodramatic bent of Miss Howard's performance.

[215] H. Chance Newton again notes that *The Indian Mutiny* (written by George Daventry himself) was toured for some years and featured the 'actor-author … [as] an Oriental villain of the deepest dye and Mrs D. [who] won all hearts, plus plenteous plaudits, as a Jessie Brown-like British heroine.' (Ibid, p. 215). *Lost in Paris* could be a variant on W. Phillips's (1867) *Lost in London* or Leonard Grover's (1896) 'Olympic' comedy-drama *Lost in New York.*

[216] The long black robe was, according to Miss Howard, 'correct, being an exact copy of the dress of some mediaeval Danish students in Racine's book of costume in the Darlington Free Library.' (*Nottingham Daily Express*, 27 October 1899.)

[217] Act III, Scene 2.

I think, omitted, and at the finish there was a very effective tableau – Hamlet leaning over a table reciting the words:

'Tis now the [very] witching time of night.

and the black velvet curtains at the back parted to reveal the motionless figure of the Ghost. The Ghost at the Grand differed a little from the one at the Royal. Its garments were shaped more like ordinary mortals' and they shone with the brilliancy of many silver spangles.

The scene with the mother was hardly taken in a right filial spirit – if Hamlet was chiefly mad 'bending his eye on vacancy.' Miss Nellie King, a rather stout lady, who was the Queen could not add any dignity to this scene. Unfortunately she would keep reminding me of the Lady queens in the 'portables' of my youth.[218]

In Act 4 Scene 2 Miss Howard made plain a point which Mr Benson it seems to me missed. I mean the little passage where Hamlet calls the King his mother.

Hamlet	Farewell, dear mother.
King	Thy loving father, Hamlet.
Hamlet	My mother: father and mother is man and wife; man and wife is one flesh; and so my mother.

The concluding words – 'For England' – were very vigorously delivered by our female Hamlet, and brought down the house. The preceding passage, 'if your messenger find him not there, seek him i' the other place yourself' had also been delivered with much unction and was [in a] new light to me.

At the end of Act 4 Scene 3 Miss Howard introduced a new reading. The King sat down and wrote a letter for Rosencrantz and Guildenstern to carry asking for Hamlet to be assassinated. Hamlet overhears this read, comes in and writes another letter, on similar parchment, asking for the messengers who carry it to be slain. Then Rosencrantz and Guildenstern appear, Hamlet asks to look at the parchment they carry, and before handing it back substitutes his own for it. For this scene the *Express* says Miss Howard has found her authority in an old folio.[219] I should like, however, to make some examination of the old texts before passing any judgement on it. At the end of Act 4 the body of Ophelia was brought in on a bier, and after Laertes' speech the curtain came down on his standing weeping over it. The applause was so great that it had to go up again, and then we saw the bier moving off with the grief stricken brother helped along after it – a very effective ending.

The churchyard scene was taken in on true low comedy vein by the two clowns. The only thing I did not like about the 1st grave digger was his slapping of the skulls with his hands which made the audience laugh immoderately. For the rest, he was rather good, and though his work was of a more common order than Mr Weir's,[220] yet in a theatre like this it was more effective, and I am half of an opinion that it was also more humorous.

The interment of Ophelia was not so well managed as at the Benson's performance, for the body was lifted into the grave in our sight. The consequence was

---

[218] See p. 34.
[219] 'The authority for Mr George Daventry's version is a 1696 folio in the possession of the Duke of Devonshire. The only other copy known is in the British Museum. The folio contains very copious notes and stage directions all of which Mr Daventry has tried to introduce.' (*Nottingham Daily Express*, 27 October 1899).
[220] George Weir, F. R. Benson's comic giant. See p. 101. There is no account of Benson's *Hamlet* in the journals; it is either missing, or Race did not make a record of it.

that the work not being done neatly, a number of the 'gods' took it into their heads to laugh, and the laughter was repeated when Laertes jumped into the grave a few minutes later and half lifted the body up again in wishing Ophelia farewell.

The message of Osric was delivered by the very nicely spoken girl I have mentioned as appearing as the Player Girl. Here, she looked very nice in her boy's suit, besides acting the part charmingly. On the program I see the name of the Player Queen was given as Miss Marie Ellerton, Osric being down to somebody else entirely, but really, I believe, she was Miss Daventry, Miss Howard's daughter. I was much pleased with her.

The last scene of all was very finely acted by Miss Howard, the death being especially well done. The fight was much more prolonged than at the Benson's performance, and the two fought with long, stout swords, not rapiers. This gave an opportunity for sparks to fly, and for our enthusiasm to grow very high, and really, though there was not the same skill shown as by Mr Benson and his companion, the combat looked a dangerous one. After drinking the poisoned cup Miss Howard fell on her knees and made a fine end of it. At the words:

The potent poison doth steal about my soul

she gave a realistic shiver, and at last seemed hardly able to gasp out,

– the rest is silence.

The stage had been darkened for this moment and a strong white light was thrown on her face to set off its agony. This was undoubtedly a capital piece of work. At the Benson rendering of the play there was so much confusion on the stage at the finish, that I have no idea how Hamlet died. It seems a point in Miss Howard's favour that her death scene should have made so strong an impression on, a least, one spectator.

Undoubtedly this Hamlet of Miss Howard's was a very interesting performance. As I have pointed out it had some strong points, and every now and then there was an introduction of impressive business, as for instance where the actress silently crossed herself at the words, 'To what base uses we may return, Horatio' (Act 5 Scene 1). Miss Howard showed herself to be possessed of a surprisingly powerful voice and she carried the whole play through with great vigour. The chief fault in the performance was that Hamlet was never made to appear mad or, perhaps as he really was, to be shamming a madness. On the contrary, he was a remarkably sane person, and one not very polite to his betters, to boot. If Miss Howard could rid herself of all traces of melodrama for this one play, and make Hamlet more of the moody scholar, she would give a capital representation of the character.

Polonius and the 1st gravedigger were taken, I think, by the same actor – Mr John Hignett, who makes a very useful player. Polonius both in looks and manner very much resembled the same individual in the Benson performance.

The King (Mr Magill Martyn), like the Queen, was too much extracted from melodrama to be satisfactory. Laertes (Mr George Daventry) was also of the common order, but acted very vigorously and much to the satisfaction of the 'house.' Mr Daventry wears a moustache and speaks with his mouth awry.

Miss Ethel King, the Ophelia, rather pleased me. She is young and the part was evidently a heavy task for her, but she managed it very nicely. The rest of the actors were a more or less feeble lot. For the first time in my experience of the stage I saw an actor (Guildenstern) who did not know what to do with his hands. Possibly, however, he was little more than a super.

There was a very good house in the popular parts to see the performance and the boxes and dress circle all had their occupants. It was quite apparent that the audience was much interested in the play, but it had not the same critical judgement as the house at the Benson performance. Here at the 'Grand' the 'gods' could not help laughing at the word 'bloody', and the noise had nearly grown into a roar before it was hushed down. At our other theatre a disturbance of this kind was not tolerated at its inception.

(P.S. The short criticism in the *Express* of this performance is rubbish.)

1900

Thursday March 29
To the Grand Theatre at 9 o'clock to see Edmund Tearle in *The Christian's Cross*.[221] *The Christian's Cross*, announced as adapted 'from Cardinal Wiseman's novel *Fabiola* by the Rev. Frederick Oakley, M.A. and revised by 'Clarke Claypole', is nothing more nor less than another version of *The Sign of the Cross* produced by Mr Tearle in the vain hope of robbing Mr Wilson Barrett of some of his multitudinous shekels. I do not know the novel, and probably should not read it if I had the opportunity, so perhaps it will be best to run briefly through the play, as I remember it, to give some idea of what the stage version is like.

When I got to the theatre, late though it was, the second act was still being played so I became an interested spectator of Cecilia, a blind girl (Miss Marion Esher, possessed of such a pretty face that she wisely kept her eyes open) who was being tortured in the presence of Tertullus, a prefect. The torture consisted of the application of an iron crown to the head of the girl who was refusing to render up certain information regarding the Christians. In the end, Sebastian, 'Chief Officer of the Imperial Guard' (Mr Tearle) rushed on to rescue the girl, but she had fallen dead at the Prefect's feet. Miss Esher was dressed wholly in white, looked lovely, and spoke nicely, but it was the voice, for all the world, of Miss Maud Jeffries.

Scenes 1 and 2 of Act 3 were taken up with interviews between Agnes, a wealthy Christian lady (Miss Millie Ford) and sundry gentlemen of evil character who desired her hand. As she refused this, she was led out to die uttering sentiments very similar to those of the heroine in Mr Wilson Barrett's piece, and comforted by, I think, Lucina, a noble lady (Miss Katherine Glover).

Scene 3 was a Roman interior in which we behold Fabiola, a Roman lady (Miss Kate Clinton), reclining at full length on a couch, and being in a very cross mood she orders her girl to send in music. Whereupon enters a harpist with a cardboard harp who – twanging the noiseless strings – sings a love ditty which makes some critic near me chuckle long and loud. I have not a musical ear but I rather fancy that the singer went horribly flat besides being possessed of a voice of very poor quality. Later enters Sebastian who takes up the rest of the scene with Fabiola. What this scene was exactly, I am sorry to say I do not remember, for as I made no notes at the time and did not feel particularly interested in the piece, my recollections have

---

[221] David Mayer discusses the intricacies of this drama – on and off the stage – in his essay 'Toga Plays', in *British Theatre in the 1890s*, pp. 71–92.

become a little misty on the point. Sebastian, I think, announces his love for Fabiola but declares himself a Christan. Fabiola thereupon takes his love but curses the whole body of Christians, and only when Sebastian has recited the articles of his faith does she recall her words and promise to be as he is. The scene is overheard by Fulvius, a spy, who denounces Sebastian to the Emperor who enters with his guards. The Emperor asks him to eat his words; he refuses; is attacked by the guards; draws his sword on the Emperor; and is finally overpowered and dragged off to prison. Either in this scene or the one that followed Miss Kate Clinton was exceedingly impressive. She is rather stout, but she moves with the air of a tragedy queen and is particularly clever in the management of her drapery. I do not remember to have yet seen anyone on the stage who walked with so much skill and managed her train with so much effectiveness as she did.

In Scenes 1 and 2 of Act 4, the spy slays Corvinus, son of the prefect (Mr Wynne) and is himself poisoned by a dark-skinned slave of Fabiola (?Miss Ellen Ashmore) – which is the end of a villain. An interlude took place in the 2nd Act where Calpurnis, a philosopher and lover of wine and women, received the reclining body of the dying Corvinus in his arms. Calpurnis was the counterpart of the like character in *The Sign of the Cross*, only that his witticisms were stale and his gait old after the antics of the gentleman who preceded him in this line. In the last scene, Sebastian stood bound to a tree with the Court before him engaged in planting arrows in the fleshy parts of his body by way of sport. At last one reaches his heart and he dies; Fabiola rushes on and supports him in her arms while the scene at the back opens and some angels (chorus girls dressed in white and pointing upwards) chant a heavenly song as the soul of the martyr leaves him.

The Christian's Cross was long, agonizing and not entrancing and I do not think that it will ever achieve the fame of its predecessor. For one thing, it suffers from its actors. Wilson Barrett on the stage – off he is a seedy-looking individual with dirty-coloured hair and clothes to match – is a handsome figure, and he can put a good deal of pathos into the character. Edmund Tearle on the other hand, is a very stout man, with a thick round head, short hooky nose, and a neck like a bull's. There is nothing meek about him, nor frail, and when he refers, as he did once, 'to this weak frame' which he was ready to submit to be tortured, you feel ready to laugh outright. Altogether there was nothing of the traditional martyr about him, and to me it seems a great mistake that he should take the part.

The Prefect of Mr A. Gow Bentinck, was a very satisfactory one. The actor has a good voice and manner, and would give a good account, I think, of any Shakesperian part in this company. He was much the cleverest of Mr Tearle's associates – on the male side at least. Mr J. W. Benson, Calpurnis, was a fair player, and should quite fill some of his other roles. Mr Vyner Edwyn is much younger than the other two, but as he has every appearance of being ambitious he should bye and bye, as he gains experience, put in some good work. His Fulvius, the spy, was very energetically acted. The rest of the company – the ladies who, as I have said, did very well – were of a very indifferent order and none of them command, I am afraid, anything approaching an extravagant salary.

In the 2nd Act, I should have said that I heard a hymn 'Guide thou our Steps' sung; it is as near as it dare be to 'Shepherd of Souls.' Miss Millie Ford, I should also have added, was very good looking, and like Miss Esher, spoke with correctness and a nice accent. Mr Tearle, at any rate, knows how to select his lady performers.

On Saturday afternoon, the play bill announces the company will give a matinee of *Julius Caesar*. Mr Tearle appears as Brutus, Mr Vyner Edwyn as Marc

Antony, Mr A. Gow Bentinck as Julius Caesar, and Mr Benson as Casca. The Cassius is Mr T. Owen Chambers who acted the Emperor in *The Christian's Cross*, in which part he was a black, and if I had been casting the play I think I should have given this character to Mr Edwyn and moved the other two actors up to Antony and Caesar respectively. I have not, however, much curiosity to see the company in the play.

The performance of *The Christian's Cross* has rather disappointed me because I had imagined that Mr Tearle and his company were of rather a different mould. Mr Tearle, I am afraid, is not capable of interpreting with much intelligence any of Shakespeare's plays though he may give a fair representation of such tragedies as *Richard III* which may be ranted. He is no elocutionist; and for the most part the acting of his company is of a very inferior order.

Monday May 21ˢᵗ
Mr Wilson Barrett in *Claudian*
This evening to the Theatre Royal to see Wilson Barrett in *Claudian*.[222] I seem fated for adventures where this actor is concerned. Three years ago I went up into the gallery, which was crowded to suffocation, to see him in *The Sign of the Cross*,[223] and this evening – though quite by mistake this time – I got into the gallery queue again and did not find out my mistake until we had begun to move into the theatre. It is curious how an audience changes with the actor. A very large proportion of those who had come to see Wilson Barrett were females of the elderly and a little too well-living persuasion, with a very fair sprinkling of young girls. Generally the members of the audience might be said to belong to the lower middle class, the cultured individuals of both sexes whom you always meet in the pit when the Bensons are playing being quite absent. Perhaps I am a little prejudiced on this subject because there was a very beery looking party seated behind me whose natural home was the gallery and who was here continually sending his 'old woman,' as he called her, out for three pennyworth of whisky while his foul breath blew on me the whole evening. Besides I do not like an audience which laughs unseemly at [gap] phrases as this did tonight when somebody on the stage was called an 'audacious wench.' It was amusing to note how the audience mistook an actor on his first entry for Wilson Barrett (whom he was not in the least like) and cheered him to the echo, afterwards making the same mistake over a person it thought was Miss Jeffries, while really fine acting from subordinates never got a round of applause the whole evening.[224] One feels consoled in thinking of these things when people declare they 'love' Wilson Barrett and – quite against your own judgement – laud him to the skies as a mighty fine actor.

---

[222] According to A. Nicoll, *A History of English Drama 1660-1900. Volume VI. A Short-title Alphabetical Catalogue of Plays* (Cambridge, 1965) the dramatists were H. Herman & W. G. Wills but, as David Mayer points out, the collaboration was far more extensive. Whilst Herman formulated the play's 'structure and narrative' and Wills created the dialogue, E. W. Godwin provided 'the archaeology of costumes, &c.' and Wilson Barrett produced the drama and took the leading role. (Mayer, *Playing out the empire*, p. 30).
[223] Actually, it was October 1898. See p. 121.
[224] They were, perhaps, members of the audience who were unused to going to the theatre. See a report by Clement Scott in the *Theatre*, No. 27 (May 1896), p. 129, that 'a considerable portion of those who witness it [*The Sign of the Cross*] are people to whom the inside of a theatre is entirely unfamiliar,' and a similar comment by G. W. Foote, who was 'struck by the novel character of the audience, which might almost be called a congregation... Most of the people appeared to be unused to such surroundings. They walked as if they were advancing to pews, and took their seats with an air of reverential expectation.' (G. W. Foote, 'The Sign of the Cross': *A Candid Criticism of Mr Wilson Barrett's Play* (London, 1896), pp. 9–10 quoted in Mayer, *Playing out the empire*, p. 16.)

Claudian is divided into a Prologue and three acts. In the Prologue, Theorus, a sculptor, finds Serena, his wife and her child, in the hands of Sesiphon, a slave dealer. He is buying her freedom when Claudian appears, outbids him and would have carried her away, but the populace, spurred on by the vehemence of Theorus, rescue her from the hands of the nobleman. Serena flys to a cave where the Holy Clement dwells and begs his protection. Claudian, following her, swears he will have the woman, and brushing aside the cross which the old man raises, stabs the Holy Clement to the heart. Then with his last breaths the holy man utters God's message. Claudian had dared the lightning to strike him; he had defied death; now let him know that he should not die, that none can kill him, that … [*pages missing*]

And now, having told the story, what of the acting? In truth, there are many actors who would have played the story better than Mr Wilson Barrett. Wilson Barrett has a fine face and a remarkably handsome appearance on the stage – where he makes himself appear much taller than he is – but his sugared accents will not let him put genuine emotion into his acting. All through the play, he speaks in the silvery monotone – often much too quickly – but passion and pity he never really exhibits. Time after time he let his opportunities slip by him for the introduction of real pathos into his playing, but always he could pose in picturesque fashion. When I see *Claudian* again, may I see an actor of heart in the part, and then perhaps I shall feel some emotion at what is really a touching story.

Miss Maud Jeffries[225] when I came to examine her face through the glasses seemed to be unable to counterfeit emotion. Miss Ellen Terry, you will remember, can shed real tears on the stage; through Miss Jeffries' troubled face you could always see the happy disposition and smiling eyes being forced down under a thick veil. Curiously enough when I saw her in *The Sign of the Cross* from the gallery, her emotion appeared to be very genuine, but I do not think I made a mistake in my judgement this evening – she acts better the bright traits of character rather than the sad ones.

The best acting in the Prologue was done by Mr Basil Gill (Theorus). He was very earnest, if a little vehement, has a strong voice, and is a good elocutionist. Mr James Carter-Edwards was very good as the Holy Clement, but I think he is burdened with too long a curse for a dying man.

The best of the characters in the play were the Tetrarch (Mr J. Wigney Percyval) and Belos (Mr Horace Hodges). The former looked a thorough oriental, and he acted up to the part splendidly. He was especially good in the scene where he throws himself down before Claudian, and begs for imprisonment, for torture, to be banished – anything but death. Mr Horace Hodges was capital as the rustic. His stupidity in fact was – if one may be allowed to use the term – beautiful. If I was forming a repertory company for old fashioned comedy – dull headed countrymen like Bannister played – Mr Hodges would be one of the first actors I should engage. The Agazil of Mr Edward Irwin was a very satisfactory performance; natural but not quite varied enough for the stage.

The rest of the cast were very fair though the company does not strike one as being anything beyond the average. One or two of the actors were sticks – as for instance Mr N. Jeffries who had a minor speaking part in the Prologue. He has not yet learned the elementary lessons for the use of his voice and hands in a theatre.

Mr Barrett's scenery and appointments are all very elaborate, so much so that after the taste which Irving and a few others show on the stage, they strike the eye as a

---

[225] See p. 126.

little gaudy. They look very costly and very rich, but seem a little highly coloured. In the vineyard scene a chorus of girls sang a very pretty song, led by Miss Cecilia Wilman.

Wednesday September 28th
The Kendals[226] in *The Elder Miss Blossom*
This evening to the Theatre Royal to see the Kendals in *The Elder Miss Blossom*. They have made a great success with this play of late years, chiefly because it has taken Mrs Kendal away from girlish parts which she had been playing too long, and on this tour at any rate they have been able to drop *A Scrap of Paper*, *The Ironmaster*, *The Queen's Shilling*[227] and other old favourites from their programme. But for all that *The Elder Miss Blossom* does not seem to me a very strong play. The theme is good, but the working out of it is amateurish. And there are one or two elements in it which are out of the picture or appear introduced without sufficient cause – such as Withers, the valet to Dr Quick and the affair of the *Hambledon Guardian*.

The story will not take long telling. Act I opens in the London chambers of Andrew Quick, a distinguished traveller, who is expected to arrive back almost immediately from a scientific expedition on which he has been absent several years. The rooms are at the moment invaded by Christopher Blossom with his sister, and daughter, the elder lady (Mrs Kendal) being under the agreeable impression that she is engaged to the home-coming scientist. When they depart, brother and sister make for home, while the younger Miss Blossom does some shopping and thinking that her father and aunt are waiting at the chambers for her, returns there to find Dr Quick arrived. Whereupon results some amusing fencing produced by the delicate hints of the Doctor's that he desires, and expects, to be allowed to salute the lady, and the surprise of the latter who imagines that his kisses should be reserved for her aunt. The end of the scene is that Andrew Quick finds that his letter of proposal addressed to Miss Blossom was received and acknowledged by the older lady, and that he has been living in a fool's paradise induced by his recollections of a girl with whom he had been charmed at a ball.

In Act 2 we behold Miss Blossom senr. in the height of (rather elderly) maiden spirits preparing for her coming marriage, and also learn early that her niece is in love with a neighbouring curate who possesses all the accomplishments and ways of the young clergyman. When Andrew Quick arrives on the scene he has the disagreeable duty of making the mistake known to Miss Blossom. It takes him some time to tell his tale because she has no thought of what he is aiming at; on the contrary, she makes approaches in a very bashful way for those little endearments which the other Miss Blossom had refused. At last, calling himself a fool and a coward, he blurts out the truth. Miss Blossom is heart-broken; everyone will know of it for the wedding presents have arrived and must be returned; and the one happy hope of her life has vanished. She cries, begs of him not to tell how he has humbled her; laughs and cries again. Then he goes out, thoroughly miserable and through the window open onto the

---

[226] Madge Kendal (Margaret Robertson) (1848–1935) and William Hunter Kendal (1843–1917). *The Elder Miss Blossom* by E. Hendrie and M. Wood (1897) was a drama entirely suited to Mrs Kendal's acting temperament and abilities. A. E. Wilson wrote that her performance was 'one of the most touching pieces of acting that I can remember … it gave the actress the opportunity of expressing poignant suffering and she was peerless in that sort of thing.' (*Edwardian Theatre* (London, 1951), p. 116).
[227] *A Scrap of Paper* by J. P. Simpson (1861); *The Ironmaster* by Sir A. W. Pinero (1884); *The Queen's Shilling* by G. W. Godfrey (1877).

lawn we hear the sound of marriage bells – her marriage bells for which the ringers are practising. She rushes to the window and drags it to, and as the sound dies away falls down with her head on her knees – sick and hurt and saddened.

In Act III the Curate and the junior Miss Blossom who have had a quarrel in the last scene become friends again by the brave help of the aunt, and Andrew Quick reappears, convinced that after all it is the elder and not the younger Miss Blossom that he loves. This most agreeable conclusion being imparted to the lady she, when convinced of its genuiness [sic], goes to his arms and so all ends happily – but we don't hear the marriage bells again as I think we ought to do.

The faults in the piece are not in its construction so much as in the working out. No explanation is given of the Doctor's sudden renunciation of the younger Miss Blossom – the fact that she is engaged, or nearly so, is not communicated to him. A greater error is that the appreciation of the elder lady's charms follows too quickly their rejection. The two have hardly seen one another before this occasion; he tells her she is not the woman he loves; goes out, walks round the stables, comes back and declares himself her devoted servant. This is too quick.

Tacked onto the story is a rather weak episode, the chief partners in which are a journalist and a retired army man, friend to Dr Quick. The newspaper man rushes into print with a column of the Major's tall stories which have been palmed onto him as gospel, and afterwards goes in fear of his life with the Major after him, his pockets stuffed with *Hambledon Guardian*s. A curious figure introduced onto the stage is the valet of Andrew Quick. He is a most extraordinary looking individual with a thin tapering nose, a head of long black hair, and a suit of old fashioned black clothes. He has a stutter, is very nervous and finds it difficult to speak properly. You think of him as a villain going about among a flock of school children, and are very much surprised to find at the end of the play that he is going to marry the Blossom's parlour maid.

Mrs Kendal looked wonderfully young on the stage, though she must be near, if not past, the fifties.[228] I do not think she has the same emotional gifts as Miss Terry, but she possesses a power over the tones of her voice almost remarkable in its naturalness. This was shown in several little asides, one of the best examples to explain being the manner in which she received the curate's wedding present. It was an ink stand of curious design – most strongly reminiscent of the gentleman's infatuation for golf – and the way in which she was first inclined to laugh and make fun of it and afterwards for the sake of the thing relapsed into the usual gushing stream of thanks, the while holding the inkstand away from her as though it was some noxious insect was most amusing. Mrs Kendal plays most easily, and one would not have to be a great critic of acting to notice how cleverly she manages her general stage deportment, and drapery. You feel that you have witnessed accomplished acting of the parlour order after seeing her – at least in this play, but you hardly think of her as a great tragic or emotional actress.

Miss Nellie Campbell who was the other Miss Blossom has no talents of a great order, but she managed very nicely the whole evening. I suppose we all envied the curate when he put his arm round her waist, and later laid his lips on hers, and I know a ripple of laugher went through the house when she came in from the lawn – leaving the gentleman among the gooseberry bushes - and went about on springs, only able to reply to questions 'I don't know, I don't know.' A healthy sample of a country blossom surely.

---

[228] She would be fifty-two.

Figure 15. Mrs Kendal

It is difficult to tell whether Mr Rudge Harding, the curate, was acting or not, but if so he gave a remarkably close imitation of the young gentleman in orders who so graces his parish during the first few years he spends in the church. All the same, it was a most harmless and agreeable impersonation.

Mr P. T. Ames, the valet, was almost too lifelike to be pleasant, and other faithful copies of their respective characters were – the caretaker of the Doctor's chambers (Mr Leonard Calvert) and the parlour maid at the Blossom's (Mrs A. B. Tapping).

Mr Kendal himself I have left last for consideration. He makes one great mistake through the play – he does not in the least look like a professor, or a scientist, or traveller, or anything of the kind. On the contrary, he is the prosperous banker, or country gentleman of town habits, to the life, and you never for a moment think of him travelling in the wilds of Australia or having been engaged in scientific research. He plays naturally and appears more like a gentleman than an actor on the stage.[229] He did not take the trying scene with the elder Miss Blossom at all badly and on the whole I quite enjoyed his performance. He and Major Twentyman (Mr Frank Fenton) and Miss Sophie Blossom in the 3rd Act participated in one of the best bits of comedy in the play – the little episode where the lady displays her aunt's wedding dress and the gentlemen acted as gentlemen always do on such occasions – handled the thing as though it were a creature from the other world.

The rest of the Company were capable, but the Kendals seem to take care not to surround themselves with 'stars'. The two were head and shoulders above their supporters in skill.

The scenery was the Kendals own and very appropriate. The second set (the Blossom's drawing room) was most elegantly furnished with modern appointments and the great French windows at the back looked out onto charming country.

There was a very fair house.

P.S. I find I have omitted to note as remarkable Mrs Kendal's manner of receiving the news that she is the wrong Miss Blossom – the little start she gives as she holds up the letter of proposal – confident that it vouches for the genuineness of her relief – and then the realisation that the ground is cut from beneath her as it is all over.

---

[229] Clement Scott said that he was 'a good sound actor, and excellent comedian' (*Drama of Yesterday and Today,* p. 135).

Figure 16. The Great Wheel, Earls Court, c. 1900

3

A London tourist

Sydney Race's metropolitan excursions

Race's trip to London was a regular event, involving a four-hour train journey from Nottingham to the capital, and a very late return. Arriving in the London, he made the most of every minute, taking in what we might now term the 'tourist sites', and always including a quota of churches and museums. This lengthy pilgrimage was conducted on foot and by bus, covering very many miles in the course of a day, and his journal records his route and an often detailed description of what he saw. Perhaps he used one of the many guidebooks or books of 'London walks' to traverse the capital in search of the noteworthy. It is not until 1897, when he is 22, that he stays overnight in London, going to the Shaftesbury Theatre to see Edna May in The Belle of New York, *and making his first visit to the great Theatre of Varieties, the Alhambra, Leicester Square.*

His London theatrical experiences prior to 1897 were confined to the spectacular shows performed at the Olympia and Earl's Court exhibitions: 'Venice in London' *(1892–3),* 'The Orient' *(1894–5) and* 'India and Ceylon' *(1895–6). These were long and complex performances, involving hundreds of performers and intricate stage and scenery manoeuvres. For example, India, was a torturous four hours long when the* Times *correspondent saw the show in August 1895! For Sydney Race, show and exhibition represented safe, rational entertainment, rather like that found at the Mechanics' Institute at home in Nottingham, or the local exhibitions he frequented (see p. 28). In the exhibition itself, the weighty Official Guidebook rationalised the foreignness of both culture and geography for the visitor, signalling 'education' over 'amusement', and complemented by the many ethnic displays of skills and industry. Colonised cultures were captured, arranged and displayed, with exhibitions of 'native crafts' and more dubious spectacles of ethno-cultural behaviours: the Harem (which caused some upset to the Turkish government) and the Singing Gondoliers, for example.[230] The exhibitions, orchestrated by the American-Hungarian Kiralfy brothers, were exercises in construction and management on a vast scale. Cites were realised in miniature – a vast Venetian canal system or a Temple of Venus, with sixteen Doric columns and a floor of Carrara marble. Real animals in menageries, real water in a canal sat beside the massive panorama of Constantinople, the Great Pyramid and an Egyptian street scene. The fine balance that was struck between rational recreation and stark commercialism was increasingly threatened in the fin de siècle moment of the 1890s. Race notes the shops selling 'fancy goods' and the increasing variety of refreshment areas, courtesy, of course, of 'Joe' Lyons. In just four years, inducements to spend over and above the not inconsiderable entrance fee were multiplying. At the 1896* 'India and Ceylon' *exhibition Race notices the 'side*

---

[230] See John Glanfield, *Earls Court and Olympia. From Buffalo Bill to the 'Brits'* (Stroud, 2003), pp. 38–39, and below p. 144. J. B. Booth recalled, with mild irony, the Venetian gondoliers singing, as they rowed, '"Remembra gondoliere,/Foor drinkita biere!"' J. B. Booth, *London Town* (London, 1929), pp. 194–195.

shows' – of the latest moving pictures, the exhibition of X-rays, alongside native jugglers and conjurors – which might be seen for an additional payment.

1892

Whit Monday June 6th
Race travels to London by train, arriving at 9.30 am. He visits the Tower of London, St Paul's Cathedral, Fleet Street, the Strand, the Law Courts, the Houses of Parliament, Horse Guards, and attends a service at Westminster Abbey.

We went to see 'Venice – the Bride of the Sea' at Olympia,[231] which is strangely advertised[232] and about which there is much talk. Everyone on paying got a numbered ticket for the performance. Inside was a big exhibition and fancy goods on sale – all presided over by well-dressed young ladies. Then we went into 'Modern Venice.' Here were rooms of houses. The illusion was good. Some were all painted others had proper doors and windows. They were on canvas with the ornaments and knockers, images of Saints made of plaster. Between them were canals of real water on which were rowed gondolas. The water was perhaps 3 feet deep – when you were directly over it you could easily see the bottom though from a side view the appearance of great depth was very good. On these the real gondolas were propelled by real gondoliers in costume.[233] Some of them singing as they went along. The charge for a row was 6d. Some of the houses were tenanted by fancy goods people – others were empty. At one spot was a big canvas representing a grand Canal and in front was a gondola fastened to some posts in which sat 3 men in boating costume. 2 played guitars and the other the fiddle. They gave some good songs and music. In another spot 3 men and one woman in costumes were singing Italian songs and we could hear a lady singing out of one of the houses but could not get near enough to see her. There were many bridges over the water and you could walk along the sides (of wood) easily but you [soon] got round the place. At one spot there were refreshment tables on the sides at which you could eat while gondolas rowed by. The canals were perhaps 12ft wide – there was a painted sky and also pigeons flying about.

The performance commenced at 8.30. The seats were Chairs numbered as your tickets – a good idea.

The performance was something after Belle Vue style.[234] The stage was crowded by perhaps over 500 performers in gorgeous costumes. These sometimes sang – the words indistinguishable led by an overpowering band out of sight – and sometimes the ballet took possession of the stage and went though their evolutions. In one scene six flat-bottomed boats very [sic] filled by soldiers and the dancers and

---

[231] Opened in 1886, first as the National Agricultural Hall, it was originally a venue for the staging of tournaments and exhibitions, as well as livestock and machinery displays. Agricultural exhibitions were quickly replaced by spectacular shows and massive set-piece exhibitions. The Irish Exhibition of 1888, complete with Blarney stone and a thatched village was followed by P. T. Barnum's 'Greatest Show on Earth' circus in 1889–90. In 1891, Hungarian Imre Kiralfy (who had worked with Barnum) was brought over from America to orchestrate 'Venice in London', which ran for 18 months from December 1891. See Glanfield, *Earls Court* (2003).

[232] Race is possibly referring to the fantastical artwork produced for posters and programmes, featuring St Mark's Square and the Grand Canal with gondolas and gondoliers.

[233] Specially-built gondolas, propelled by real Gondoliers, operated on the canal network.

[234] Opened in 1836 by John Jennison as Zoological Gardens, Manchester's Belle Vue, with its acres of grounds, exhibitions centre, gardens and amusement park, offered a very similar kind of spectacular entertainment.

rowed out onto the water and then various motions were performed. The scene before St Marks was very good. A bell was heard tolling and then a great crowd assembled and an uproar took place in the Market. There were some gorgeous Ecclesiastical processions of men in all dresses. Part 2 was the better one. In one scene many gondolas rowed in till the whole space of water was covered. These were of gorgeous colours and filled with girls in beautiful costumes formed into striking groups. Then there was a scene representing a banquet with terraces behind filled with people watching the spread. In this scene the whole stage – said to be 450 ft long – was covered by a row of dancers – some women in male attire who went through various movements as one body.

1895

Tuesday July 2
Race takes advantage of a local day excursion to the Nonconformist Festival at the Crystal Palace in London to make a trip to the capital. Departing from Nottingham, he had a carriage to himself on both the outward and return journeys, and writes: '[I] managed to travel in my usual suit and change into my best one for the Metropolis. I found this, and especially the slippers I wore, a very comfortable mode of travel and particularly so when coming back'!

On arriving at King's Cross at 8.15, Race has a 'wash and brush up' and breakfast and sets out for St Paul's on foot. He takes a bus down Holborn and Chancery Lane to Fleet Street, and another to St Paul's, after which he walks to Smithfield, through the Cattle Market, goes to the churches of St Bartholomew the Great and St Saviour's, Southwark, and on Tower Bridge. He returns to St Paul's by bus, has lunch in a restaurant in Fleet Street, then takes in Bow Church and the (closed) Temple Church, Lincoln's Inn Fields, visiting Sir John Soane's Museum[235] – 'the object of my visit'. *He returns to Temple Church (now open), and inspects the British Museum*:

'I also by obtaining a ticket at the entrance was allowed to stand just inside the Reading Room and gaze round the mighty dome and see the crowd of readers at the tables. The next time I come I must do the Museum more thoroughly; oh that I could join the number of daily readers in its magnificent library!'

He then takes a bus to Trafalgar Square and visits the National Gallery. Having walked around Trafalgar Square, he takes a bus to Westminster Abbey and arrives there, just before six o'clock, when it is closing. He walks through Deans Close to the Houses of Parliament where he is frustrated in his efforts to sit in the Strangers Gallery. He walks back along the Embankment, having 'a good cheap tea' *of coddled eggs and a pot of tea on the way, and then along Piccadilly, Bond Street and Oxford Street to Marble Arch.* 'This was a long walk,' *he writes,* ' and I was pretty tired by the time I got to the Arch.' *Taking a bus to Hyde Park Corner, he was* 'greatly surprised by the large number of diners out (many of them ladies in evening dress) who passed us in hansoms.' *Another bus journey delivers him to the Brompton*

---

[235] An eclectic mix of art and artefacts preserved in the private residence of Sir John Soane in Lincoln's Inn Fields. The collection includes Hogarth's *A Rake's Progress,* three paintings by Canaletto, Sir Robert Walpole's desk, numbers of Roman marbles, and sections of the fourteenth-century House of Lords and Prince's Chamber. See the Museum website at http://www.soane.org.

Oratory where he looks around, afterwards walking to the South Kensington Museum (the 'V. and A.'), past the Natural History Museum, the School of Science and the Imperial Institute.]

I take my last London bus ride[236] from here [South Kensington] and that to Olympia. The Show this year is 'The Orient'[237] succeeding Constantinople which followed Venice. It has not been a success and the last performance will be given next Saturday. The Directors have exhausted all the Capital after a great deal of discussion by the Shareholders tried to raise more money on further shares but found the game useless and had to give it up.[238]

The interior was arranged like the last show I saw here. There was an outer corridor in which were refreshment bars and stalls for the sale of fancy goods and a little further on was Constantinople itself. That is to say there was a large collection of shops all occupied for the sale of fancy articles, in appearance like old houses and the streets they stood in were of worn stones apparently and wound in and out up bridges and over canals. At one place there was a harbour with quite a number of ships in and from here you could have sailed in a boat along the canals and into the Hall of One Thousand Columns.[239] This latter I suppose was a very deceptive arrangement as by the aid of mirrors it was made to appear an immense size. The water was two or three feet in depth. However I never saw anyone on these boats of which there did not appear to be many quite different from at Venice. This must be partly the management's fault as no price was up for the ride and further I noticed that there were no catalogues for sale under a shilling.

There was also the Tower of Galatea here which seemed an immense height up as you went along its passages. At the further end was a panorama of Constantinople. The back part of it was the painted canvas and in front the roofs of houses were imitated in wood. Thus one at the top of a high tower seemed to be looking down onto a big city at one's feet.

In addition to the stage entertainment there were two novelties – the Temple of Venus and a Representation of a Harem. In the former of these, which was like the interior of a beautiful marble building with several steps to it 4 or 5 girls lay or sat in various postures. One or two of them were fairly good looking and all were well painted to make them appear so. They were dressed in full length Classical costumes but had the arms bare. They kept pretty nearly the same position, though one of them who was lying on the ground must have felt rather tired, all the time they were on show but they talked to one another and did not hesitate to move their heads etc occasionally. The Harem was a more natural affair and here the young ladies reclined on hassocks, couches, etc. They were in Turkish costume but like the others had their arms bare. One of the girls here was rather good looking but generally they were not a

---

[236] Race travelled by horse-drawn omnibus, of course, which was still the cheapest mode of transport in the city.

[237] The canals and buildings used in the 'Venice in London' exhibition were re-used for 'Constantinople, or the Revels of the East', which opened on Boxing Day 1893, orchestrated by Imre Kiralfy's brother, Bolossy. In fact, much of the Constantinople exhibition was retained, including 'the Tower of Galatea, the Bridge of Boats, the scenes from the "Arabian Nights", the water trip and the Hall of the Thousand and One Columns.' (*Times*, 27 December 1894). There is no record of Race visiting the 'Constantinople' exhibition. He either did not visit London in 1894, or the journal entry is missing.

[238] The 'Olympia' Company was compulsorily wound up on 1 July with debts of over £25,000. (*Era*, 27 July 1895).

[239] This represented the fourth-century Cistern of Constantine, an immense underground chamber, the vaulted roof of which is supported by 336 marble columns.

fascinating lot. They must have had an awful cheek though to sit out there so often to be stared at and have remarks passed on them.

Each of these places was enclosed with glass so that we could not hear anything said inside.

The stage entertainment had commenced by the time I got in, (about 8.30). The place, which is of course a monster open [area], was perhaps a little more than half filled the people sitting in a flat semi circle round the stage. This time the band was placed in front of the stage but low down so as not to obstruct the view.

The first part of the entertainment represented an Eastern scene with the ballet girls dressed in Oriental costumes. The figures and colours of this were most pretty and as a 'finale' a wooden platform came out from under the stage right into the water meeting far out in a semi-circle and on this the long row of girls came dancing. This produced a splendid finish. Most of the dresses worn by the dancers were rather scanty. They had no petticoats on but their skirts reaching below the knee on one side were on the other open to the hip so that when they whirled round almost the full length of the leg was seen. However as the distance was great no harm was done. When this was over a 'cloth' came down bearing a good view of the Sphinx and Pyramids by moonlight. A party of Arabs came in with camels and after some sports to music of tom-toms tents were pitched and some of the men went in and otherwise slept out round the tents. Then a long white robed Bedouin comes in stealthily, looks round, discovers the state of affairs and goes back bringing on his tribe who come rushing in on horseback. Then the camp is awakened and a hand to hand combat takes place. Eventually the sleepers are beaten and pursued off the ground by their mounted enemies.

After an interval the big curtain rose on a view of a street in Old London with gates at either end. Enter merry apprentices with their sweethearts and they all have a merry time dancing round the maypole and at old English sports. At our end of the stage a man was exhibiting a performing donkey and poodle each being a 'property' animal. After a show of profound wisdom on the part of the donkey and an amusing imitation of the usual jumping performance from the poodle the two animals push their master into the water from which he escapes swimming. A like fate befell several men at the other end of the stage and there were also boat races and swimming matches in the water. Several men had also an exciting race on a wooden animal something like an ostrich in the water. These objects are very unreliable ones and upset several riders just as they were reaching the goal.

Then on land there were tight rope dancers and jugglers and also races on foot and on horseback. These last were very exciting affairs as the horses made a great clatter as they went along. The course was several times round which necessitated them going behind the scenes and the noise of the horses' hoofs could therefore be heard like thunder getting louder and louder as the animals got nearer. All the racers wore coloured jackets like jockeys to distinguish them.

Afterwards came a grand procession which was really a treat to watch. It was headed by a jester on horseback and after him came about 100 pike men in full armour and 10 mounted trumpeters blowing a loud blast. Then there were bowmen and other soldiers and men on horseback. There were also 4 or 5 companies of girls all marching in perfect time and beating drums. Each company was in a colour of its own – heliotrope, lavender, etc and the effect was charming. Then there were many banners borne along and other people whose distinctive dress I have forgotten. Last came the King and Queen riding on horseback under a palanquin. Then there was more dancing including some by a troupe of girls in Highland Costume. Lastly gorgeous barges of the City Companies filled with girls and men came rowing in. Some of these had sails set and others carried fine banners. They were occupied by different trades. On one were the bakers and on another the Smiths. The latter sang a song with deep bass voices as they proceeded slowly along beating time on their anvils. This effect was very pretty indeed. After singing all the people on the stage joined hands and the curtain fell on a long row of dancers. This last scene was very pretty especially the procession which presented a fine effect as it came down onto the stage through a massive gateway. The barges too were very handsome and the groups on them well arranged.

This performance was over about quarter past ten.

Race returns to King's Cross, has supper, catches his train and arrives back in Nottingham at just after 4 o'clock. 'An eventful day this,' *he writes, with no trace of irony!*

1896

Whit Monday May 25th

A very similar itinerary to his visit to London the previous year (except that he goes with Will and E.[240]*), taking in the Foundling Hospital, the British Museum, Hazlitt's epitaph in Soho,*[241] *Trafalgar Square, the Strand, plenty of churches, and Newgate:* 'It is a long, black looking place, well representing its character. As we looked at it we remembered that it contained four murderers condemned to death: Millsom, Fowler Seaman, Mrs Dyer.'[242] *Then London Bridge, the House of Commons, Westminster Abbey, Whitehall, Horse Guards Parade, Brompton Oratory, South Kensington Museum, ending up at Earls Court where the India and Ceylon Exhibition is taking place.*

From here [the South Kensington Museum] we took a bus to the India and Ceylon Exhibition, Earl's Court where we arrive just after nine. On getting inside W. begins to examine some side shops minutely but as I was not interested in them we agreed to separate for an hour. On going back to the rendezvous they turn up a little late and I found they had been round the Great Wheel.[243] The journey had only taken 20 mins and I had never thought of going on it thinking it would take an hour or two to do it. Tonight the wheel was lighted up with electricity which gave it a very pretty effect. It seemed a marvellous and beautiful piece of engineering and it greatly impressed me with its height. A 1/-[244] was charged for the journey round it.

---

[240] Probably Emily, Race's older sister.

[241] In St Ann's Churchyard, Wardour Street, Soho.

[242] Albert Millsom and Henry Fowler were hanged on 9 June 1896 for the murder of William Smith of Muswell Hill, on the same scaffold as William Seaman, who had murdered John Levy and Sarah Gale. The following day, Amelia Dyer was hanged for the murder of a four-month old baby. She was engaged in the illegal practice of 'baby farming', receiving money to care for unwanted babies. It was thought she had murdered at least six other babies – and had been paid to do so.

[243] Begun in 1894, the Earl's Court Giant Wheel was 300 feet high, carrying 1,200 passengers at a time. Obviously W. and his friend were not put off riding on the wheel by the incident which took place only four days earlier when, with over sixty people on board, it became stuck for 15 hours, from 9 in the evening until the next day. Those stranded were supplied with refreshments by 'ex-sailor attendants' who scaled the massive structure to deliver them, and were entertained throughout the evening by the Guards Band. See Glanfield, *Earls Court*, pp. 69–70.

[244] 1/-: one shilling.

In the exhibition were two large circular courts ingeniously erected of canvas and painted wood to appear like stone. In the centre was a band stand and the band, sides, and ground were, in each case, lighted with innumerable lighted glass cups. The first court was surrounded with shops where fancy Indian [*word missing*] etc., was sold, the air being perfumed with a peculiar scent. Chairs were laid round the band stands and, near the sides, were little tables at which visitors were sitting having refreshments. The other court was a little more select and there was a railed off space for members in which all the seats were wicker easy ones. Both courts were laid out with flower beds (somewhat artificial ones) and were filled with a fashionable throng parading to the music. As in London itself, I was struck with the 'Frenchy' style in which the ladies dress. The hair and headgear have this appearance, particularly.[245]

There were some 6 or 8 elephants, and half a dozen camels parading about on which folks were riding and Japanese carriages pulled about by natives who ran a long shouting at the top of their voices. In another part of the exhibition were several rows of streets of native shops with real Ceylonese at work painting, glass blowing, etc. The men were noteworthy by reason of their small size.

There were in addition any number of side shows for which an extra charge was made. Among them were the following: the Princess[246] Theatre (an enormous spectacular affair), a panorama of Ancient Rome, a captive balloon with rides at 5/- per head, like Olympia; nautch girls[247] and native jugglers; a menagerie; an exhibition of a conjuring marvel; the X-rays[248] and a place where the performances at the chief Theatres and music halls could be heard. There were several of Edison's Kinetoscopes;[249] several elaborate shooting galleries; and a switchback set among painted scenery.

The place was certainly a fine one and required a good day and a long purse to do it thoroughly. We had only an hour and a half in it and then had to catch a train back to Kings Cross from an adjoining station. I daresay that Earl's Court has with Londoners the kind of reputation that Vauxhall had but everybody was well behaved tonight.[250]

Race and his friends leave King's Cross at midnight and arrive in Nottingham four hours later.

---

[245] As always, Race is acutely aware of women's fashions, noting here the difference between the provincial look in Nottingham and the more up-to-date costumes of London. The 'Frenchy' style he notes for hats and hair is a comment on elaborately dressed creations which used feathers and ribbons, huge artificial flowers and spotted veils as decoration. Fashionable women's dress was notable for the 'wasp waist', long train and 'leg-of-mutton' sleeves.

[246] Race presumably means the re-built Empress Theatre, a magnificent structure, with a 315 foot-wide stage, and equipment with which to facilitate spectacular productions. See Glanfield, *Earls Court*, p. 66.

[247] Professional dancing women from India.

[248] Although X-ray imaging had been discovered 10 years earlier, it was only in the previous 3 years that the technology had become more widely known, and in March 1896 that Thomas Edison developed the fluoroscope for medical use. In the same year, Friese Green was performing matinee X-ray Exhibitions at the Oxford Music Hall. See Richard Crangle, 'Saturday Night at the X-rays: The Moving Picture and the New Photography in Britain, 1896', in *Celebrating 1895* ed. by John Fullerton (Sydney, 1998), pp. 138–144.

[249] See p. 50.

[250] Vauxhall Gardens which, during the early part of the nineteenth-century, was notorious as a resort for promiscuous behaviour. There is no record that Earl's Court developed the same reputation, and it is difficult to see from Race's account, what might have been objectionable, other than the lively behaviour which such a venue might encourage.

1898

Friday September 2ⁿᵈ
Another trip to London where Race follows a similar itinerary to previous years, but this time he elects to stay overnight, securing accommodation in Fleet Street.

The Guildhall unfortunately was not open so I had to go back the way I had gone and en route I came across a shop in which were being exhibited a number of cinematograph views all worked by turning a handle after putting up a penny in a slot. The things were doing a roaring trade; no admission being charged to the place but a fellow walking about to give full change to anybody short of coppers. Many of the views were of a shady character, at least as shady as they could openly be. One showed a painter painting from the 'nude.' Immediately the picture started you saw the painter step up to his model and arrange her, and then for the rest of the time the latter stood like a statue. Another, which I did not patronize, represented the now familiar subject of a 'lady' preparing for a bath.[251]

More description of sight seeing, then to the Shaftesbury Theatre, Shaftesbury Avenue[252]*...*

... where I took my stand in the queue of people waiting to hear The Belle of New York.[253]

As with *The Shop Girl* I watched this piece in such an uncritical spirit that really I can write very little about it. Indeed when I wanted to write a paragraph about it for *City Sketches* last month, to my annoyance I could not find anything to say of it.

The piece of course has very little plot, but *The Belle* is a gay young creature who becomes a demure Salvation Army lassie to entrap into marriage Harry Bronson, son of Ichabod Bronson, 'President of the Young Mens Rescue League and Anti-Cigarette Society of Cohoe;' at least that is who I believe it was. The women make the play; and of them the most interesting was the Belle herself. Miss Edna May. Miss May's photograph is all over London. She has a very demure – it is the only word – face, and in the photographs generally wears a large Salvation Army poke bonnet etc which, as she has her hair parted down the middle, sets it off to perfection. In other pictures she has a bodice cut very low, and skirts much abbreviated. On the stage, one does not notice these things so much. She makes her first appearance in a red frock, in which she dances and shows her lingerie; afterwards she wore her Army dress and was very circumspect; and lastly she came on as a French music hall singer – black dress, cut low, skirts short, black lingerie – to sing what was described as a naughty French song, but which did not sound particularly wicked in the amphitheatre where I

---

[251] By 1898, coin-operated moving picture machines were becoming popular in arcades, bazaars and, as here, in shop shows.

[252] Built in 1888, to a design by C. J. Phipps, it was destroyed by bombing in 1941, and should not be confused with the current Shaftesbury Theatre.

[253] *The Belle of New York*, a musical comedy, ran for over a year from April 1898, having transferred from New York where it had little success, running to only 64 performances. It made Edna May a star, and Race's note that her photograph was 'all over London' testifies to her immense popularity. Postcards of her portraying the demure Salvation Army girl, Violet Gray, were particularly abundant (see www.peopleplayuk.org.uk for a reproduction of postcard). A programme for the first night of the show, dated 12 April 1898, can be found at http://www.arthurlloyd.co.uk/Shaftesbury/ ShaftesburyProgramme.htm with a further link to a page showing a photograph of the Shaftesbury Theatre, and a seating plan.

sat. The Shaftesbury has two galleries only – balcony and gallery – and the amphitheatre is the row of four or five seats in front of the gallery.

Miss Edna May has only a remote idea of acting; and she has very little voice for singing, but her songs, particularly because they come from a little, pretty mouth, have a peculiar attraction. Generally she gave me the impression that she had played the piece so often that she was thoroughly sick of it. There was very little life in her performance.

Some of the other actresses were very fine women – who knew it. In the last scene one wore a very décolleté dress and as she had a particularly fine bosom and a handsome pair of shoulders to display, considerably showed us both by turning her back on us for a while so that we might examine it. Another girl had a romps part to play, which means that we saw much white underlinen at intervals. In fact the ladies were particularly liberal, so far as my recollections go, in displaying their charms, but I was not affected by them and I have nearly forgotten quite what they were.

The gentlemen were a harmless and feeble lot, and the only one among them to get any applause that evening was the lucky individual whose lot it was to sing a topical song such as we get in every pantomime. Really there was little genuine applause the whole evening, and no hearty laughter. People seemed to have heard it was a good show and so gone to see it, and when they were arrived found the dresses and the scenery quite enough to occupy their thoughts. Two gentlemen – called 'twin portugese brothers' on the programme[254] – had some idiotic business to do in which the chief part – at one period – was to fire a pistol, and another couple – official designations 'a polite lunatic' and 'a mixed-ale pugilist' – were fitted with some equally clever business. Most of us preferred I think to watch the ladies of the play.

Saturday September 3
[pages missing]
… Of course getting so late to the Alhambra[255] and it being Saturday night there was not a seat to be had. I had intended sitting in the Pit stalls but these were all full, and so was the Pit of which there were only a few rows. So I took my stand in the promenade and leaning over the wooden balustrade which goes round in a semi circle has a fair view of the performance. The Alhambra is a large place, much larger than our Theatre Royal, and nearly the size – in the interior ring – of our Mechanics' Hall, I should think. It is so far as I could see very prettily decorated, but the details I could not describe from the little I could catch sight of. The orchestra stalls – which were very sparsely filled – looked very luxurious. The audience seemed a respectable one, chiefly men, and in the part where I was there were few, if any, bad characters of the female sex. Before each row of seats – or rather on the back of every one – is a little shelf, wired round, large enough to hold two glasses, and waiters in uniform go in and out for 'orders.' I noticed that the individual who looked after the pit was not afraid to ask for a tip.

When I got in some dogs were performing and very clever they seemed to be. Then there was an orchestral selection, following which came two American safety

---

[254] The opening night programme shows that Count Ratsi Rattatoo and Count Patsi Rattatoo were played by Mr William H. Sloan and Mr William Gould. Karl Von Pumpernick, 'polite lunatic', was Mr J. E. Sullivan, and Mr Frank Lawton played 'Blinky Bill' McGuirk, the 'Mixed Ale Pugilist'. (Thanks to Matthew Lloyd for this material. See his excellent website http://www.arthurlloyd.co.uk.)
[255] The Alhambra, burnt down in 1882, was rebuilt as a music hall, becoming famous for its ballets and the prostitutes who populated the promenade. Race clearly relishes the former and, taking his place in the promenade, is not *un*aware of the latter! The consumption of alcohol was still allowed in the halls.

trick cyclists, the renowned Kilpatrick and Barber. One of these was a lady, and both were dressed very elegantly in pale blue tights. They did some clever feats with safety tricycles, and received a lot of applause. The next item was supplied by Wood and Shepherd, who were two very smart (artificially) coloured gentlemen. One was dressed in a fashionable grey suit, and the other had on an outrageous costume consisting of very wide trousers in a neat (!) pattern, waistcoat to match and a voluminous coat. They did some funny tricks with various musical instruments, interladed (?) with much comic business and some good banjo playing. Most of the comic business was done by the outrageous gent, and one of his best tricks was when he took off his watch – a thing the size of a dinner plate with a great chain attached – and threw it into the wings where we heard the works going at a tremendous rate until they went off with a loud crash. At the finish the smart gentleman played a capital cornet solo and then bowed himself off. Afterwards his partner (apparently) gave us another solo, equally good, and was bowing <u>himself</u> off very effusively when the other appeared to claim the solo as his own, to the outrageous gent's great disgust.

The next item was a 'ballet divertissement' called *Jack Ashore*[256] and I think I shall be only speaking the truth to say that I have never before seen such lovely costumes on the stage. The piece had a little plot. Jack was about to marry Nellie but his rival Cecil Bertram appears, gets a 'long shoreman' to have the successful lover captured by a press gang and is just going to have him carried off to sea when the news comes that peace has been proclaimed and that no more pressed men are wanted. Then the plot is exposed and Bertram is hustled off with much indignation by the sailors.

The scene showed an Inn on one side, with an arbour on the other, docks in the rear, and the sea in the distance. It was beautifully painted: the Inn – an old time one for the piece was dated at the beginning of the century – had a quaint look with it, and the arbour, where was hung a parrot in a cage, looked a place of real trees. As the piece progressed a realistic effect was produced on the 'sea.' Several ships sailed it; the night grew dark and the moon arose; and all along the quayside little lights appeared. It was capital.

---

[256] Devised and produced by Chas. Wilson, music by George W. Byng. Jack was played by Lytton Grey, Cecil Bertram by Philip Sefton, and Nellie by Grace Arundale. Her sister, Sybil Arundale, played Naomi, the Gipsy Girl. Though the story was in the mode of the nautical melodrama of 40 years earlier, the Alhambra ballet was designed, like the Olympia and Earl's Court productions, to privilege the spectacle rather than the narrative. For a thorough discussion of the neglected topic of music hall ballet, see Alexandra Carter, *Dance and Dancers in the Victorian and Edwardian Music Hall Ballet* (London, 2005).

4

'Tours in Town and Other Sketches'

two articles by Race published in the Nottingham Argus

These two essays published in the Nottingham Argus – *'The Circus' (January 1896) and 'Shows in Shops' (April 1896) represent Race's youthful ambition (never well-hidden) to write for the local press. They relate specifically to two popular entertainment forms in Nottingham, and illustrate not only his now-matured writing style – one nicely attuned to the readership of a provincial journal – but also the eclecticism of his interests. These two essays and the range of amusements covered in the rest of his writings offer the reader a rare glimpse of performances that existed both within and, perhaps more importantly, outside local licensing laws and conventional theatrical and exhibition venues. The conventional approach to the circus – that sentimental resort of the family – has a sharper edge in Race's hands, with descriptions of the audience of Mr and Mrs Largefamily, the swells, the old folk and the 'giddy girls' as well as the circus acts. More unusually, Race writes about the shop shows to which he was a frequent visitor, and which existed in every major British city during the nineteenth and early twentieth centuries. These temporary entertainments lie so far outside the scope of journalism and published anecdote that the detail of performers and performance has up to now been negligible.*

The Circus[257]

The Circus is certainly one of the Englishman's favourite amusements. It enjoys a reputation – we would not whisper that it is an undeserved one – among a certain class of the community that the theatre has not; it is an entertainment, or rather an institution, of which the great British public is justly proud.

We must confess that we always enjoy a circus ourselves, and that at each performance we attend we evoke a blessing on the memory of Philip Astley,[258] the great originator of this kind of entertainment. The name of Astley – one of the *Sketches by Boz*[259] describes a visit to his establishment – was for years a household one in London, just as Sanger is now in the provinces. And following Astley are there not the glorious names of Ducrow, Clarke, Cooke, Hughes, Batty, Ginnett and Hengler,[260] names to conjure with – names concerning which we could write

---

[257] Published 11 January 1896.

[258] The 'father of the modern circus'. See John Turner, *Victorian Arena*.

[259] 'Astley's': one of Charles Dickens's 'Sketches of London', first published in the *Evening Chronicle*, 9 May 1835, and collected in *Sketches by Boz* (1836). See Charles Dickens, *Dickens' journalism:* Sketches by Boz *and other early papers, 1833–39.* ed. by Michael Slater (London, 1996), pp. 106–111.

[260] For details of these circus proprietors see John Turner, *Victorian Arena* or the *Dictionary of National Biography.*

columns? Has not the profession of a clown been one to which every right-minded individual at some portion of his career aspired? Of course it has. What better place then for a tour could we find than Mr Gilbert's circus now in Nottingham? None! say the readers of the ARGUS. And so think we, and, as we know that we shall not be able to curb our eloquence on this subject, let us immediately without detailing the history of circuses in general, and our own knowledge of them in particular, proceed with the description of a visit we paid to it.

Behold us, then, making our way to the Victoria Hall, Talbot-street, with a joyful look in anticipation of the performance we are about to see, and, joining the crowd outside, we are not ashamed to say, the pit entrance. We always patronise the pit, and desire no greater pleasure than to sit with the good folks who do likewise. There is one bar, however, to our enjoyment tonight, and that is the early door, whereby certain well-favoured individuals appropriate the best seats. On the present occasion, fortunately, there were not many early door patronisers, but such as there were must have noticed the scowl in our eye. People who take this mean advantage generally have a shame-faced look – at least so it seems to us.

As seven approaches the crowd begins to get anxious and to make preparations for a crush. Hats are adjusted by the gentlemen, hair arranged by the ladies, children hoisted higher by fond parents, money placed in handy pockets by the male portion of the crowd, sticks and umbrellas grasped more firmly by all, and injunctions to 'keep close by me' scattered broadcast by everybody. The gentleman who has been announcing the advantages of the early door shouts, 'This way for comfortable seats and no crushing' with increased energy. He is endeavouring to catch a few late comers, but knows the game is nearly up. Still he clings on a little after time, and has to bear the expostulations of the crowd who want to get in.

Hallo! the door is being gently opened. Steady, now, steady; mind the children. Keep close to me, my dear. Look out, Tommy. Oh my! don't they crush? In we go. Where's your money? Have you any change? One and two halves. Two shillings, please. No two and a half! Then half a-crown, quick. Now pass on, sir, you are keeping the people. Here? No, there. Well make haste or we shall get nowhere! Such are the exciting stages by which we are at last landed on a front seat in the promenade at exactly seven and a half minutes past seven, with over thirty minutes to wait before the performance begins.

As we have so long a time to spare we must amuse ourselves by looking round. Many people read their evening newspapers; a good number eat oranges. The polite gentlemen accompanied by ladies engage themselves in frivolous talk; the impolite smoke on in silence. A little variety is imparted into the monotony by the efforts of the ringmen to find seats for late comers in all sorts of imaginary openings. One couple in this manner squeeze into a full row, and are compelled to sit cramped up half the night before their neighbours, who received them with very long faces, choose to make a little more room for them. This being an evening performance, children are not very numerous, and paterfamilias, with ma and the children, is conspicuous by his absence. Mr Largefamily knows better than to bring Mrs L and all the little L's here on a night in Christmas week. Still there are one or two little girls in company of father with a few small boys in charge of their maternal parents. This is the invariable order we'd have noticed when the youngsters go out. A more frequent sight is the boy of 12 or 14. He generally comes with a 'pal', arrives early at the doors, and takes a front seat in the sixpenny places. These young men are very knowing and confer seriously together as the show progresses; it does not take a close observer to find that they are very frequent visitors here. When required they have no hesitation in immediately volunteering to assist our old friend the clown in the ring. Other visitors are old folks who are giving themselves a Christmas treat, and giddy girls who spend most of the time in chattering loudly. The latter have a way of looking earnestly into one another's faces, and occasionally darting glances at the male folks near that is very refreshing. The promenade is largely occupied with swells who smoke cigarettes, stand on anything at the back of the crowd, and generally interest themselves in everything but the performance in the ring.

Before the time for opening the programme we have a little music. It is a good band and members of it seem jolly fellows. We wonder, though, if Mr Gilbert treats them as old Astley treated his players. One day a performer suddenly ceased playing. 'Hullo!' cried Astley, addressing the delinquent, 'what's the matter now?' 'There's a rest,' answered the other. 'A rest,' Astley repeated angrily; 'I don't pay you to rest, but to play!'[261] We noticed that the band did indulge in several 'rests,' but they seemed intervals, which they filled in by telling tales to one another. How we wished that we could have heard those tales.

However, 7.45 arrives at last, and immediately – for punctual time is kept by Mr Gilbert – seven or eight gentlemen in evening dress (sleeves generally a little too short, but hands encased in capacious white gloves) appear and range themselves in two rows by the entrance to the ring. They are forming a guard of honour for Mdlle Rubini, who is about to open the performance by walking on a telegraph wire. In she comes with a bounce, a nice-looking girl of 16 or so clad in tights. Her walking on the wire is superintended by an elderly gentleman, presumably her father, and is very clever for such a young performer. Not only does she dance, but she also runs on the wire and turns round and round on it after the manner of a teetotum.[262] Further she picks up a handkerchief that rests on the wire at her feet, and does several other clever feats, all of which are duly appreciated by the audience. In return we are rewarded with kisses blown along the pretty arms of the fair young lady. The performance is greatly superior to that with which, in our younger days, we were regaled by Mdlles Topsy, Violet and Rose, and other experts in travelling circuses. These young ladies performed on a rope, termed a 'corde-de-elastic' about the size of their wrist, on which we have at times imagined an elephant might have walked, and further, they carried an enormous balancing pole, whereas Mdlle Rubini was content with the occasional assistance of a Japanese umbrella. But how we used to laugh when the ringmaster, having chalked this 'corde-de-elastic' to prevent, as he explained, the young lady from slipping off, the clown would take the chalk and rub it along the bottom of the rope to prevent, as he also explained, the young lady from falling up!

After the departure of Mdlle Rubini, Mr Johnson appears in an act of horsemanship. Mr Johnson is dressed in cowboy costume, and comes in flourishing a lasso. The most daring of his feats is to hang from the saddle right down over the horse's back, preserving his safety by keeping one foot in a convenient loop. He makes his exit by urging his horse at a furious pace round the ring, the while discharging a revolver in the air, and uttering cries after the Indian manner (as detailed in tales of adventure in 'the Far West'.) Later on we have another performance on horseback – this time from Mr Harry Yelding in the character of an Epsom jockey. This gentleman is very expert in standing up on his horse as it goes along at a good rate. He slips the saddle off by gradually working it down with his feet and then stands on the horse's

---

[261] This is a well-known anecdote told about Philip Astley, although it is sometimes also attributed to Andrew Ducrow. See A. H. Saxon, *The Life and Art of Andrew Ducrow and the Romantic Age of the English Circus* (Hamden, Conn., 1978).

[262] A top, with a fine point, on which it was made to spin.

bare-back with the same unconcern as before. He is also very clever at jumping on his horse when it is at a full gallop and clearing gate, bars and other obstacles. While these various feats are in progress we are entertained with the antics of a clown. How the 'gods' laugh when he walks in with an innocent look on his powdered face. And how two little girls in the front chairs clap their hands and laugh when he gives us some of his witticisms. Mr Clown has his innings when Messrs Johnson and Yelding are resting after a spell at riding, but we fancy that the latter had rather that he had given us a little less of his fun. Now with the ladies the case is different, for they are always contented to sit panting and smiling and casting sweet glances all round. To see them smile on the clown and the other gentlemen in the ring, as the groom guides their horse along at a slow walk, is to make one's heart burst with envy. We must confess to a feeling of disappointment that no fair equestriennes (they are always termed either graceful or daring on circus programmes) appeared this evening. We should greatly like to have seen the beautiful Signoretta Isabella, the champion lady rider in the world, again in her dashing leaps on to a running horse's back, or that Russian lady, clad in a costume more suitable for a tropical clime than her own country, in her charming flights over banners and through drums and rings. But this was not to be tonight.

Next we have a performance by two gymnasts on the horizontal bars, and following them the Great Villions appear. They are a troupe of bicyclists, composed of a stout gentleman, and a thin gentleman, a tall girl, a small girl, and a little boy. The first four are in a very pretty costume, the prevailing colours being yellow and mauve, and the last named is attired as a clown. This family do a large number of wonderful tricks on various makes and shapes of bicycles, on which they seem as at home as the Epsom jockey was on his horse. For instance, they not only ride a bicycle that is minus its back wheel, but they also trundle one along which has no shaft at all; and, further, they treat an ordinary cart wheel in the same manner. Then they ride a while with a flat side, a wheel shaped like an egg, and a wheel with no shape at all. The elder girl starts and works a machine backwards way about, and afterwards plays a violin solo standing on a wheel alone, while her sister, riding a tiny bicycle, takes flying leaps through paper hoops. The stout gentleman when going at full speed keeps three plates spinning round on three sticks held in his mouth, with another stick and plate in his right hand, and a large hat revolving on a stick in his left. He holds one of the girls up in the air at the full length of his arm while she keeps on working her machine, and to conclude, he and his bicycle act as horse to a miniature dog-cart, in which the clown is seated. As they drive out the wheels of the cart come off and are immediately appropriated by the girls and used as bicycles to carry them off. Such are some of the feats these clever Villions did, and they had to respond several times to the applause that followed their exit.

Last came Mr G. Holloway (he used to be called The Great George, but is evidently advancing in the social scale), who was dressed as a sailor, his costume, as is usual with the British tar, being of brilliant blue. A large stand having been arranged after a great deal of trouble by the gentlemen in evening dress, assisted by a contingent of other ring men, Mr Holloway mounted a large ladder which was placed on it, and, keeping it rocking, was enabled to reach the top and come down on the other side without it being supported. Time getting on, we fancy that Mr Holloway had to cut his performance short, as we have a remembrance of having seen him to the edification of the public generally, divest himself of his nautical garments at the top of the ladder and appear in the ordinary costume of gymnasts, viz., tights.

The late George Augustus Sala[263] on one of his visits to America was commissioned to supply an account of a certain length of the Niagara falls. Mr Sala sat down to write, and after some time found that he had reached the stipulated length of the article without having said a word on the falls – he had filled up his paper with a description of the people in the car, the scenery on the way to the falls, etc. So he wrote at the end of his article: - 'P.S. I forgot to mention that there are some excellent falls in the neighbourhood.' Now this is exactly our position. We have exhausted all our space without having said a word of Mr Gilbert's great Christmas pantomime, 'A Royal Garden party,' so *we* will add a postscript.

P.S. There followed a capital pantomime. We greatly regret to take this course as we know we could have waxed eloquent on the pantomime. But the editor is inexorable, and we shall have to leave to the reader's imagination the sight the ring presented when it had been transformed into a garden illuminated with electricity, how a large number of notables, male and female, including foreign emperors and republican presidents, political celebrities (Mr Gladstone was one, in his shirt sleeves, and carrying a woodman's axe), representatives of various nations in gorgeous costumes, and a 'New Woman,'[264] appeared and made obeisance to her Majesty the Queen, who was accompanied by the Prince and Princess of Wales, the Duke and Duchess of York and 'the latest' (vide the announcement of a gorgeous flunkey). Nor can we tell how a stately minuet was danced by 8 children in old-time costume, how the 'four merry maids' in a dance, and the Lizette Troupe in acrobatic gambols pleased the gentlemen and shocked the ladies, how there was a grand review of Life Guards, highlanders, lancers, artillerymen, Grenadier Guards, Robin Hoods, and Indian troopers; and how, finally the Queen made her exit seated beside Britannia in a chariot drawn by half a dozen sailor boys.

We do not know if the circus, like the great auk, will become extinct. We hope not; but if it does, Lord Macaulay's New Zealander will certainly give us thanks when he discovers this true and particular account of a circus performance in the year of grace 1895.

Shows in Shops[265]

We feel that no apology is needed for an article on the above subject. The showman does not stand on the same rung of the professional ladder as the actor, who possesses a literature all to himself, yet his life has often been described by the novelist. By other writers too it has been specially treated; that painstaking journalist, Thomas Frost, compiled a book on *Shows and the old London Showman*, while *The Memoirs of Bartholomew Fair* are contained in a thick volume written by Henry Morley.[266]

---

[263] George Augustus Sala (1828–1895), journalist, essayist and one of 'Mr Dickens's young men.'

[264] The late nineteenth-century 'New Woman' might have been recognisable by her lack of corsetry and simple, comfortable clothes, outward demonstrations of women's rights to liberty and self-realisation. See Angelique Richardson and Chris Willis, *The New Woman in Fiction and Fact: Fin-de-siècle Feminisms* (London, 2002).

[265] Published 18 April 1896.

[266] Thomas Frost, *The Old Showmen and the Old London Fairs* (London, 1874); Henry Morley, *Memoirs of Bartholomew Fair* (London, 1859).

Only a few weeks ago we had in our hands a paper on 'Fairs' which had been read before a learned society in a city that prides itself on its intellectual position. With, therefore, the above examples before us, we think that a few facts in reference to Shows and Shops may well find a place in these 'Tours in Town.'

Dwarfs are frequently to be met with. Two years ago a tiny woman was exhibited in High-street, under the name of the Princess Paulina.[267] She was said to be only eighteen inches in height, and though this may not have been quite correct she could have been but little taller. Her features, which were almost those of a Mulatto, and her limbs were quite in harmony with her size, and she appeared fully the age she was stated to be, viz. twenty. She answered several questions in English with a foreign accent (she was of Dutch nationality), shook hands, and for a performance coquetted with a fan, lifted a heavy dumb-bell, and (strange feat!) stood on her head several times. In the daytime she was carried out for an airing in infant's clothes. She was a genuine midget, and quite different from a man and woman of stunted growth who were shown in a shop on Derby-road in 1887. These were, perhaps, three feet in height, and the chief thing they did, if we remember rightly, was to sing the then popular song, 'We're all very fine and large,' after which they indulged in a jig.

To the same shop in High-street we were attracted by a very flaming picture which represented two children, joined together after the manner of the Siamese Twins, walking on a platform.[268] The Prince of Wales and other members of the Royal Family, several gentlemen in military uniform, an admiral or two, and a crowd of civilians were gathered around the platform expressing their astonishment in various manners, the chief of which seemed to consist in elevating the palms of the hands in the air. Outside the shop a man was describing in a loud tone this modern marvel, and so we passed inside to the accompaniment of a barrel organ and a kettle-drum. On a platform we found arranged a little wooden house, wherein we fondly imagined the twins dwelt. Presently a woman came and drew back the curtain forming the door of the house with a great parade. Then she whipped a cloth off a big round bottle and exposed to view, preserved in spirits, a child, which could never have lived, that was something like the representation in the picture![269] The audience were invited to walk round and view the monstrosity from all sides, but we preferred to make a quick exit from the place. These same people afterwards rented a shop on Long-row, where they exhibited, in succession, an armless lady, who wrote with her toes; General Dot, a midget; a performing seal, and a fine art gallery; and a performing dog, the property of Miss Flora Bell. A performing seal was, if we mistake not, once shown in Clumber-street. The seal has a wonderfully human look, and deserves better treatment than we suspect it generally gets at the showman's hands. It can be trained to shake a fin, make a noise in answer to questions something like the human voice, fire a gun, and do several other clever tricks. As a rule it goes under the title of the Wonderful Mermaid, though sometimes it descends to the more commonplace description of the Talking Fish.

---

[267] See p. 33. Race seems to be recalling his earlier account.
[268] Large and fanciful paintings were, indeed, part of the exhibition culture of shop shows and freak shows, many showmen stipulating that prospective exhibits brought with them 'good paintings'. Such paintings were not, as Race indicates above, necessarily true to life, and indeed were often fanciful in the extreme. See Sir Frederick Treves' account of the painting outside Joseph Merrick, the Elephant Man's, exhibition in a shop on the Mile End Road reproduced in Michael Howell and Peter Ford, *The True History of the Elephant Man* (London, 2001). Siamese twins: Chang and Eng Bunker (1811–1874) who were joined at the chest.
[269] Again, this seems to be a re-working of Race's earlier account, p. 24.

Figure 17. 'Jolly' Fat Girl, promotional postcard c.1900

In Goose-gate there were exhibited, some years ago, two 'fat' women, but we had not the pleasure of seeing them. This couple, shortly afterwards, when riding to a station at Bradford broke down the axle of their cab. To complete their misfortunes the Railway Company, the same day, sent their luggage astray. In an action brought against the company, the exhibitor of the 'fat' women stated that he engaged them at £1 a week each with board and lodgings, and that on a good day, at a well patronised fair, he expected to take £20 at the doors. Much amusement was created in court by the statement that the 'fats' travelled as passengers, but a certain excess in weight was treated as luggage and charged accordingly![270]

Following the 'fat' women came a strong man, who modestly termed himself 'Samson', the conqueror of all strong men. This strong man did various feats with heavy dumb bells, but his performance was eclipsed by a buxom young woman, dressed in tights, who, placing a strap in her mouth, attached the loose end of it by a hook to a barrel filled with weights, which she then swung round in the air. At the conclusion of the performance Samson informed us that his expenses were so heavy that he was forced to make a collection, which he thereupon did, while most of the audience became interested in the ceiling or gazed earnestly into space. There was one comfort in the vast expense, viz., that it was not incurred in buying that luxury, soap, for neither the strong man nor his partner were over clean in the face or dress. We confess to coming out of this show with a 'hope-nobody-will-see-us' air.

About seven years ago the shop at the bottom of Mount-street, now in the occupation of Messrs Boots, was given over to shows.[271] The full strength of the dramatis personae was only three (two men and a woman), but at each performance a tragedy and a farce were given. The men were very old stagers, and had evidently descended the professional ladder. They had quite an aristocratic appearance (we used especially to admire one in a Roman costume with his cheeks roughed [sic] a little), and we remember reverently following for some time one of them whom we saw on Beastmarket-hill. Though his clothes had fallen on hard times he still sported a tall hat.

After the Ghost Show had departed, the shop was taken to exhibit a Zulu. Dressed in a very ferocious costume and carrying a large assegai this 'savage' showed, firstly, how he prayed to his gods; secondly, how he stalked and killed wild animals; thirdly, how his people rejoiced at a marriage; and fourthly, and lastly, how Zulus said goodnight. This Zulu (he was a genuine black, though rumour hath it that at times savages exhibited in shows have been detected frauds) was very fond of a kind of foghorn with which he made a big noise, and when he went hopping about with this in his hands most in the shop took care to give him a wide berth.

Here was also an exhibition of juggling and knife-throwing. At the latter we have noticed that most ladies grow very frightened and, if they are under male escort, cling closely to their companion. A skeleton woman and clock-eyed girl were also shown here. On the usual highly-coloured picture the clock-eyed girl was depicted as having the figures of the hour in Roman numerals marked on her eyes. For the sum of one penny we were allowed to gaze closely at her, and we certainly found that she had

---

[270] Tales of 'fat' people breaking their carriages was commonplace. In a similar account, the weight of two giant children, exhibiting at Reynolds's Waxworks in Liverpool, broke the springs and destroyed the floor of the cab taking them home (*Era*, 4 May 1895).
[271] Race's description of a shop adapted to theatrical performance has precedents elsewhere. Montagu Williams, for example, describes the conversion of an East End undertaker's shop to a penny show (*Round London: Down East and Up West*, (London, 1892)), and Tom Norman's autobiography, *The Penny Showman*, in which he describes taking over empty shops located on Nottingham's Long Row.

some curious marks round her eyes just above the pupil, but they were not figures nor letters.[272]

In Pelham-street in 1890 Professor England exhibited his 'marvellous troupe of trained and educated fleas.' The fleas were held in captivity by what appeared to be gold wire no thicker than a human hair. One of them pulled a hansom cab in which a brother flea was seated as driver; another dragged along a log of wood fixed on a tiny model of a dray, while several others were harnessed to a stage coach. A third was fastened to a kennel, which he guarded after the manner of a watch dog, and by an ingenious arrangement another of these little insects drew a miniature bucket up a well, and the 'great military flea' fired off a cannon. It was certainly very interesting to watch these fleas, but speculation as to their mode of training and living was useless; the ordinary animal-trainer would have been unable, we are sure, to make anything out of them. Two years afterwards we came across this exhibition in another town, and found that flea education had developed. "an entirely new and original novelty," the funeral of a flea, had recently been added! Professor England informed his audiences that the fleas groused on his arm at night, and that each flea lived six weeks in captivity. For the benefit of the nervous members of the public his bills contained the reassuring announcement that every flea was securely chained![273]

Waxwork exhibitions are of a slightly different order of show from those we have been dealing with. There was one in High-street in 1892 which, though most of the figures were old, contained several good tableaux.[274] Chief of these was the grave scene from 'Hamlet'. Another represented Joe, the crossing-sweeper in 'Bleak House', lying dead in the snow. In Bridlesmith-gate in the previous year, a shop whose locality we cannot now remember, was showing an ancient collection of waxwork figures, of which a ghastly representation of a murdered family remains impressed on our memory. There was also a scene representing the death of Napoleon III. The emperor lay on a bed, the posts of which were covered with gold paper. By the side were the Empress, the Prince Imperial, and two Sisters of Mercy. At a table, which bore two candles and a cross, stood a Roman Catholic priest, properly vested, reciting the last offices. Attached to this show was a marionette exhibition, where the renowned play of *Spring-Heel Jack*[275] was performed for our edification. The best waxwork exhibition we have seen in Nottingham was that of Ernest Gambart, which occupied a shop on Long-row in 1891. This man exhibited a really good collection of figures, and had further, a life-size representation of 'The Last Supper.'[276]

In our wanderings in Showland we have encountered many varieties of the showman. Of him and his life we could say much, but for the present we refrain. Of course, there are worthy and unworthy members of the profession. We here enter our determination that the worthy members, who are many, we will never despise, and we invite you, reader, to do the same.

---

[272] Again, Zulus, skeleton woman and the clock-eyed girl were 'exhibits' featured in Tom Norman's memoirs. See *The Penny Showman* (1985).

[273] Professor England's Royal Exhibition of Educated Performing Fleas visited Nottingham's Goose Fair in 1892. For Flea Circus history, see Ricky Jay, *Jay's Journal of Anomalies* (New York, 2001).

[274] See p. 33. Race recalled seeing Violet's Waxwork Show in High-street in 1892.

[275] The story of Spring-heeled Jack was ripe for adaptation to marionette performances, depending as it did up the 'superhuman' antics of Jack who frightened, robbed and in some cases attacked his victims.

[276] Ernest Gambart Baines (1858–1920) inherited the waxwork show from his mother, Clementina.

Bibliography

Archives
Race, Sydney, 'Memorable days at the Mechanics' Hall' [by S. Race] Sm4fo.
  Scrapbook I, 128–31; 164–6. Local Studies Library, Angel Row, Nottingham.
  – Journals 1892-1900 (ref. M24480), Nottinghamshire Archives.

Books
Allen, Fred and Williams, Ned, *Pat Collins, King of Showmen* (Wolverhampton,
  1991).
Altick, Richard, *The Shows of London, a panoramic history of exhibitions 1600–1862*
  (Cambridge, 1978).
Archer, William, *William Charles Macready* (London, 1890).
Assael, Brenda, *The Circus and Victorian Society* (Charlottesville & London, 2005).
Auerbach, Nina, *Ellen Terry: Player in her Time* (London, 1987).
Balzer, Richard, *Peepshows: a Visual History* (London, 1998).
Barnes, John, *The Beginnings of the Cinema in England 1894–1901; Vols.1–5*
  (Exeter, 1996-1998).
Bingham, Madeleine, *Henry Irving. The Greatest Victorian Actor* (London, 1978).
Boaden, James, *Memoirs of the Life of John Philip Kemble, Esq: including a history
  of the stage, from the time of Garrick to the present period* (London, 1825).
Bogdan, Robert, *Freak Show: Presenting Human Oddities for Amusement and Profit.*
  (Chicago & London, 1988).
Booth, J. B., *London Town* (London, 1929).
Booth, Michael, *English Melodrama* (London, 1965).
Booth, Michael R., *Theatre in the Victorian Age* (Cambridge, 1991).
Braithwaite, David, *Fairground Architecture* (2nd rev. ed.) (London, 1976).
  – *Travelling Fairs.* Shire Album 17 (Aylesbury, Bucks, 1976).
Braithwaite, Paul, *A Palace on Wheels: a History of Travelling Showmen's Living
  Vans with an A-Z of Manufacturers 1860–1960.* Fairground heritage series; no.4
  (Berkshire, 1999).
Brand, Ken, 'Unhealthy Areas in Victorian Nottingham: the Rookeries', in
  Nottinghamshire Past. Essays in honour of Adrian Henstock, ed. by J. Beckett
  (Nottingham, 2003), pp. 155–171.
Bratton, Jacky 'What is a Play? Drama and the Victorian Circus', in *The Performing
  Society: British Theatre in the Nineteenth Century*, ed. by Tracy C. Davis and
  Peter Holland (Palgrave Macmillan, forthcoming).
  – and Featherstone, Ann, *The Victorian Clown* (Cambridge, 2006).
Brown, Frances, *Fairground Strollers and Showfolk* (Taunton, 2001).
Brown, Richard, 'The Kinetoscope in Yorkshire', in *Visual Delights: Essays on the
  Popular and Projected Image in the19th Century*, ed. by Simon Popple and
  Vanessa Toulmin (Trowbridge, 2000), pp.105–115.
Carter, Alexandra, *Dance and Dancers in the Victorian and Edwardian Music Hall
  Ballet* (London, 2005).
Church, Roy A., *Economic and Social Change in a Midland Town: Victorian*

Nottingham, 1815–1900 (London, 1966).

Clarke, Sidney W., *The Annals of Conjuring*. ed. by Edwin A. Dawes and Todd Karr, (Seattle, 2001).

Crangle, Richard, 'Saturday Night at the X-rays: The Moving Picture and the New Photography in Britain, 1896' in *Celebrating 1895*, ed. by John Fullerton (Sydney, 1998).

Dickens, Charles, *Dickens' Journalism:* Sketches by Boz *and other early papers, 1833-39*, ed. by Michael Slater (London, 1996).

Encyclopedia of Early Cinema, ed. by Richard Abel (Oxford, 2005).

Featherstone, Ann 'Showing the freak: photographic images of the extraordinary body,' in *Visual Delights. Essays on the Popular and Projected Image in the 19th Century* ed. by Simon Popple and Vanessa Toulmin (Trowbridge, 2000), pp. 135–142.

Forbes-Winslow, D., *Daly's. The Biography of a Theatre* (London, 1944).

Foulkes, Richard, *Performing Shakespeare in the Age of Empire* (Cambridge, 2003).

Fried, Fred, *A Pictorial History of the Carousel* (New York, 1964).

Frost, Thomas, *The Old Showmen and the Old London Fairs* (London, 1874).

Frow, Gerald, *'Oh yes it is!': a history of pantomime* (London, 1985).

Ganzl, Kurt, *The British Musical Theatre*. Vol. 1 1865–1914 (Basingstoke, Herts,1986).

Gardner, Viv 'Provincial stages, 1900-1934: touring and early repertory theatre,' in *The Cambridge History of British Theatre. Volume 3. Since 1895*, ed. by Baz Kershaw (Cambridge, 2004).

Gillies, Midge *Marie Lloyd. The One and Only* (London, 1999).

Glanfield, John *Earls Court and Olympia. From Buffalo Bill to the 'Brits'* (Stroud, 2003).

Goodall, Jane R. *Performance and Evolution in the Age of Darwin: Out of the Natural Order* (London, 2002).

Granger, James *Nottingham Mechanics' Institution. A Retrospect* (Nottingham, 1912)

The Green Room Book and Who's Who on the Stage (London, 1907).

Hare, Augustus J. C. *Walks in London. Vol 1*(7th ed.) (London, 1901).

Higson, Andrew (ed.), *Young and Innocent? The Cinema in Britain 1896–1930* (Exeter, 2002).

History of the Nottingham Mechanics' Institution 1837–1887. Published by the Committee on the Occasion of the Fiftieth Anniversary of its Foundation, November 1887 (Nottingham, 1887).

Holland, Charlie, *Strange Feats and Clever Turns* (London, 1998).

Howard, Diana, *London Theatres and Music Halls 1850–1950* (London, 1970).

Howell, Michael and Ford, Peter, *The True History of the Elephant Man* (London, 2001).

Iliffe, Richard and Baguely, Wilfred, *Victorian Nottingham. A Story in Pictures*
  – Volume 3. (inc.) *Magic Lanterns to Living Pictures* and *The Grand Theatre, Hyson Green* (Nottingham, 1971).
  – Volume 4. *Goose Fair* (Nottingham, 1972).

Jay, Ricky, *Jay's Journal of Anomalies* (New York, 2001).

King, W. D., *Henry Irving's* Waterloo. *Theatrical Engagements with Arthur Conan Doyle, George Bernard Shaw, Ellen Terry, Late-Victorian Culture, Assorted Ghosts, Old Men, War and History* (Berkeley, 1993).

Lane, Michael, *Burrell Showman's road locomotives : the story of Showman's type road locomotives manufactured by Charles Burrell & Sons Ltd* (Hemel Hempstead, 1971).

Le White, Jack and Ford, Peter, *Rings and Curtains. Family and Personal Memoirs* (London, 1992).

McCormick, John, *The Victorian Marionette Theatre* (Iowa City, 2004).

Macqueen-Pope, W., *Marie Lloyd: Queen of the Music Halls* (London, 1947).
  – *Gaiety: Theatre of Enchantment* (London, 1949).

Mander, Raymond and Mitcheson, Joe, *Pantomime. A Story in Pictures* (London, 1973).

Mayer, David *Playing out the Empire*: Ben Hur *and Other Toga Plays and Films, 1883-1908. A Critical Anthology* (Oxford, 1994).
  – 'Toga Plays,' in *British theatre in the 1890s: essays on drama and the stage*, ed. by Richard Foulkes (Cambridge, 1992).
  – *Henry Irving and* The Bells. *Irving's personal script of the play by Leopold Lewis* (Manchester, 1980).
  – *Harlequin in his Element: the English pantomime 1806–1836* (Cambridge, Mass: 1969).

Melville, Joy, *Ellen Terry*. (London, 2006).

Middlemiss, J. L., *A Zoo on Wheels: Bostock and Wombwell's Menagerie* (Winshill, 1987).

Morley, Henry, *The Journal of a London Playgoer* 2nd ed. (1866) reprinted, with an introduction by Michael R. Booth (Leicester, 1974).
  – *Memoirs of Bartholomew Fair* (London, 1859).

Ned Farmer's Scrap Book; Being a Selection of Poems, Songs, Scraps, etc. etc. Enlarged and Revised 3rd ed. (London, 1863).

Newton, Henry Chance, *Cues and Curtain Calls* (London, 1927).

Nicoll, Allardyce, *A History of English Drama 1660-1900. Volume VI. A Short-title Alphabetical Catalogue of Plays* (Cambridge,1965).

Norman, Tom, *The Penny Showman: Memoirs of Tom Norman "Silver King,"* with additional writings by his son, George Norman (London, 1985).

Nottingham in the eighteen eighties: a study in social change. Compiled by I. Casterton et al, ed. by Helen E. Meller (Nottingham, 1971).

The Nottingham Mechanics Institution. Fifteen Years Record being the History of the Institution from 1912 to 1927 (Nottingham, 1928).

Oettermann, Stephen, *The Panorama: History of a Mass Medium* (New York, 1997).

The Oxford Encyclopedia of Theatre and Performance, 2 vols. ed. by Dennis Kennedy (Oxford, 2003).

Philips, John, *The Ghost! the Ghost!! the Ghost!!!* (London, 1998).

Pilbeam, Pamela, *Madame Taussaud and the History of Waxworks* (London, 2003).

Popple, Simon and Kember, Joe, *Early Cinema: from Factory Gate to Dream Factory* (London, 2004).

Reynolds, Harry, *Minstrel Memories. The Story of Burnt Cork Minstrelsy in Great Britain from 1836 to 1927* (London, 1928).

Richards, Jeffrey, *Sir Henry Irving. A Victorian Actor and His World* (Hambledon and London, 2005).

Richards, Lily May, *Biography of William Haggar: Actor, Showman and Pioneer of the Film Industry* (n.d.) (Pamphlet held in the National Fairground Archive, University of Sheffield).

Richardson, Angelique and Willis, Chris, *The New Woman in Fiction and Fact: Fin-de-siècle Feminisms* (London, 2002).

Sanger, 'Lord' George, *Seventy Years a Showman* (London, 1927).

Saxon, A. H., *The Life and Art of Andrew Ducrow and the Romantic Age of the English Circus* (Hamden, Conn., 1978).

Scott, Clement, *The Drama of Yesterday and Today*. 2 vols. (London, 1899).

Scrivens, Kevin and Smith, Stephen, *The Travelling Cinematograph Show* (Tweedale, 1999).

Shakespeare in the Theatre. An Anthology of Criticism ed. by Stanley Wells (Oxford, 1997 (2000).

Singleton, Brian, *Oscar Asche, Orientalism, and British Musical Comedy* (Westport, CT, 2004).

Speaight,George, *A History of the Circus* (London, 1980).

Sullivan, Jill, 'The business of pantomime: regional productions 1865 to 1892' (unpublished PhD), (University of Nottingham, 2005).

Taylor, George, 'Svengali, mesmerist and aesthete' in *British Theatre in the 1890s* ed. by Richard Foulkes (Cambridge, 1992).

The Theatres Trust Guide to British Theatres 1750–1950. A Gazetteer, ed. by John Earl and Michael Sell (London, 2000).

Toulmin, Vanessa, *Electric Edwardians. The Story of the Mitchell and Kenyon Collection* (London, 2006).

– *Pleasurelands: All the Fun of the Fair*. (Sheffield, 2003).

– 'The Cinematograph at the Goose Fair, 1896-1911', in *The Showman, the Spectacle and the Two-Minute Silence* ed. by Alain Burton and Laraine Porter (Trowbridge 2001), pp. 76-86.

– *A Fair Fight. An Illustrated Review of Boxing on British Fairgrounds* (Oldham, 1999).

– *Randall Williams, King of Showmen. From Ghost Show to Bioscope* (Sheffield,1998).

Trease, Geoffrey, *Nottingham: A Biography* (Otley, West Yorkshire, 1984)

Trewin, J. C., *Benson and the Bensonians* (London,1960).

Turner, John, *Victorian Arena*. Vol. 2 (Formby, 2000).

– *Victorian Arena* Vol. 1 (Formby, 1995).

Weedon, Geoff, *Fairground Art: the Art Forms of Travelling Fairs, Carousels and Carnival Midways* (London, 1981).

Williams, Montagu, *Round London: Down East and Up West* (London, 1892).

Wilson, A. E., *Edwardian Theatre* (London, 1951).

– *Pantomime Pageant. A Procession of Harlequins, Clowns, Comedians, Principal Boys, Pantomime-writers, Producers and Playgoers* (London, 1946).

– *The Story of Pantomime* (London, 1949).

Journals

Braithwaite, Paul, 'The rise of waxwork shows: a short history', in *Living Pictures: Journal of the Popular and Projected Image before 1914* 1:2 (2001), 36–58.

Brown, Simon, 'Early Cinema in Britain and the Smoking Concert Film', *Early Popular Visual Culture* 3:2 (2005), 165–178.

Featherstone, Ann, '"There is a peep-show in the market": gazing at/in the journals of Sydney Race', *Early Popular Visual Culture*, 3:1 (2005), 43–57.

Haggar, Walter, 'Recollections. Early Days of show Business with a Portable Theatre in South Wales', *Dock Leaves*. n.d.

Hoffman, Kathryn A., 'Sleeping Beauties in the Fairground. The Spitzner, Pedley and Chemisé exhibits', *Early Popular Visual Culture* 4:2 (2006), 139–159.

Bibliography

Pedley, Catherine, '*Maria Marten, or the Murder in the Red Barn*: the Theatricality of Provincial Life', *Nineteenth Century Theatre and Film* 31:1 (2004), 26–38.

Popple, Simon, 'Photography, Vice and the moral dilemma in Victorian Britain', *Early Popular Visual Culture* 3:2 (2005), 113–133.

Purcell, Edward L., 'Trilby and Trilby-Mania: the Beginnings of the Best-seller System', *Journal of Popular Culture* 11:1 (1977), 62–76.

Toulmin, Vanessa '"Curios Things in Curios Places": Temporary Exhibition Venues in the Victorian and Edwardian Entertainment Environment', *Early Popular Visual Culture* 4:2 (2006), 113–137.

Newspapers and Periodicals
City Sketches
Dock Leaves
The Era
Midland Jackdaw
Notes and Queries
Nottingham Argus
Nottingham Daily Express
Nottingham Evening News
Nottingham Evening Post
Nottingham Journal
Nottingham Owl
The Nottinghamian
Nottinghamshire Guardian
The Times
World's Fair

Websites
John Turner's Circus Biography http://www.circusbiography.co.uk (accessed 26 February 2007)

Library of Congress, http://www.loc.gov (accessed 26 February 2007)

Matthew Lloyd's comprehensive website about his music-hall ancestor Arthur Lloyd, but also much useful material on theatres in London and the provinces http://www.arthurlloyd.co.uk (accessed 26 February 2007)

National Fairground Archive, http://www.shef.ac.uk/nfa (accessed 26 February 2007)

Sir John Soane Museum, http://www.soane.org. (accessed 26 February 2007)

The Theatre Museum, London www.peopleplayuk.org.uk (accessed 26 February 2007)

Index